The Intimate Life of the last Tsarina

The Empress Alexandra

The Intimate Life of the last Tsarina

Princess Catherine Radziwill

With an introduction by

John Van der Kiste

A & F Reprints

First published by Cassell 1929
Published with a new introduction by A & F 2017

Introduction © 2017 John Van der Kiste

A & F Publications
South Brent, Devon, England TQ10 9AS

Typeset 11pt Georgia

ISBN-13: 978-1546383468
ISBN-10: 1546383468

Cover: *The wedding of Nicholas II and Alexandra Feodorovna*, after Laurits Tuxen

Printed by CreateSpace

CONTENTS

APPENDICES

Illustrations appear between pages 119 and 132

INTRODUCTION

PRINCESS CATHERINE RADZIWILL was born in St Petersburg as Countess Ekaterina Adamovna Rzewuska on 30 March 1858. She was the only child of Adam Adamowicz Rzewuski, a general who had fought in the Crimean War, and his second wife Anna Dmitrievna Dashkova, who died in childbirth. Her father later married a third time and in due course she had three half-brothers. In 1873 she married Prince Wilhelm Radziwill, a Polish officer in the Prussian army, and they settled in Berlin, where they raised a family of four sons (two of whom died in infancy) and three daughters.

She began her writing career pseudonymously in 1884, when the French journal *Nouvelle Reveu* published a series of articles written as letters to a young diplomat by the supposedly elderly and previously unknown aristocrat Count Paul Vasili. These were highly critical of society in Berlin, which was portrayed as a decadent and immoral city, and contained much damaging gossip about the Imperial court. Once the series had completed its serial publication, the features appeared in book form under the title *Berlin Society*. The writer evidently knew the imperial family well, and an investigation named Auguste Gérard, the French reader of the Empress Augusta, as the guilty person. Although he protested his innocence, he was dismissed from court. Only in 1918 did Princess Radziwill confess to having been responsible. She had however fallen under suspicion, and felt it only wise to leave Berlin. She and her family moved back to St Petersburg, where she became a close friend of the imperial adviser, Constantin Pobedonostsev, whose reactionary politics greatly influenced Tsars Alexander III and Nicholas II, and had an affair with General Alexander Cherevin, a trusted confidant of Alexander III. On the latter's early death in 1894 her position at court waned sharply, and she became estranged from her husband and children. Noted for her lavish lifestyle, she soon fell into debt and was only able to offset this in part by writing articles for the American press on British and European society.

In 1899 she left Russia for South Africa, where she briefly became a close friend of Cecil Rhodes. After further financial troubles, she became estranged from him, was found guilty of forging his signature on several promissory notes, and served a prison sentence. In 1906 she was divorced by her husband and a few years later she married Karl Emile Kolb-Danvin, a Swedish engineer and entrepreneur. Once again she (and her husband) lived in St Petersburg, where she took up writing again. *Behind the Veil of the Russian court*, published in 1914 under her old byline Count Paul Vasili, revealed the previously closely-guarded secret at court that the Tsarevich was afflicted with the incurable bleeding disease of haemophilia. Although it was said that the Count had passed away, she was soon unmasked and deported by the Russian police. Her second marriage did not last long, although it probably ended in separation rather than divorce and Kolb-Danvin died a few years afterwards. She lived in Stockholm for a while where she turned out a prodigious number of books, mostly of her sometimes rather dubious memories of court life in Russia, Germany and Austria, and two volumes of fiction. Some of her detractors might have been forgiven for suggesting with a note of cynicism that all her books contained at least a sprinkling of fiction. After the war she visited the United States, where she decided to remain. After being admitted to hospital in New York with a fractured hip, she died there in 1941, aged eighty-three.

Altogether she wrote more than twenty books, mostly under her first married name. Several more may have appeared under various additional pseudonyms, although the only one which can be attributed to her – albeit with some doubt – is that of Hildegarde Ebenthal. They included at least two volumes of autobiography, several on the Russian court, a couple on Germany, and one on Cecil Rhodes.

The Intimate Life of the Tsarina was her second volume on its subject, the first having been published in the year of her death. Although Radziwill's books have to be treated with caution, her portrait of Empress Alexandra Feodorovna rings true enough, and it can be assumed that her research was on the while based on material from reliable sources. It is a portrait which combines a measure of sympathy and understanding with fierce criticism. The Tsarina was a 'Poor, poor, distracted woman .... to be pitied rather than blamed', but evidently her own worst enemy, who would not hear a word against 'our friend' Rasputin, who accepted his verdict that the death of Earl Kitchener at sea in 1916 was 'good for us', as 'he might have done Russia harm', and who even in the first years of her married life was the despair of Queen Victoria as she refused to listen to advice. In her summing up of her subject and the final verdict of history (or as near

4

to a final a verdict as can be pronounced on someone who has been dead for only a decade) in Chapter X, Radziwill writes that

> it is impossible to deny that bad luck pursued her from the very first day of her marriage, but then this bad luck was in many cases her own fault, the fault of her pride, of her obstinacy, of the falsely exalted idea which she had of her own importance, and also of the violent dislike she had taken to those of the Russian aristocracy, in whom she saw her direct and personal enemies.

As a recent historian, Brian Roberts, has observed, in Princess Radziwill's books, 'fact is so mixed with fiction, [and] it is necessary to check whatever she says'. Her views are sometimes contradictory, changing between one book and another, all too often reflecting the news reports and hearsay on which they are based.[1] Nevertheless her portrait of the Tsarina in the present volume rings true on the whole. While it is impossible to prove that her account of events at the Russian court over a hundred years ago is completely accurate, the record of posterity suggests that it is one of her more truthful books, and as a biography, her version of facts is supported by more recent biographers whose credibility has never been open to question.

NOTES

1 Roberts, Brian, 'Princess Razzle-Dazzle'. In *Royalty Digest* 25, July 1993, pp. 21-23

John Van der Kiste

PREFACE

THIS is neither an apology nor an indictment of the last Empress of Russia. Either would be in bad taste, because, while it is impossible not to try to defend her from baseless accusations which have been hurled at her head, yet it is equally out of the question to attempt to absolve her from a very large share of responsibility in regard to the terrible collapse of Russia.

Yet it is debatable whether any other woman in her place would have been able to avert it, or even to hold it back for a while. It is a question most difficult to answer when one reflects that, although the reign of Nicholas II was at the same time the saddest and most tragic in the history of Russia, the catastrophe in which it culminated had been slowly preparing itself for years. It was the result of the rotten system of government under which the country had been struggling ever since the period of the "great reforms" by Alexander II had come to an end after being arrested in development by the crime of a few and the ignorance and intriguing spirit of the many.

Alexander III had shown strong character and uprightness: he had succeeded in bringing back peace to an intellectually troubled land in leading it towards a prosperity none had expected it would ever reach. He was, moreover, respected and trusted, and his subjects, as well as the rest of the world, knew that he not only never broke his word, but he admitted his mistakes when these were demonstrated to him. With his son it was different. He was of the type of those Greeks of the Lower Empire to which the great Napoleon had compared his predecessor on the throne of Russia, Alexander I, and, like the latter, was considered insincere and untrustworthy. He was weak, moreover, while believing himself strong, and towards the end of his reign had succeeded in alienating not only every class and section of Russian society, but also his own family.

The individuality of Nicholas II was undoubtedly one of the leading features in the discontent which gradually overshadowed the throne of the Romanoffs and then shook it until it perished. Even without the War Nicholas would never have been able to maintain his high position, although he might perhaps have escaped his tragic fate. He had no backbone and little sincerity of character. With it all, he was absolutely indifferent to what went on around him, and nothing could ever shake a composure which was not strength of mind but an utter incapacity for apprehending the purport of events. His diary, recently published in Berlin, is the most formidable indictment that could ever have been penned against him.

From this diary, which he kept for a number of years, until the eve of his murder in fact, it is manifest that he never experienced the least sign of emotion in the various great moments of his life. All he notes is the number and names of the people he received each day, and when faced with political events or movements of the greatest importance, he acknowledges their existence only so far as they touch upon his daily occupations. This explains how futile it was for anyone having matters to report to him, to keep his attention riveted on the subject they were trying to bring to his knowledge. He listened to everybody in silence, and with an absolutely indifferent expression. As a man who knew him well, and had the opportunity to see him almost daily, Prince Serge Yolkonski, — who for two years was director of the Imperial theatres and had to leave owing to intrigue, — writes about him in his memoirs, one had the feeling, when talking with him, that "one stood in the presence of an empty place."

A man with such a character ought to have had a wife capable of stiffening his character. Instead, she was as narrow-minded as he, far more authoritative in her ideas, ill-balanced in her mind and inclined to every superstition. Unfortunately, too, knowing his defects and, having a high opinion of her own qualities, she tried to impose her will and to make him an instrument of her despotism. Then, as well as Alix, whom it has now been proved he adored and whose demands he never could resist, the dancer Kchessinska, with whom he had a long and close friendship, kept plying him with constant demands and advice, and, through her new lover, the Grand Duke Serge Michailovitch, continued to exercise her influence over him. Surely a curious situation!

This was the main reason of the tragedy which culminated in the basement room at Ekaterinburg where a dynasty was butchered in cold blood. It would be unjust to make the Empress alone responsible for it, but it would not be right to ignore her share in the disaster. In the Russian Revolution as in the Great War, everybody was guilty, and no one was innocent.

All these considerations, therefore, make the history of Alexandra Feodorovna a curious study, one that deserves to be approached without prejudice because it is so largely a pathological complex as well as a political problem. She was not normal, and she did not live in normal times: a fact which goes far to explain that supreme tragedy of which she became the most tragic victim.

The reader may perhaps feel that I have made too many quotations from the Empress's letters, from the book of her favourite, Madame Viroubova, and from the Emperor's diary; but in my desire not to write a fantastic story, I searched for the truth. Where could I find it elsewhere and better than in those authentic effusions of souls "living in great times, without any grandeur in their characters wherewith to meet them"?

GENEALOGY

ALEXANDER II m. Marie Alexandrovna
1818-81   1824-80

|

ALEXANDER III m. Dagmar (Marie Feodorovna)
1845-94   1847-1928

|

NICHOLAS II m. Alexandra Feodorovna
1868-1918   1872-1918

|

Olga (1895-1918)
Tatiana (1897-1918)
Marie (1899-1918)
Anastasia (1901-18)
Alexis (1904-18)

PART ONE

CHAPTER I

EARLY YEARS AND MARRIAGE

ALIX VICTORIA HELEN LOUISE BEATRICE OF HESSE was born on June 6, 1872, at Darmstadt, and was the youngest child of the Grand Duke Louis IV of Hesse, and of the Princess Alice Maud Mary of Great Britain and Ireland, the second daughter of Queen Victoria. She lost her mother when she was only six years old, and was partly brought up by her grandmother in England, and partly at Darmstadt. Her sisters were all much older than she, and she had no real companions of her own age, growing up an isolated, sad little girl, needing a mother's care and a mother's love to counterbalance a naturally haughty disposition and difficult temper. Her father had never given much attention to the education of his children, and the Queen had always treated her family with the severity of a sovereign who requires to be obeyed rather than as a tender parent. She was, moreover, far too much engrossed in cares of State to be able to give much time to the timid, sensitive child who, wherever she went, found herself *de trop*.

Alix, as she grew up, developed a temper which made her difficult, but she knew how to keep it under control, and in the presence of her father or of her grandmother she was always submissive and dutiful in words as well as in conduct. But she suffered from the subordinate position in which she was kept, especially by her elder sisters, one of whom had married her cousin. Prince Louis of Battenberg, while the other had become the wife of the Grand Duke of Russia.

This Russian marriage had been the one great social triumph of the House of Hesse, who saw in it a perpetuation of the old tradition and old ties which had existed since the day when the Princess Marie of Hesse had married the Emperor Alexander II of Russia. In consequence, the Princess Elizabeth was looked upon as the star of the Hessian dynasty. From time to time her German relatives went to see her in St. Petersburg and Moscow, and on their return had long tales to relate concerning the splendour with which she was surrounded, the atmosphere of luxury and riches amidst which she moved. The fact that all this pomp and wealth had brought her no

Ella

13

happiness was not taken into consideration: if it had been, little Alix might have avoided the terrible fate which became hers many years later.

In the year 1892 the Grand Duke of Hesse went to St. Petersburg to see his daughter, and for the first time since her sister's wedding Alix accompanied him. Rumours about the possibility of her becoming the wife of the heir to the Russian throne had already been current, and it was an open secret that the Grand Duchess Elizabeth did all in her power to help it to success. But the Empress Marie did not care for the idea of having a German daughter-in-law. St. Petersburg society took its cue from the sovereign, and the Princess Alix was pronounced awkward, disagreeable, impolite, and, last but not least in such smart society as that of the Russian capital, abominably dressed. In consequence, Alix found herself neglected, and it even happened that at Court balls she did not find partners, owing probably to the fact that she danced very indifferently. The visit from which she had expected so much, passed off rather like a nightmare, and the young girl must have sighed with relief when she found herself back in her old home at Darmstadt.

And now comes the first enigmatic incident in her career. According to the rumours which were going the rounds in St. Petersburg, the Princess Alix had neither captivated the Tsarevitch,[1] as her family and Queen Victoria had hoped she would do, nor had she succeeded in making herself liked by those whom she met. At least, so it was said everywhere. On the other hand, it seems, judging from some letters and documents which have come to light recently, that she had inspired a violent passion in Nicholas, from the very first moment he had set his eyes upon her, a passion which, she returned and shared. When at last the Tsar's consent to his son's marrying the Princess Alix was granted, the Grand Duke Nicholas did not lose a moment in proposing. This came at the psychological moment. Since the death of the Grand Duke of Hesse, the Princess Alix had queened it at Darmstadt. All her sisters were married, and she was the only princess who could carry out for her mother the honours of the little Hessian Court. She enjoyed the importance to which she had risen. The new Grand Duke had always been fond of his little sister, was glad to have her beside him as a companion and friend, and allowed her a free hand in all the internal arrangements of their household. This pleased Alix, and, strange to relate, she never thought that in course of time there was bound to be a Grand Duchess of Hesse; least of all did she expect that he would marry a girl with whom he would be really in love. Yet this is what actually happened.

During a visit which the new Grand Duke paid his grandmother,

Queen Victoria, at Balmoral, he met one of his cousins, the Princess Victoria of Edinburgh, and forthwith fell in love with her, encouraged by the Queen, who had romance in her nature and was, in spite of her denial, a matchmaker at heart. She accordingly favoured this idyll, doing her best to induce her grandson to come to a decision in **regard to a union** which suited her so well from every point of view, and with which he was only too eager to comply.

The Princess Alix had not accompanied her brother to Scotland, and consequently knew nothing of what went on in the Highlands. When she received the telegram announcing the Grand Duke's betrothal to his cousin of Edinburgh, she was so angry that only with great difficulty her ladies-in-waiting persuaded her to send congratulations to the young couple. She hated the idea of having a sister-in-law at Darmstadt to snatch from her a position which, no one knows why, she had imagined she would keep as long as she lived. When his sister treated him to a scene on his return home, the Grand Duke of Hesse quietly told her that his marriage was none of her business, and that if she did not wish to continue living at Darmstadt, she could go to one of his shooting-boxes with a lady-in-waiting, and he was ready and willing to settle a small allowance upon her.

This did not suit Alix, so she submitted to the inevitable and condescended to write a nice little note to her future sister-in-law, wishing her joy and happiness. But when she had to start for Coburg, where the marriage was to fake place, she did so in a sullen frame of mind. It was while she was in this mood that the Tsarevitch arrived at Coburg and, in accordance with a stipulated programme, almost immediately asked her to become his wife.

At this moment it is illuminating to observe the feelings of the young man who was so soon to become one of the mightiest monarchs in Europe. He himself writes in his curious diary, on December 21, 1891, two and a half years before his betrothal to the Princess Alix:

"My dream is one day to marry Alix of Hesse. I have loved her a long time, but more deeply and fervently since the year 1889, when she spent six weeks in Petersburg. I have struggled for a long time against my feelings, and tried to persuade myself that it was an impossible thing, but since Eddy[2] gave up the idea of marrying her, or was refused by her, it seems to me that the only obstacle standing between us is the religious question. There is no other one, because I am convinced that she shares my feelings. Everything is in God's hands, and, relying on His mercy, I await the future with calm and humility."

One month later he returns to the subject, and writes, on January 29, 1892:

"During a conversation with mamma this morning, she made a few allusions to Helene, the daughter of the Count of Paris, which rather put me into a strange frame of mind. Two roads seem to be open to me. I myself want to go in one direction, and it is evident that mamma wants me to choose the other one. What will happen?"

This last admission is very significant, because it substantiates rumours which were going about at that time, in Paris and Petersburg drawing-rooms, concerning the advisability of a union between the Tsarevitch and the French princess who was later to become the Duchess of Aosta, rumours which were energetically denied in competent quarters. Whether the fate of Nicholas II would have been happier had he married the Princess Helene is another question. For her it was a blessing that this plan came to nothing, yet perhaps her presence beside Nicholas II on the throne of the Romanoffs would have averted the catastrophe, or at least given to it a dignity of which it was deprived by the fatal character and strange conduct of the Empress Alexandra.

This, however, is but a digression; to return to this strange betrothal, and the manner in which it affected Nicholas II. He writes about it in his diary in all kinds of detail, but in such a childish manner that involuntarily one is reminded of the words of Alexander III to Count Witte when the latter asked him to entrust the chairmanship of the committee for the construction of the trans-Siberian railroad to the then heir to the throne. He then exclaimed, surprised: "Do you know what it is you are asking? The Tsarevitch is still a boy, and his judgments are those of a perfect child!" Yet, two years later, this same child was to become the Emperor of Russia.

People had begun to realize that this was to happen soon when the Grand Duke came to Coburg, ostensibly for the purpose of attending his cousin's marriage. A numerous family gathering was assembled for this auspicious occasion. It included Queen Victoria, who passionately wished her granddaughter to become Nicholas's bride. Every facility was granted to the young man to press his suit, and the day after his arrival he was given an opportunity to be alone with the Princess Alix.

This is how he describes his conversation with her;

"I found Alix grown ever so much prettier since I had seen her, but she looked extremely sad. We were left alone together and then began between us this talk which I wished so much to take place, while dreading it at the same time. "We spoke until twelve o'clock, but without any result, because she could not bring herself to accept a change of religion. The poor thing cried a lot, but had quietened down a little before we separated."

Three days later, on April 8, 1894, the young princess allowed herself to be persuaded by her lover, and this is how he tells it to us:

"A beautiful day in my life, which I shall never forget, the day of my betrothal with my dearest and incomparable Alix. About ten o'clock this morning she came to Aunt Michen[3] and after having talked with her we came to an understanding together. My God, what a joy, what a load of anxiety was lifted from my shoulders! With what joy I shall be able to gratify dear papa and mamma! I remained the whole day wrapped in a kind of cloud, and could not realize what really had happened to me. Wilhelm[4] sat in the next room, with my uncles and aunts, awaiting the result of our conversation. I went immediately with Alix to see the Queen, and then Aunt Marie,[5] where there was a long scene of tenderness, and we all kissed one another. After lunch we went to Aunt Marie's private chapel, where a service of thanksgiving was celebrated. I cannot believe yet that I have a bride."

The days which followed were days of general rejoicing, and Nicholas's diary is full of expressions of love for the beautiful princess. Yet he had not broken off his friendship with the dancer Mathilde Kchessinska, whose influence over him was to continue until the very day of his abdication. A strange character, surely!

The engagement of the Tsarevitch and the Princess Alix of Hesse was, of course, an event of almost international importance, and everybody, beginning with Queen Victoria, was delighted that it had at last become an accomplished fact. The young girl was made much of, and found herself suddenly transformed into a most important personage, not only in her own eyes (that she had always been), but in those of the whole of Europe, which hailed her as a future Empress of Russia. In this general enthusiasm, the bride in whose honour this family gathering had assembled at Coburg was forgotten, and Alix, instead of having to play second fiddle to her new sister-in-law, as she had feared she would be compelled to do, found herself the object of general adulation by the large circle of royalties that had gathered for the nuptials of the Grand Duke of Hesse and the Princess Victoria of Edinburgh.

That Nicholas was really delighted is evident from what we find written about it in his diary. On April 12th she writes:

"I awoke to the knowledge that another beautiful day was beginning. At 10 o'clock we went with Alix to the Queen to breakfast together with her. Now I am to call her 'Granny.' A military band played under the windows during the meal. I replied to some telegrams in Alix's room. At eleven o'clock I went to church. We lunched at three o'clock with the Queen. We drove later with Alix to the Rosenau, where a large company was assembled to play lawn tennis and drink tea. I sat in my beloved fiancee's room until 8.15. With the permission of Aunt Marie, I moved out of the castle into a little house of hers in the park close to the villa where Alix lives. I occupy the rooms of Alfred, who left to-day for Potsdam. They are very comfortable, and, what is more important than anything else, I am close to her, my beloved!"

"Saturday, 16th April.' — A cold and rainy day. We all breakfasted together at Aunt Marie's. At 10 o'clock we were suddenly summoned with Alix to the Queen to have breakfast with her. At eleven o'clock I went to church. At five o'clock there arrived a special messenger from home who brought me lovely letters, the decoration of St. Catherine, and a superb and wonderful present for Alix from papa and mamma, together with Easter eggs. What joy this was to us both! I read her my parents' letters, so full of warm love, and joy, and satisfaction! At 6 o'clock we went to the castle to say good-bye to the Queen. She left for England, accompanied to the railway station by her German regiment of dragoons. After dinner I sat with my dear and beloved Alix!"

Queen Victoria was perhaps the person who was most pleased at the turn which events had taken. She liked the idea of her own granddaughter becoming the sovereign of one of the greatest empires in the world, and she had, besides, a sincere personal regard for the Tsarevitch, who had won her heart by the deference which he had always shown her. She believed that this marriage, which would ally the future Tsar with half the reigning houses of Europe, was a guarantee that the peace of Europe would not be disturbed for years to come, and that, in particular, the old differences which, ever since the Crimean War, had divided Russia and England would at last be smoothed over. So not only did she show all the pleasure which her grandchild's betrothal had given her, but she forthwith made plans for the Princess to spend part of the coming summer with her, and for the Tsarevitch to come to Windsor for a long visit at the same time.

All this was smooth enough, but then suddenly there arose difficulties connected with the religious question. The Princess Alix was a devout Protestant, and it was imperiously necessary for her to adopt the Orthodox faith. She at first absolutely refused to entertain the idea of what she called apostasy. Circumstances, however, together with her affection for her future husband, proved too strong for her. The tact and diplomacy of Father Yanischeff, the Tsar's confessor and a most able man, who was sent on purpose to England with the mission of converting the Princess Alix to Orthodoxy, succeeded in winning her goodwill, and she decided at last to examine seriously the differences which existed between the religion of her youth and that of the land over which she was one day to reign. Finally she was won over by the astute priest, and promised to accept the creed of the Romanoffs.

It is a curious fact, which, so far as I know, has never yet been noticed in any of the books and newspaper articles dealing with the personality of the late Empress, but this determination of hers to change her religion after having protested so energetically against the very idea of doing so, was one of the things that did most to set St. Petersburg society against her. At that time there was a strong vein of Liberalism running through Russian society and a feeling that liberty of conscience ought never to be interfered with. Part of it was the outcome of the general antipathy which existed against M. Pobedonostseff, the then powerful Procurator of the Holy Synod, who was credited with a mastery over the mind of Alexander III; and after it had become known that the young girl whose hand the heir to the Russian throne was seeking in marriage had declared she would accept only if she were allowed to retain the creed in which she had been born and bred, general sympathy went out to her, and she was pronounced a wonder. Then, suddenly, things changed, and the public was told that the Princess Alix had become reconciled so far as to promise to listen to the arguments of Father Yanischeff, and later to accept the Orthodox faith. This dispelled the glamour, and Russian society began to wonder whether its future Empress was really the paragon she had been made out to be. It aroused a feeling of animosity against her, to which no one would have owned but which became in time very real, even before people had had opportunity to become personally acquainted with Alix.

In the Imperial family, opinions were divided as to the marriage. The Empress Marie frankly said that she did not like it, and yet she had failed to find for her first-born anyone who answered to the requirements expected of a Tsarevna, for this was to be the title of the Princess Alix. The different grand duchesses also looked upon the Hessian princess more or less as an intruder, and thought some other bride, better fitted to become the second lady in the land than this silent and, in certain respects, uncouth child, might have been discovered. They all feared that with her arrival in Russia, English influence would become supreme in affairs of State, and England at that time was most unpopular — an unpopularity which was fanned by the French party, then extremely powerful in Imperial circles. Added to all these considerations was the far more serious question of the Emperor's health, which was failing rapidly, but the real condition of which was not allowed to become known to the public, although it was well known to his family and to others in his immediate surroundings. If he were to die before, or immediately after, his heir's marriage, the Princess Alix would not pass through any stage of preparation for the exalted position she was to occupy, but would be thrust into it without warning, ignorant of many things she ought to know, and was supposed to know, before she ascended the throne of all the Russias.

People talked and talked, and somehow no one seemed satisfied when the news of the betrothal of the Tsarevitch was officially announced. He was said to have been compelled to marry by his parents and in accordance with the wishes of the country, which was not true, because whatever has been said and whatever was said at the time, Nicholas was truly in love with, the beautiful girl who was to share his throne as well as his tragic fate, and there was no compulsion at all in his wooing her. The marriage, on his side at least, was entirely one of affection, whatever it may have been on that of the young Princess. The question whether, rather than love, she was dazzled by the splendid position awaiting her, has never been answered in a satisfactory manner.

There was a good deal of weariness, as well as of vanity, which had probably influenced her when at last she had said "yes" — weariness of her life, which was not only dull and uninteresting, but also mortifying to a certain extent. Hers was not a nature that liked to play second fiddle, and the thought of having to do so in the presence of her new sister-in-law, for whom she had never felt any great sympathy, was certainly distasteful, while her vanity was pleasantly tickled at the idea of finding herself raised to a position so far above that of most of her relatives and friends.

At the time of which I am writing, it was still considered a great thing to be an empress, and Alix would have been more than human if she had not felt elated at all the flatteries which were poured into her ear as to the importance she had assumed in the eyes of the world, and at the wonderful presents which were offered to her by the enamoured Tsarevitch as well as by his parents, who were continually sending her magnificent jewellery and priceless laces and furs. The

Empress Marie, too, started to consult her in regard to the trousseau which, according to tradition, was to be offered to her by the Russian Court. It was to be on such a splendid scale as to overwhelm an impressionable girl who all her days had been yearning' for pretty things which her people could not afford to give her.

Yes, those were idyllic months, in that summer on the banks of the Thames during which the young lovers wandered about in the gardens and fields, and forgot everything but the one supreme fact that they were happy. What did it matter to them that the world talked? And it did talk; tongues wagged eagerly.

Queen Victoria watched this love affair with interested eyes. Nothing pleased her better than to see her granddaughter the heroine of what seemed almost a fairy story. Nevertheless she was more awake than anyone in Russia as to what ought to and might follow upon this marriage in which she felt so much pride. The Queen was perhaps the best politician and diplomat of her time, and she could see at once the advantages which Great Britain might derive from a better understanding with Russia, her traditional enemy and antagonist. And then she loved her beautiful granddaughter, though not blind to her faults, and the thought of seeing her seated on the throne of the Romanoffs was essentially pleasing; so pleasant, indeed, that for once the Queen closed her eyes to certain ominous signs which might have told her that Alix was not going to have it all her own way in St. Petersburg.

The family of the young Princess was very much divided in opinion concerning her and the possibilities of her proving a success in Russia. The Empress Frederick, one of the cleverest women in Europe, was perhaps the one who judged better than most people the character of her niece. Speaking to one of her friends about her, she expressed herself as being apprehensive in regard to the future. And she discouraged any ideas of the friend in question, a Russian by the way, in regard to the Liberal opinions of the bride of the Tsarevitch. "You will find that they are exactly the reverse," she said. "Alix is very imperious and will always insist on having her own way; she will never yield one iota of the power she will imagine she wields; I use the word 'imagine' advisedly," added the Empress, "because my niece is given to very exaggerated ideas as to her own cleverness and importance."

The Empress Frederick, however, was about the only person who talked so openly in regard to the Princess Alix. To the world in general Alix appeared surrounded by a halo which, had she only shown herself the least tactful, she might have preserved very easily. St. Petersburg — intellectual society in particular — looked upon her with sympathy and interest, and as it was the moment when people were beginning to be just a little weary of the iron rule of Alexander III, the betrothal of the latter's son and heir to the granddaughter of Queen Victoria, Alix of Hesse, had their approval, and her arrival in Russia was eagerly looked forward to, in the hope that she would acquire a good influence over the Tsarevitch and induce him to fulfil the wishes of all intelligent and well-meaning Russian patriots, by beginning his reign with the granting of constitutional government to his country.

Although not known among the general public, the health of the Emperor Alexander was failing fast, because of an incurable ailment. In Court circles people were aware that the Tsar was doomed and that his days were numbered; their eyes, therefore, began to turn towards the hitherto little known personality of the heir to the throne. What would he do when he found himself called upon to wear the diadem of the Romanoffs ? Would he understand that times had changed since the day his father had inherited it that the hour had come to start Russia upon a new road, a road that might lead it to as much prosperity as when Peter the Great began his great reforms?

Those who knew the young man well realized that he would never understand anything of the politics of the future, but they hoped that his wife might — she who had been in the atmosphere of the British Court, who knew what constitutional government meant, and who had seen how it worked. The Princess was credited with a strong intelligence, was said to be of an earnest, upright character, devoted to her family and to her duties, an ideal woman for the difficult role of empress, and consequently the greatest sympathy for her was expressed in Liberal circles as soon as the news of her betrothal became public.

Of course there were some who said that it would be better to wait before passing a definite judgment upon the future Empress of Russia, These same people expressed regret that she might not have to pass through the initial stage of a Grand Duchess Tsarevna, with all the restraints this position implied, and which might have prepared her for the more important station that was awaiting her. They also remarked that her betrothal had been in part the work of her sister and brother-in-law, the Grand Duke and Grand Duchess Serge, and as *they* were known as violent reactionaries, their influence over the Princess Alix, if allowed to remain unchallenged, might have consequences of immense magnitude. All these, however, were voices crying in the wilderness — never expressed too loudly. The general public, as well as a large part of St. Petersburg society, was filled with enthusiasm for the young and beautiful girl about to become their future empress, and they looked for miracles such as no one being could accomplish, a fact which perhaps had something to do with the unpopularity she so quickly acquired.

Meanwhile the idyll in Windsor went on undisturbed. The Grand Duke, who had returned to Russia immediately after his betrothal, arrived in England on June 8th, and spent two days with Prince and Princess Louis of Battenberg in their home on the Thames, where he was welcomed by them and by the Princess Alix. He then proceeded to Windsor Castle, where the Queen received him warmly and affectionately. Diming the month which he spent under her roof, his tenderness for his future bride seemed to grow with every hour that passed, and his diary is full of his passionate love for her. She seems to fill all his thoughts, and to acquire more and more influence over his mind. He showed her this journal of his daily experiences and thoughts, although she did not at that time understand Russian, and she also wrote in it, almost daily, remarks that give us an insight into her strange character. They are mostly passages from books she had read, English, French, and German, and breathe that strange romanticism which was hers, as, too, the deep religious feelings of her curious nature. For instance, she quotes:

> "That His peace may tend you.
> And His love caress you.
> Is the wish I send you
> In the words, 'God bless you.'"

And a little farther we read:

> "*La nuit, j'aime être assise,*
> *Etre assise en songeant,*
> *L'œil sur la mer profonde,*
> *Tandis que pâle et blonde,*
> *La lune ouvre dans l'onde*
> *Son éventail d'argent!*"[6]

On another page:

> "*Es gibt Tage und Momente, die Strablen werfen konnen über Jahre.*"

"April 20th, Easter night. — Shall we ever forget it, O my kind, sweet manikins!" Under the words is drawn a heart, with the words in French, "*toi, toi, toi, toi!*"

On July 6th she writes : "I dreamt that I was loved, I woke and found it true, and thanked God on my knees for it. True love is the gift which God has given, daily stronger, deeper, fuller, purer."

Of course her head had been more or less turned by the extraordinary change which had taken place in her life, and she is not to be blamed for it; most girls would have been the same in her place. In the deference which was shown to her by her grandmother's Court, so different from the carelessness with which it had treated her formerly, Alix could see unwonted attentions, and for a person with whom vanity was almost an ailment, it was quite natural she should at last come to believe that she was the perfect being she was told she had become; the one woman whose influence in the history of her future country was to be kind and beneficent and conducive to great things.

And yet, even in this chorus of eulogy there were a few discordant notes, and some critically-minded people who said, or rather whispered, that the Princess could be more amiable, could show herself more interested in the various persons whom she met. Although she did not go out in society, which might have been embarrassing for her under the circumstances, she attended, nevertheless, a few afternoon receptions and garden parties during those summer months when the London season was at its height. A few Russians who also happened to be there were presented to her at their request, eager to pay their respects to their future empress, and they complained that she had received them most coldly, hardly saying three words to them. Of course this might have been timidity and shyness, but old ladies who remembered the arrival in Russia of the Empress Marie Feodorovna related that although she also was shy and timid, she had contrived to impress with the charm of her personality every one she had met. The Princess Alix was not amiable, and did not seem to wish to be so. She kept herself entrenched within an atmosphere of disdain and icy aloofness, which somehow jarred on the nerves of all who had tried to break down the barrier of haughty reserve she seemed to have put between herself and the world.

All this, however, might pass. People meant to be kind and indulgent to her. Things would be different when the Princess was in Russia and when she had learned to know the people and the country. No one, during those summer months, thought that the death of the Tsar was so near. Her German relatives also had become most attentive to her, and the Kaiser sent her many letters of affection and good advice, while even her own brother had begun to regard her as a person of great importance. The young princess would have been more than human if she had not been influenced by all these circumstances, for which the life she had led until then had so little prepared her.

And so the days of sweetness on the banks of the Thames went their course, heedless of the hands of fate slowly moving round the clock of life.

It may be asked what were the feelings of Nicholas during those beautiful summer days when he was wooing his lovely bride under the shade of the great oaks of Windsor Park ? His diary will again reveal something of the state of his mind. From the first he seems quite absorbed by his love for Alix, as his diary reveals.

Alix also liked to confide to his diary her expressions of love for her future husband, to whom she began to ascribe every quality he did, or did not, possess.

Whether she was genuine in her expressions of unbounded love and admiration where was little to admire, and very little to love, is another matter. Some people, later, were to say that her enthusiasm for her affianced husband was purely affectation, used only to allow her to obtain complete influence over him, and to control his mind, but it is difficult to accept this theory entirely. Very likely the young Princess was really becoming attached to the man who had laid so much at her feet, while she had so little to give him in return for his unbounded devotion.

Perhaps, also, the romantic and mystical trend of her mind was already then beginning to assert itself, because there is certainly a good deal of foolish enthusiasm, as well as religious superstition, in the remarks she wrote down in this diary of Nicholas. She puts in it all kinds of quotations from the various books she is or has been reading, all of them of the same trend, and sentimental when not tender. For instance, she writes: "My thoughts are ever with you, and my love grows deeper day by day"; then, in another place: "Let those love now who never loved before; let those who have always loved love more — yes." And, a little farther: *Fidèle toujours l'attendre, toujours l'aimer, ouvrir les bras, et toujours les lui tendre . . . . Sur cette page blanche, que ne puis-je y graver un seul mot: le bonheur!"* Then she becomes ever so much more tender:

"Never forget your own ever true old Spitzbub, who loves you so deeply! My own boysy-boysy dear, never changing, always true, have confidence and faith in your girly dear, who loves more deeply and devotedly than she can say. Words are too poor to express my love and admiration and respect; what is past is past, and will never return, and we can look back on it with calm — we are all tempted in this world, and when we are young we cannot always fight and hold

25

our own against the temptation, but so long as we repent and come back to the good and on to the straight path, God forgives us. 'If we confess our sins, He is faithful and just to forgive us our sins.' God pardons those who confess their faults. Forgive my writing so much, but I want you to be quite sure of my love for you and that I love you even more since you told me that little story; your confidence in me touched me, oh, so deeply, and I pray to God that I may show myself worthy of it. God bless you, beloved Nicky!"

All through the weeks he spent in England, Nicholas seems to have become more and more absorbed in his affection for the young princess. He sees nothing outside of her, and little seems to affect him but what concerns her. For instance, when the present Prince of Wales was born, the Tsarevitch simply writes:

"Yesterday, at ten o'clock in the evening, a son was born to Georgie and May, to the general joy. In the morning I went with Granny [the Queen] and Alix to Frogmore for breakfast; then I sat with my betrothed in the garden enjoying the summer weather. We went driving together, and returned home at one o'clock. We lunched at two, then drove with Granny to Bagshot, where Uncle Arthur and his wife are living. "We had tea in the tent, and looked over the handsome house and its Indian room. We returned to Windsor with Granny. The beauty of the rhododendrons in the park impressed me immensely. We dined at half past nine o'clock. I put on for the first time the so-called Windsor dinner coat with a red collar. I stayed with dear Alix the whole evening."

While all this was going on, Alexander III was slowly succumbing to file disease that was destroying his strong frame, and the question arose whether the marriage of the heir to the throne ought to be celebrated before his father had passed away, or postponed. And among the persons in close attendance upon the Empress Marie and her dying husband, it was suggested that it would be better to let the whole matter fall into abeyance for a time. There is the possibility that at the bottom of the heart of all these people was a secret hope that something might yet happen to prevent the marriage from taking place. This hope was shared by the anti-English and pro-French party at Court, which was very powerful and feared the advent of an empress who was German by birth and English by education; indeed, it was openly said in certain drawing-rooms in St. Petersburg that it would be to the advantage of the Tsarevitch not to be hurried into a marriage with a girl reared in ideas so entirely different from those in which he had been nurtured. On the other hand, the Liberal elements in the country, of which there were far more than the government suspected, were all in favour of the match, and declared that an unmarried sovereign would be exposed to so many temptations and unpleasantnesses that the only thing to do was to hurry the wedding of the young Grand Duke, even if it could not be celebrated with the pomp usual on such an occasion. And although some members of the Imperial family favoured a postponement of it, and tried to influence the Empress Marie in that direction, others, among whom the most prominent were the Grand Duke and Grand Duchess Serge, declared, on the contrary, that the only thing to do was to ask the future bride to hurry to Russia and be married there without delay.

Finally it was they who won, much to the joy of Nicholas. The Grand Duchess Elizabeth Feodorovna, together with her husband, the Grand Duke Serge, took the opportunity of an interview which they had with the dying Tsar, to persuade him to send a message to his future daughter-in-law inviting her to come at once to Livadia, and the Grand Duchess herself hastened to the Russian frontier to bring her sister over to the Crimea as quickly as possible. Commenting upon it, the Tsarevitch writes:

"October 5th, Wednesday.— Papa and mamma have allowed me to bring my dearest Alix over here from Darmstadt. Ella and Uncle Serge are going to bring her. I was deeply touched by the love they showed me and by their desire to see her. What a happiness to meet her again so unexpectedly! It is only sad that this meeting takes place under such circumstances."

A few days later he says:

"I woke up in beautiful warm weather. Uncle Vladimir and Aunt Michen arrived early this morning on the *Saratoff* from Odessa. At half past nine we started with Uncle Serge for Alouchta, where we arrived at one o'clock in the afternoon. Ten minutes later my incomparable Alix arrived from Sympheropol with Ella. We sat down to lunch in the house of General Goluboff. After lunch I seated myself with Alix in an open carriage, and we started together for Livadia. My God, what happiness to meet her in my own country and to have her near me! It seems to me that half my troubles and anxieties have been lifted from my shoulders. At every station we were met by Tartars with bread and salt. On the frontier of the Massandra domain, Lazareff, Olive, and Viazemsky were waiting for us; our carriage was decorated with flowers and bunches of grapes. I was terribly nervous when we entered the room of my beloved parents. Papa was weaker to-day, and Alix's arrival together with an interview he had with Father John, tired him. At the door of the palace stood a guard of honour of His Majesty's rifle regiment. We went to church, where a short service of thanksgiving was celebrated. I remained with Alix until dinner. We spent the evening as usual. I took her to her rooms."

The young princess, in the meanwhile, was going through one of the most critical moments of her life. She was weighed down with a feeling of crushing responsibility while preparing herself for her future position and its various duties. Indeed, one of her great mistakes consisted in thinking only about these duties. She had forgotten entirely the fact that the consort of a sovereign has also social obligations to perform and that she must observe them, whether she likes to or not. She had not realized that she would not be called upon to rule Russia, but would have to content herself with reigning over it, a vastly different thing, and that in fact an empress, instead of attempting to play a political part, ought to avoid politics as much as she could, and to realize that it was not her work to try to reform society otherwise than by setting it a good example.

Alix of Hesse was in fact far too serious, too ambitious, and too much absorbed in the thought of all that she imagined she would have to initiate in order to elevate Russia and Russian society to the ideal she considered they should attain. In regard to these plans of hers, she feared the future, feared that she would not be allowed to execute them. She had studied with real attention and great sincerity of intention the Russian Orthodox faith, and during her conversations with Father Yanischeff, the Imperial chaplain, she had struck him by her self-importance and her conviction that, once she was married, she could never do anything wrong — that in fact it would then be the duty of all Russia to admire whatever she did or said. The shrewd priest, instead of discouraging this natural tendency of the Princess Alix to consider herself quite above the rest of mankind, had in a certain sense ministered to it, and by his words strengthened her conviction that an empress of Russia could never do anything wrong, a conviction which was never to leave her, and which was to lead her to the terrible doom towards which she walked without the faintest suspicion that it could ever overtake her.

In Germany her approaching marriage was looked upon with disfavour. Popular feeling was averse to the change of religion; moreover, there was at the time a distinct feeling of distrust in the country against Russia and everything that was Russian. It was believed that the Princess was being forced into this union against her will, and that, left to herself, she would have preferred to remain in Germany, a belief which, as we have seen, was absolutely erroneous, because Alix had been very unhappy at home since her brother's marriage to Princess Victoria of Saxe-Coburg, whom she disliked intensely, and was very conscious of the grandeur that awaited her in St. Petersburg, and of the importance of the position she was about to occupy. This, however, was not known in her native land, and on the day she started for the Crimea, the principal paper of Darmstadt published an article full of regret for her departure and of apprehension as to the fate that awaited her in the land over which she was to reign. The following lines of the article referred to have since acquired a sinister and prophetic importance in view of the fears they expressed for the future of the girl whose approaching marriage had inspired them:

"It is only with feelings of deep grief and pity that the German people can follow during her journey to Russia the gracious and beloved Princess Alix. We cannot banish from our thoughts the secret forewarning that this Princess, who wept such bitter tears when she left Darmstadt, will have a life full of tears and bitterness on foreign soil. One need not be a prophet to foresee what conflict of thoughts and impressions will crowd within the heart of the august bride during these decisive weeks. Human law requires that a young girl follow the husband of her choice into the unknown.

"But the German people cannot consider this marriage with joy nor with the charm of things where the heart alone is in question. The German people cannot forget the old saying of the poet: 'Princes are only the slaves of their position; they must not follow the leanings of their own hearts.'

"If we cast a glance upon the Tsar fighting against the throes of death : upon the   'private life' of the bridegroom; upon the renunciation of the Evangelical faith by the Princess, a faith to which she has belonged to this day, sincere and convinced as to its truth, we consider that only a heroic nature can overcome all these terrors.

"After the German people had, until the last hour, reckoned on the rupture of this union, which cannot bring any happiness for the bride, so far as it is possible to judge of these things in advance, it only remains to feel ashamed that, in the country of liberty of conscience and of convictions, political considerations require the sacrifice of one's faith and of one's heart.

"One would learn with a deep joy in Germany that the Princess has found by the side of her husband real and lasting happiness. In the meanwhile we can only indulge in wishes for her welfare, and hope

29

for the best in a dark and uncertain future."

This article is quoted not so much because of its prophetic words as because it shows how little sympathy the marriage of the Princess Alix had inspired in Germany, or at least among those German people who were not swayed by political considerations. Except in England, where everything went off quite smoothly, and where in a certain sense the betrothal of the Queen's granddaughter with the heir to the throne of all the Russias was popular, as likely to put an end to animosities no reasonable person wanted to see persist, the marriage was nowhere the object of enthusiasm — neither in Russia, where the idea of a German bride was distasteful, nor in that bride's own country, where Russia was so intensely disliked.

In spite of all these prophecies of evil, the Princess Alix did not lose heart on the day when she began the long journey which was to bring her to her new home. All the German princesses who had started on such a pilgrimage in the past had done so with great pomp, solemn leave-takings, cannons booming, and crowds cheering their farewell. With her it was different. She was hurrying to a death-bed, and no one knew on that dark November morning which saw her enter almost furtively the railway carriage that was to bear her away from her beloved Darmstadt, whether she was leaving it for ever or whether she would return soon, after having been introduced to her prospective parents-in-law. The young girl had red eyes and looked sad when she departed, and as she herself told one of her friends, she felt that she was going into an unknown which at times terrified her.

In Berlin the Kaiser met her at the station and talked to her in the train for more than an hour. It was presumed that he offered advice and tried to obtain, in exchange, promises to try and maintain good relations between him and the future Tsar. But even with William II the Princess Alix maintained an icy reserve and confined herself to vague phrases that meant nothing at all; the cousins parted with great cordiality but without any effusiveness, and the Princess began the second stage of the journey to Livadia quite alone, except for a lady-in-waiting, and with a more than heavy heart. At the Russian frontier she found her sister, the Grand Duchess Elizabeth, awaiting her, and a guard of honour in command of an officer, together with a few civil functionaries, who greeted her with words of flattery and presented her with flowers. She accepted the flowers but hardly replied to the compliments, and seemed to be in a hurry to have done with attentions which evidently embarrassed her. She felt that, in spite of their official character, they differed from what they would have been had she really been a bride coming to Russia to be married, and at heart she resented and realized the difference.

In the meanwhile, at Livadia, gossip was rife concerning the coming arrival of the bride of the Tsarevitch, and people wondered whether her marriage to him would be solemnized as soon as she reached the Crimea. Even in the Imperial family, the eventuality that this might be the case was discussed with curiosity and interest. But at last the question was settled by the Emperor, who said that his son could not be married in a semi-private manner, but only with all the pomp indispensable to the nuptials of an heir to the Russian throne. This closed the matter and stopped the tongues of the busybodies, and the world ceased to trouble itself about the Princess Alix when it discovered that she was likely to remain the Princess Alix as long as she stayed in the Crimea.

Alexander III, nevertheless, gave orders that his future daughter-in-law should be received with every possible honour and ceremony, and on the day she reached Livadia she was met at the palace door by the whole Imperial family, who had assembled in the Crimea in expectation of the Emperor's death, with the exception of the Empress Marie, who would not leave her sick husband. As well, there was a guard of honour, with music and colours flying. The Tsarevitch had gone as far as Alouchta to meet her and her sister, and there an incident occurred which, though trivial, was nevertheless typical in its way, and a forerunner of certain difficulties that later on dogged the steps of the Princess Alix.

As she got out of the train prior to entering the Imperial carriage which stood in readiness to convey her to Livadia she somehow stepped out before her sister. The Grand Duke Serge, noticing it, pulled his wife by the sleeve, and almost compelled her to place herself before the Princess Alix, thus reminding the latter that until her marriage she was not entitled to the precedence of a Russian Grand Duchess. The tears came into the girl's eyes, and one could see that she was terribly hurt, but she merely drew in her lips and said nothing; but after that she always refused to come forward, and resolutely placed herself behind every lady belonging to the Imperial family. She did not intend to allow anyone to show her a second time what was her proper place.

In his sick-room at Livadia, Alexander III, who, in spite of his failing strength, had insisted on having himself dressed in his gala uniform, raised himself in the armchair where most of his time was spent, to welcome his future daughter-in-law. The young girl knelt before him to receive his blessing, and then was warmly embraced by the Empress, who tried to show herself as cordial and affectionate as possible, after which she was taken to the apartments that had been prepared for her.

No wonder poor Alix felt unhappy and cheerless. She was all alone in a strange country, with no one of her own kin near her, except a sister, whom perhaps she feared more than she loved, to remind her of her old home and childish associations. She felt herself discussed with anything but kindness by people whom she hardly knew and did not at all understand. She could not yet speak Russian, and her knowledge of French was indifferent, while German seemed to be a banished language at the Russian Court.

At the same time she was keenly alive to the fact that she ought to induce her future husband to assert himself and to realize his important position. She inaugurated, during those first days, that system, which she pursued until the last day of her tragic existence, of always telling Nicholas to impose his will and not to allow others to forget who he was. On October 15th, five days after her arrival in the Crimea, she writes in the Tsarevitch's diary these significant sentences:

"Sweet child, pray to God. He will comfort you; don't feel too low. He will help you in your trouble. Your Sunny is praying for you and the beloved patient. Darling Boysy, me loves you, oh, so very tenderly and deep. Be firm and make the doctors, Leyden or the other, G., come alone to you every day and tell you how they find him, and exactly what they wish him to do, so that you are always the first to know. You can help to persuade him then, too, to do what is right. And if the doctor has any wishes or needs anything, make him come direct to you . Don't let others be put first and you left out. You are Father's dear son and must be told all and be asked about everything. Show your own mind and don't let others forget *who you are*. Forgive me, lovy."

A week passed, and then the Emperor died as he had lived, every inch a sovereign, whose dignity and courage never deserted or failed him, even in the presence of the great Reaper. And Alix knew, after she had seen him breathe his last, that the man she was engaged to marry was no longer the relatively insignificant personage she had loved, teased, and played with, under the shade of the trees of Windsor Park, but the all-powerful Tsar of all the Russias.

How did he himself look upon this colossal change? Did he realize all it meant, all the responsibilities which had been laid upon his young and inexperienced shoulders? Did any awe fill his heart at the thought of the future which was before him, of all he would have to do and to achieve? An hour after his father's death, this is what he wrote in his diary:

"October 20th, Thursday.— My God, my God, what a day I The Lord has called to Him our beloved, adored papa. My head is turning round and round; one somehow does not want to believe it, because it seems such an impossible, terrible fact. "We spent the whole morning beside him 1 His breathing was impaired, and we had to administer oxygen to him the whole time. At about half past two he received Holy Communion. Soon after, slight convulsions began, and the end came quickly! Father John remained more than one hour standing beside him, holding his head. It was the death of a saint! Oh, God help us during these dreadful days. Poor, dear mamma! — In the evening, at half past nine, we had prayers — in that same room, I felt as if I were dead myself. My darling Alix's feet have again begun to hurt her!"

This last phrase is in itself a revelation. Any comment would be out of place. The only one that could be made concerning it is contained in Nicholas II's diary twenty-four hours later, which continues his feelings at this important and solemn moment of his existence:

"October 21st, Friday. — In our deep sorrow and misfortune, the Lord has granted us a quiet but radiant joy. At 10 o'clock this morning, in the presence only of our family, my beloved, dear Alix was received into our Church, and after mass we partook of Holy Communion with her, my dear mamma, and Ella, Alix made her responses, and read the prayers wonderfully well. After lunch we had a service for the dead, and another one at nine o'clock in the evening. The expression of dear papa's face is beautiful; he looks as if he were about to smile. I spent the whole day replying to telegrams together with Alix. . . . Even the weather has changed; it was cold and stormy at sea."

Not one word of anxiety in regard to the difficulties of his new position, not one of doubt as to his strength to cope with his new duties! All he thinks of is his future wife. We do not find ourselves in the presence of a sovereign who has just ascended his throne, but of a boy, boyishly and ardently in love.

An hour after the Emperor Alexander III had breathed his last, and while the guns of the men-of-war at anchor in the harbour of Yalta were still thundering their last salute to the dead sovereign, an altar was erected on the lawn in front of the Palace at Livadia, and the confessor of the Imperial family, Father Yanischeff, clad in golden vestments, came out of the gates and solemnly administered to the attendants, courtiers, high officials, and civil and military functionaries hastily assembled for the purpose, the oath to the new sovereign. From her windows the Princess Alix could see the ceremony and realize something of the responsibilities resting from that minute on the young and inexperienced shoulders. He was the Emperor, the Little Father of a country numbering a hundred and eighty millions of inhabitants, prostrated in adoration before him.

The pomp of power must have overwhelmed her at that moment, must have touched her with its deceptive splendour, and evidently she must have been impressed by such a sight, as well as by the death-bed she had just attended, that death-bed at which so much serenity had presided, such trust in God, such confidence in a future life ; because although, up to that moment, she had always put off the ceremony of her reception into the Greek Church, she suddenly expressed the wish that it should take place as soon as possible, and in accordance with that desire, the first to which she had ventured to give expression since she had reached Livadia, she was, on the very next day, led by her future husband and by her sister into the private chapel of the Imperial palace, and there abjured in the presence of Father Yanischeff the Protestant religion in which she had been born and reared, for the faith of her new country and of the man whose bride she was to be. The Princess Alix of Hesse disappeared, and in her place stood the Grand Duchess Alexandra Feodorovna, with the precedence which it conferred immediately after her reception into the Church of which she was in time to become one of the most fanatical adherents.

She was no more the insignificant little German princess. People began to gather around her and to try to win her favour. Perhaps it would have been better for her if she had not discouraged them, but she had retained her shyness, and appeared to have but one wish, — to be left alone. To tell the truth, she had not been well impressed by all that she had seen at Livadia. Her earnest, too earnest, nature had been horrified to find that, for the numerous people gathered round the Imperial family, life was going on as usual although an emperor lay dying close to them. She taxed them, and, together with them, the whole of Russia, with frivolity and lack of feeling, and, unfortunately for her, she allowed the world to guess the state of her mind and feelings on the subject. Her unemotional, stern Anglo-German nature failed to comprehend the subtleties of the Slavo-Byzantian character; she did not realize that the Court over which she was to preside was more Eastern than European. Its whole turn of mind was Byzantian, and she revolted at the many petty intrigues going on around her, the more so since she attached far too much importance to them by viewing them too seriously. The whole atmosphere of the palace seemed to her unwholesome, and she could not bring herself to enter into its small interests and its innocent gossip. She committed the great mistake of judging Russia according to what she saw of it in this little Crimean town, transformed for a few weeks into an annexe of the great Winter Palace of St. Petersburg.

She scarcely saw Nicholas, whose entire time was taken up with his new duties and the many details connected with the funeral of his father; and the Empress Marie, entirely absorbed in her own grief, did not seem to have struck the right chord in the heart of Alix of Hesse, who somehow could not get rid of a certain fear of her future mother-in-law, whose criticisms she particularly dreaded. The other ladies of the Imperial family, who might have helped her with their advice, did not like her. They kept away from her, partly out of jealousy, partly because when they had tried to make advances to her at first, they had been repulsed rather ungraciously. The fact of the matter was that the cold, unsympathetic manner of the future Empress made her, from the outset, more enemies than she need have had, and that even those who had had preconceived notions about her and her great qualities of heart and mind, had found that she did not respond to the feelings which they had fried to express to her. The world began to talk, and as it must always look for a reason for everything that does not please it, the Grand Duchess Elizabeth, and especially her husband, the Grand Duke Serge, were credited with the desire to keep Alix under their exclusive influence and, in order to retain it, to prejudice her against all the people for whom, for one reason or another, they did not care.

This had its bad effect later on, because Alexandra Feodorovna never got over those first impressions, but allowed them to guide her in after life, with pitiful results, as we shall see. It was then that she acquired the coldly disdainful manner which later procured her so many enemies. Russia had appeared to her in sinister colours, more in the light of an antagonistic country than anything else. She could never bring herself to look upon its sunny side, although, as her letters prove, she loved it fervently, with an almost passionate devotion, equal only to the one that she cherished for her son. But the world never gave her credit for it, and indeed one can hardly see how it could have done so, considering that, with very rare exceptions, nearly every one who came in contact with the wife of Nicholas II had some good reason to feel offended with her for something she had either said or done.

Under different circumstances the Empress Marie might have helped her daughter-in-law and guided her amidst the intricacies of

St. Petersburg society. But the Empress was entirely absorbed in her own grief for her husband, a grief which she felt more inclined to share with her numerous personal friends than with the young, timid, and coldly disdainful girl who was to take her place upon the throne. Alexandra therefore acquired preconceived notions as to the people who had surrounded the late Emperor and were still clustering about his widow, and her imagination endowed them with all lands of vices and defects they did not possess. Here again, her undoing, because this is what it came to in the long run, was due to her far too serious temperament, which made her see crimes in what was often nothing but peccadilloes, and also to that exaggerated sense of her own importance which required all the world to weep whenever she happened to be shedding tears.

The late Empress's greatest and only friend, Madame Viroubova, in some memoirs which she has published, tells us that Alexandra was most unhappy the first year she spent in Russia, and that it had left upon her mind sad impressions which no later circumstance could efface. As proof of the state of her feelings, she gives us the text of a letter written by the Empress, after her marriage, to one of her friends in Germany, the Countess Rantzau, lady-in-waiting to Princess Henry of Prussia, in which among other things she says:

"I feel myself completely alone, and I am in despair that those who surround my husband are apparently false and insincere. Here nobody seems to do his duty for duty's sake, or for Russia, but only for his own selfish interests and for his own advancement. I weep and I worry all day long, because I feel that my husband is so young and so inexperienced. He does not realize how they are all profiting at the expense of the State. "What will come of it in the end ? I am alone most of the time. My husband is occupied all day and he spends his evenings with his mother."

This last remark is not altogether correct and sets one wondering whether even in these early days after her marriage Alexandra had already assumed that role of a much persecuted, abused, and misunderstood woman, to which, in after years, she was to adhere so persistently, or whether she was so jealous that she even grudged the few hours — they were very few — which her husband sacrificed to the welfare of the State by attending to its business; because when we glance through the Emperor's diary, we find that far from leaving his wife alone, he used to spend most of his time with her. Day after day in this diary we read entries as the following:

"December 2nd, 1894, — Count Scheremetieff lunched with us; then, at half past two, in the big ball-room, I gave up dear papa's uniforms to the different regiments of which he was honorary chief. Afterwards we drove out with dear Alix. We dined at eight o'clock, and then played four hands on the piano in bur own rooms."

"December 4th, Sunday.— After our morning coffee, we went with Alix in the garden for a walk. The morning was fine and clear, 12° of cold. At eleven o'clock we went to mass, and then lunched with Xenia, Sandro, and Kostia. We drove out, and on our way stopped to see Aunt Eugenie. We had tea and remained alone in our room downstairs until eight o'clock. I had a lot of papers to read which bored me to death, because I would so much like to have more time to give to my beloved little soul Alix."

"December 29th, Thursday.— To-day we got up early, and on that account I was able to get through in the morning with all I had to do, and then to go out for a walk. I received Dournovo, Fredericks, Richter, and Avellane. We had to lunch in a hurry at half past twelve, with Alix. Then I went to the Academy of Sciences for its yearly meeting, which was not remarkably interesting but lasted a little under an hour, so that at two o'clock I was back home. I received Rennenkampf, then we went with Alix for a drive, and at half past four Aunt Sania came to see us. We had tea alone together, and dined at eight o'clock with George, who was on duty. Afterwards we went with my dear little wife for a drive on the islands and as far as the point. The evening was beautiful and the drive most pleasant. "We reached home at half past eleven o'clock."

On March 15, 1895, too, we find the following remarks in this amazing record of a sovereign's life and way of spending his time:

"Alix did not feel well all day, and lay on her sofa in her room. We went for a drive together. . . . We dined at eight o'clock, afterwards sat in my study, and I read aloud to her. I cannot express the happiness I find in those quiet evenings, alone with my dearly loved wife. And my heart makes me thank God for having granted me such happiness, complete beyond words."

This does not tally at all with the complaints of the young Empress to her German friend, but her letter to the Countess Rantzau discloses the curious state of her mind, which had begun in the Crimea and had become acute during the long journey through Russia, in the funeral train which was bearing towards the grim fortress of St. Peter and St. Paul, in St. Petersburg, the mortal remains of Alexander III, a journey of which the weariness was beguiled by numerous small intrigues that might have developed into importance but for the presence of the then Prince and Princess of "Wales, who had arrived post-haste from England to be with the Princess's sister, the Empress Marie, during this supreme trial of her life. The Prince was perhaps the only man in complete possession of his common sense during this trying and painful ordeal, and it was said at the time that but for his tactful intervention, more than one family quarrel would have robbed the funeral of Alexander III of its dignity. It was also rumoured that it was he who, together with the Princess of Wales, had persuaded the widowed Empress that the best thing for everybody would be to have the marriage of the young Emperor solemnized after his father's burial had taken place, in spite of the mourning period imposed upon the Court for the late Tsar. Finally his advice prevailed, and the Princess Alix, as people persisted in calling her, in spite of her new title of Grand Duchess, was told to prepare for her nuptials, which were going to be celebrated almost immediately.

She did not reply to this communication. Probably she knew already that the young Emperor had been but too glad to accept his uncle's suggestions on this important subject, but she had also begun to realize that the best thing she could do in her own interest was to remain silent. So she merely bowed her head and said nothing, appearing perfectly willing to submit to everything that was being decided for her. She raised no objection to the plans which were proposed to her, and she appeared as the very incarnation of absolute submission to the decisions of her new relatives, tier manner all through the sad days that had followed upon the demise of Alexander III was absolutely perfect, but it always gave one the impression of not being natural. She seemed constantly to be repeating a lesson which she had learned by heart, but the sense of which she had not grasped. There was neither kindness nor spontaneity in her actions; they were all performed in an automatic fashion, which robbed them of the very effect she wanted to produce, and although her dignity left nothing to be desired, one would have liked her to be less of a statue, and more frank and familiar toward those with whom she was to live. Still, there existed at the time a firm determination to find everything she did or said quite right, so criticisms, when they were heard, did not meet with any response.

Nevertheless, the fact that such criticisms had been launched against her somehow reached the ears of the future Empress, and they rankled. She was a woman of quick impulses, with a vindictive nature, who rarely went back upon the judgments she had once uttered. She took for granted that everybody in Russia, as she wrote to the Countess Rantzau, was thinking only of selfish interests and personal advancement. In this appreciation she was vastly mistaken, because at no period of her history was Russia so free from the vice of greed as during the short reign of Alexander III, whose friends and entourage had always been absolutely above suspicion, a fact for which Alix of Hesse gave them no credit at all; which was her misfortune, not theirs. By her conduct she alienated the sympathies of faithful servants of the Romanoff dynasty, and the result of her unjust suspicions was that as time went on she surrounded herself with persons who were guilty of the very sins she had falsely attributed to those who had displeased her, but who knew how to conceal them under the cloak of flattery and abject adulation.

There was one thing that the future Empress did not understand, and which probably she would have grasped had she had a few years' probation as the wife of the heir to the Russian throne. For years, nay, centuries, there were certain families who had enjoyed Imperial favour uninterruptedly, and who had acquired through it a certain independence of thought, conduct, and speech. It was not expected of a Count Vorontzoff or a Count Scheremetieff or a Prince Dolgorouky that he play the sycophant before the Tsar or keep silent when he thought he had some good advice to offer him. They were men who were friends of their monarch as well as devoted and faithful subjects, and they were far too high-born to stoop to the position of flatterers, or to adopt a servile attitude. In that they differed from German nobles, whose manner toward their sovereigns was far more respectful and far more tinted with obedience than those of Russians descended from the old Boyars. Alix of Hesse did not realize the difference, and she resented what she considered a lack of deference. Very likely, as I have said, she would not have done so had she gone through the initial stage of a Grand Duchess Tsarevna and learned through personal contact to know and understand Russian society before she was called upon to take its lead. This last circumstance had a great deal to do with the total misunderstanding which finally divided her from the people who would have proved the firmest supporters of the throne when danger threatened it if she had known how to conciliate them and how to keep their affection.

Then again, she had too much time to brood over matters which disturbed her equanimity. During those sad days in Livadia, she was left alone most of the time ; her sister was the only person in whom she could confide freely, and even with her she did not feel entirely at her ease, having discovered that the Grand Duchess Elizabeth, and especially the latter's husband, the Grand Duke Serge, would have liked to play an important part at her Court and to influence her, and through her the Emperor. This was precisely what the Princess Alix did not intend to allow them, or anyone else for that matter, to do, because she wanted her own influence to be paramount. She was clever enough to have discovered the weak points in the character of her future husband, and she had made up her mind, if not to rule him, at least to lead him to look at things from her own special point of view. At the same time she lacked the intelligence to judge of men and of things with a broad mind, to make allowances for differences of opinion and of breeding, and to recognize, in her eagerness for reforms, that before attempting to lay down the law to others, one must learn to know people, to understand their idiosyncrasies, and, above all, to avoid wounding their vanity or their hearts. This motherless girl had lacked a mother's tenderness all through her childhood and youth, and had always more or less been thrown upon the mercy of strangers. This, of course, left its mark on her character, and if one adds her immense sense of her own importance, one cannot be surprised if she failed to attract the Russian people, and herself to be attracted by them.

Then it must also be conceded that her position during those weeks which preceded her marriage was an extremely embarrassing one. Here she was, the future sovereign of one of the greatest realms in Europe, yet a nobody, completely eclipsed by her mother-in-law, aunts, and cousins. Her fiancé was not a man on whom she could rely, and altogether she seemed to occupy the place of a sheep about to be led to slaughter. This did not please her; indeed, she would not have been human had she not resented it. Yet this much justice must be rendered her: she did her very best to accommodate herself in silence to circumstances, displaying a spirit of meekness which surprised the few in St. Petersburg who knew her. She allowed others to fix the date of her wedding ; she did not object when the question of her trousseau came to be discussed and she found that it would have to be ordered in accordance with fixed rules, without being permitted to say whether or not she liked the things it contained. She regularly received religious instruction from Father Yanischeff, which seemed to interest her, and she tried to efface herself as much as possible. Again, when the question of her residence came up and the Emperor suggested that they might live in the Anitchkoff Palace with his mother, until their own apartments in the Winter Palace were ready for them to occupy, she immediately consented, with the nice remark that of course "it would not do to leave mamma with another empty place at table so soon after her great sorrow and loss." All this was very pretty and sweet, but perhaps not quite so well meant as spoken.

This lack of a separate establishment was one of the greatest mistakes made at the beginning of the married life of Nicholas II and his young consort. One fails to understand why things could not have been arranged differently. Surely there were apartments in the immense Winter Palace which might have been got ready for them until their permanent ones had been redecorated and furnished. This living in four small rooms, because this is what it practically amounted to, was not conducive to harmony, and perhaps the relations between Alexandra and her mother-in-law would have been better if the two ladies had not spent these months under the same roof, criticizing each other and more or less thwarting each other in the daily details of their life in common; and, besides, there was a lack of dignity in this arrangement which the youthful Empress naturally resented as time went on. It could not have been pleasant to her, for instance, whenever she had to give an audience, to have to ask the Dowager for the use of one of her drawing-rooms for the purpose. It could not have been agreeable to find that she had not even sufficient room in her apartment to store her trousseau and other possessions, and that her maids were put more or less under the orders of those of her mother-in-law. All this was irritating, to say the least. On the whole, Alexandra showed herself extremely patient, but friction could not be altogether avoided, friction that would never have occurred had a suitable residence been set apart for the Emperor and his bride from the very first day of their marriage.

This day had been awaited with eager interest by St. Petersburg society as well as by the whole of Russia. For one thing, it was the first time since Peter the Great that a reigning sovereign was leading a bride to the altar. Then again, it was generally felt that this new reign was bound to bring about some reforms in the internal administration and government of the country. Autocracy had outlived itself, and the intelligent part of the Russian people realized, with very few exceptions, that the time had come when old traditions would have to be set aside and the country put upon the same plane as other European countries where parliamentary rule had proved beneficial rather than the reverse. The fact that the new Empress had been educated in England spoke in her favour in the eyes of some, and while perhaps it was not so acceptable to others, yet it gave all parties the idea that she would never prove a stumbling-block in the way of intelligent reforms. Then, if the truth must be told, there was in the air a feeling of distinct relief at the removal of the iron hand of Alexander III, although this feeling was confined exclusively to the upper classes and to what was called the intelligentsia, because the peasants sincerely loved and mourned ,the dead Emperor, shrewder in this than the well-educated people, who did not realize till much later all that the land had lost by the demise of one of the best monarchs it had ever known, and certainly the most honest one.

Altogether there was a great deal of curiosity concerning the new reign, and especially the new Empress. People had seen her in the fortress during the funeral ceremonies for the dead Tsar, when her slight, deeply veiled figure had stood behind the Empress Marie, in an attitude of humble submission. She had, of course, spoken to no one, and no one had been able to approach her, but the quiet dignity of her whole demeanour had been very striking and had won her the sympathy of many, so that on her wedding-day crowds gathered round the Winter Palace to catch a glimpse of her, while in the palace itself not only the whole of Court society in St. Petersburg and Moscow, but also representatives of all classes of the nation, who had come from far and near, were assembled, awaiting the lovely bride who they all hoped would become just as popular as her mother-in-law had been during the years when she had sat next to Alexander III on the Russian throne.

And yet, in spite of this eagerness to welcome the new Empress, there was something exceedingly sad in the atmosphere of the palace. People who noticed it attributed it to the unusual circumstances under which the marriage was being celebrated, but when remembered now, one cannot help thinking that it was one of those premonitions of evil which take place sometimes and awaken the hearts of people to the sense of an approaching danger. A cloud of some sort seemed to hover over everybody and to damp the enthusiasm of the public. But when the bridal procession appeared, it vanished for one brief moment in the sudden enthusiasm inspired by the transcendent beauty of the bride.

This wedding-day of hers was the one supreme tour in Alexandra Feodorovna's life, the one great tour of triumph she was ever to know. As she walked slowly, led by the Emperor, through the vast halls and galleries of the "Winter Palace, in her silver brocade gown with a long mantle of cloth of gold trailing from her shoulders and carried by chamberlains and Court officials, and with the diamond crown of the Russian Grand Duchess on the beautiful gold hair of her head, wrapped in the folds of her lace veil, she was a vision of loveliness. Everybody was dazzled with the beauty of her figure and face, with the grace of her movements, the dignity of her whole demeanour. One exclamation greeted her, in which there was not one discordant voice: "How beautiful! How perfectly beautiful!" And in that minute of intense emotion, the love of a whole nation was thrown at her feet; would that she had only known it or understood how to appreciate the homage.

The marriage itself went off according to the ceremonial, and nothing occurred to mar its magnificence. A long array of illustrious guests came from afar to attend it, among others the Prince and Princess of Wales, the Queen of Greece, and most of the relatives of the bride and bridegroom, including the former's brother, the Grand Duke of Hesse, with his young wife, who did not guess that one day she would find herself the consort of the pretender to her sister-in-law's newly acquired throne. The Empress Dowager also did not deny herself the joy of witnessing her son's nuptials, and, laying aside the robes of her widowhood for the day, walked on the arm of her aged father, the King of Denmark, dressed in plain white, but with a firm step, in spite of the intense emotion which must at times have overpowered her. She it was who first came to congratulate the newly wedded pair; she it was also who, an hour later, awaited them at the head of the stairs of the Anitchkoff Palace, and who tenderly led them to the rooms which they were to occupy for about a year, as, for some mysterious reason, their apartments in the Winter Palace could not be ready for them earlier.

Before her marriage and during the few days previous which she had spent in St. Petersburg, the Princess Alix had been living with her sister and brother-in-law, the Grand Duke and Grand Duchess Serge, and somehow the distrust which it was said she had felt in regard to them when she arrived in Livadia disappeared. She became very affectionate towards them, and seemed to listen to their advice more than had been expected, which fact was quickly discovered and commented upon by the numerous enemies of the Grand Duke, who immediately launched against him the accusation of trying to rule Russia through his sister-in-law. Whether true or not, this reproach clung to him and brought him into conflict with another member of the Romanoff family, the Grand Duke Alexander Michailovitch, the husband of the Grand Duchess Xenia, the sister of Nicholas II, who in his turn, through his wife, did his very best to influence the young Emperor. Thus, from the very outset, Alexandra Feodorovna found herself confronted with a palace intrigue, the significance of which her ignorance of Russian society prevented her from realizing, so that she herself finally became entangled in it; against her will, to be sure, but entangled none the less.

NOTES

1 Appendix I.
2 The Duke of Clarence.

3 The Grand Duchess Marie Pavlovna.
4 The Kaiser.
5 The Duchess of Edinburgh.
6 Victor Hugo.

CHAPTER II

THE NEW EMPRESS

A NEW reign had begun, and after its first hours of emotion had passed away, people began to wonder how it would develop. St. Petersburg was full of rumours, and of people from all parts of Russia to be present at the obsequies of the late Tsar, and who had stayed on to witness the nuptials of his successor. Deputations from all provinces of the Empire had flocked to the capital in order to congratulate the new sovereign on his accession to the throne, and of course had brought along with them handsome and valuable presents. The question arose how to present them, and requests for audiences came pouring in, so that the young Emperor, in spite of the seclusion in which he had announced it was his intention to remain during the whole period of mourning for his father, had perforce to say he would receive at least the representatives of the nobility and of the various *zemstvos*, or local councils of the country.

Just at this moment an incident took place which at first was kept quiet, and which for the sake of everybody it would have been well to leave unnoticed. The *zemstvo* of the government of Tver, always known for its Liberal tendencies, sent an address of condolence to Nicholas II, and of good wishes on his accession. This address[1] when one reads it now in the light of subsequent events, seems very mild indeed, and even then sensible, reasonable people could not find anything in it that was wrong or disrespectful. Nevertheless, it caused quite a flutter in official circles, where some Ministers declared that it formulated an attack on the very principle of autocracy. This, however, was far from being the case, though it must be conceded that the document in question was in its way a remarkable one, being the first attempt on the part of the Russian public to try to bring its monarch to the comprehension of the real needs of the nation over which he ruled.

This address as a whole was irreproachable, but a few words in it excited the anger of the then Minister of the Interior, who reported on them to the Emperor, and qualified the entire document not only as a dangerous precedent but as an instigation to revolt against autocracy. Nicholas II, always so easy to influence, took to heart this so-called attempt to question his rights and privileges, and declared that the *zemstvo* of Tver ought to be taught a lesson by some expression of his displeasure being conveyed to its members. The Minister added to the Imperial words a few of his own, embodying his personal feelings on the subject, and very soon the whole of St. Petersburg became aware of the incident, and of course freely commented upon if. If the government had been wise, it would have passed it over in silence, as absolutely devoid of any significance. But then governments are not only seldom wise, but generally the last to see the writing on the wall, which prophesies the fall of dynasties and the destruction of the mighty.

Looking back on this incident of the address of the *zemstvo* of Tver and what followed upon it, it is impossible not to connect it with the final tragedy which swept the Romanoffs off their throne and led to the murder of Nicholas II and his family under the atrocious circumstances now known to the world. This incident proved to be the beginning of the end; it was the first spade-thrust in digging the grave into which so many things one had thought eternal were buried for ever.

St. Petersburg talked, but still it was not prepared for the consequences of this unlucky address. People had believed that the many comments to which it had given rise would die a natural death, as so many other things widely discussed had done in their time. The attention of the public was drawn to the announced reception of the various delegations that had come to the capital to congratulate the newly married Imperial pair, and one wondered how it would pass. It entered no one's head that Nicholas II would choose this occasion to administer his first rebuke to his people, and do it in such a ruthless manner. The delegations were received in the throne room of the Winter Palace, and when the sovereigns entered it, the first thing that struck and painfully surprised the assembly was the mourning worn by the Empress. There existed a superstition in Russia against a bride receiving congratulations in a black dress; white was the colour generally chosen for occasions of the kind. When one saw Alexandra Feodorovna appear in her crepe gown and long veil, a murmur of disapproval ran through the throng, and some persons whispered that she who had entered her capital in mourning and behind a coffin was surely going to bring misfortune along with her; that wedding bells mixed with funeral's tolling meant a bad omen for everybody, the country included.

The Tsar and his consort took their places in front of the throne, and the Minister of the Interior presented the various deputations from the different Russian provinces, who humbly and dutifully offered the monarch the traditional bread and salt, on wonderfully beautiful silver and gold plates. Then there was a moment of silence which at last was broken by Nicholas II, who, after glancing at a paper he had at the bottom of his cap, addressed himself to the assemblage in the following words:

"I am glad to see here the representatives of all the different classes of the nation, gathered to express to me their submissive and loyal feelings. I believe in those feelings, which are felt in every Russian heart. But it has come to my knowledge that during the last months there have been heard in some assemblies of the *zemstvos* the voices of those who have indulged in the *senseless dreams that the zemstvos could be called to participate in the government of the country*. I want every one to know that I will concentrate all my strength to maintain, for the good of the whole nation, the principle of absolute autocracy, as firmly and as strongly as did my lamented father."

M. Izvolsky, former Russian Ambassador in Paris and Minister of Foreign Affairs, in his book of interesting memoirs, tries to excuse Nicholas II for this extraordinary outburst, and in the desire to clear the memory of the unfortunate sovereign, tells us that the young Emperor had hesitated a long time before speaking *so firmly* and thus offending irremediably the delegates of the *zemstvos*; but that it was M. Pobedonostseff who had persuaded him that he owed it to the memory of his father solemnly to affirm his intention to keep intact the principle of absolute autocracy. He adds that it was the same M. Pobedonostseff who had "written the text of this unfortunate speech and handed it to Nicholas II as the latter was entering the throne room, without having given him the opportunity of reading it beforehand.

One can understand and admire the loyalty of M. Izvolsky, who fries to defend the memory of the monarch whom he served, and from whom he received many proofs of kindness, but the facts were entirely different from what he says, and this unfortunate speech of the young Tsar, which, as M. Izvolsky himself is obliged to admit marked the beginning of the misunderstanding that all through his reign never ceased to exist between the sovereign and the Russian nation, was entirely composed and written out by Nicholas II himself, and this against the advice of his mother., uncles, and the one or two people to whom he had spoken of his intention, and, last but not least, against the advice of this same M. Pobedonostseff, who had wanted the Emperor merely to thank the different delegates he was receiving for their loyal sentiments, without going at all into politics. This was told me by the Procurator of the Holy Synod himself, who was the first to deplore an "outburst of temper" as he called it, which was to arouse such bitterness throughout the Empire and to give rise to so many useless discussions, which only helped to destroy the prestige of the sovereign and of his dynasty.

Three days after this memorable discourse the Emperor asked General Tcherevine, the head of the Okhrana, and the most trusted friend and adviser of Alexander III, what the public had said and was thinking about this speech, to which question he received the following diplomatic reply: "People generally think that it was a notable feat." That is just what I wanted," said the Tsar; "I only expressed my personal ideas."

It would be difficult to convey the impression produced all over Russia by this first public utterance of the young monarch in whom so many hopes had been centred; the world, surprised and grieved, tried immediately to find a scapegoat on whom it could throw the responsibility for this unlucky performance. As fate would have it, it was upon the young Empress that fell the suspicion of having instigated it. Vague rumours concerning her haughtiness of temper and arrogance of character, and her dislike of contradictions, suddenly took form, and she was accused of prompting her husband to show himself a tyrant. She was said to dislike Russia, to feel contempt for it and for its traditions and customs, and such trifles as her not having discarded her mourning on the day when she was receiving congratulations on her marriage were cited as examples of her indifference to Russian prejudices and to Russian ways. Society judged her harshly, and while the public feeling all over the land revolted against the menace contained in her husband's words, the smart set of St. Petersburg, and of Moscow, discussed her personal conduct, accusing her of having tried to avenge herself for supposed slights by trying to make the people feel that she and the Emperor were their masters, and harsh ones if the need ever arose.

The loyal elements of Russian society had been staggered by the rebuff they had received. They felt bitterly ashamed that such a reproof should have been administered to them before foreigners, as Poles and Germans were considered. They began to question the future, and to wonder what it held in store for them, for the country in general, and for the dynasty in particular. The *intelligentsia* recalled the wise if strong rule of Alexander III. At least with him people knew what to expect; he would never have thrown so ruthlessly at his subjects the gauntlet of discord and strife. A general sense of consternation prevailed everywhere ; one effect was rousing to action the extreme Nihilist and Anarchist parties, who had kept quiet during the preceding reign, but who now saw an opportunity of trying to overthrow the dynasty, and tried to use it.

One week after the admonition of Nicholas II to his subjects, an open letter was addressed to him by the Revolutionary Executive Committee of Geneva,[2] the chiefs of which hastened to return to Russia to begin again the work they had been compelled to keep in abeyance. Thousands of copies of this letter were scattered all over the country, and one day the Emperor found one on his desk, without the person who had put it there ever being discovered, a sure proof that even in the vicinity of the sovereign the extreme parties had servants ready and willing to fulfil their mandates.

Read to-day in the light of all that followed upon it, this letter may be considered as the first warning of the terrible events that finally drove the Romanoff dynasty from its throne. It also sounded the knell of any hopes some people might have had that the reign of Nicholas II would prove the beginning of an era of those reforms Russia so much needed. It began the misunderstanding which, after that fatal speech, never ceased to exist between him and his subjects. Russia ceased to believe in her Tsar, while the latter was only angered by the general disapproval of his actions, which he felt existed all over the country, though at that time no one dared to hint to him that such was the case. Two systems had stood face to face for a few minutes, and challenged themselves to a mortal duel, as was said in this memorable letter, and it became henceforward a question of strength and endurance between them, until the moment when one of them would succumb.

Whether as a consequence of the speech, or for some other reason, troubles broke out a few days later in the University and Technological Institute in St. Petersburg, and angry students made a great disturbance in the streets, even before the Anitchkoff Palace, the residence of the Emperor.

These manifestations were quickly subdued by the police, but they left a feeling of great uneasiness behind them. Discussing the situation at the time with General Tcherevine, one of my best friends, who, being at the head of the political police of the Empire, could judge better than anyone else the intricacies of the situation, I asked him whether he thought that a revolutionary movement had any chance of succeeding in Russia. "Not now," he replied, "but in another twenty years it will be a different thing, and if we get entangled in a foreign war, which God forbid, then perhaps it will be even sooner that changes will take place in our land." A strange prediction, almost uncanny in its accuracy, because it was exactly twenty-two years later that Nicholas II signed his abdication in the ancient city of Pskoff, driven to it by the unpopularity of the political system which he incarnated in his person, even more than by the reverses of the War.

"While all these things were taking place, the young Empress had kept very quiet; no one heard her express any opinion as to what was going on around her. Perhaps she did not feel sure of her ground, and was afraid to say anything, in view of the fact that she had her mother-in-law at her elbow. The Dowager Empress was the most popular personage in Russia, beloved by everybody, and her word carried immense weight. It was but natural that her son should consult her rather than his young wife, still a stranger in her new country, and he was supposed to do so far more than was really the case. The fact of the matter was that Nicholas II was one of the most secretive beings on earth, and although he may for convenience' sake have sought his mother's advice, he certainly did not act upon it. The Empress Marie had been one of those whom the young Tsar's speech had most painfully impressed. Moreover, she knew extremely well all that was going on in St. Petersburg society, and was perfectly aware of the storm of indignation that her son's words had aroused. She made no secret of it among her special friends, with the result that the rumour was started that it had been Alexandra who had persuaded her husband to express himself in such strong language. In reality she had had nothing to do with it, but it is not easy to fight against preconceived opinions and ideas, and the world began to regard the wife of Nicholas II as his evil genius. Somehow she came to realize that she was unpopular, and, being possessed of the best intentions, she could not help being dreadfully hurt by the injustice of which she was the victim. This did not add to her affection for the society of St. Petersburg, whom she taxed with frivolity and unkindness. Unfortunately she lacked the tact to keep this opinion to herself.

Family frictions added to this feeling of discontent which was growing upon her. All kinds of petty matters cropped up to embitter her relations with her mother-in-law and with other members of the Imperial house, with whom she did not get on at all, principally because she had tried to impress them with the importance of her own position. The grand duchesses began to question the right of this young and inexperienced girl to dictate to them, and they resented the fact that she would not receive them when they called upon her unless they had previously asked her to do so. She was accused of trying to estrange her husband from his relatives, and unfortunately there was some truth in this reproach. Then again, she could not get on with her own ladies-in-waiting, of whom she changed several in the course of a few months, until at last it was generally felt that she was neither easy to please nor easy to serve, and that she treated her ladies just a little worse than she did her maids.

The result was that when it came to find someone to replace the Countess Lamsdorff and the Princess Bariatinsky, who in turn had been in attendance on the Empress, it was some time before anyone willing to undertake the job could be found. At last a charming woman, the Princess Obolensky, accepted the position, and contrived, thanks to her tact, to maintain her position until the Revolution, but towards the last even she had become impatient with the difficulties of the situation and would have asked to be relieved from her duties if the War had not caused her to postpone her decision. She did not belong to those who desert a sinking ship.

Of course all the ladies who composed the cream of St. Petersburg society had asked to be presented to the new Tsarina. She received a few, in an icy manner, and they did not return from their interview with favourable feelings for the consort of their sovereign. Then there was held one solemn drawing-room in the "Winter Palace at which the whole official and smart world was presented to Alexandra Feodorovna, but she hardly said a word to anybody, and people, when they returned home, complained of her lack of graciousness, and of the insolent manner in which she had received them. St. Petersburg society had been used to different things; they had always been treated with a kindly familiarity by the last two empresses, who knew everybody, their family connexions, and their family history, and who gave themselves much trouble always to say something nice to all the ladies who had come to pay their respects. Alexandra Feodorovna, instead of going to any trouble, contented herself with saying two or three words to those who were introduced to her, and not always even this. She had an official way of extending her hand to be kissed which used to exasperate those whom this action seemed to invite to a gesture of humility that had entirely gone out of fashion, except for young girls on their first presentation. Little by little, all these small incidents did their work of adding something to the growing unpopularity of the young Empress, while all those whom she had wounded or hurt turned toward her mother-in-law, and declared that she, and she alone, was and would always remain *their* Empress. As for this haughty, cold German, she had better learn that Russian ladies were not meant to be treated like dirt under her feet!

There were, of course, other persons who maintained that all this was not true, and that, on the contrary, Alexandra Feodorovna was a charming, amiable woman, who all through was being cruelly misunderstood, but somehow their number became smaller and smaller every day, until at last they could be counted on the fingers. Some more level-headed people said that it was impossible to judge of the young Tsarina until she had become more familiar with Russian life and customs. She had been handicapped by the sad circumstances surrounding her marriage, and it would be wiser, before passing harsh judgments upon her, to wait until the Court mourning was at an end and she had been allowed to take her place in society, when she would be able to show what were her intentions in regard to its leadership.

But in the meanwhile two incidents occurred which again set tongues wagging and drove people to take a stand for or against their new sovereign's wife. The first was connected with the precedence which was to be given her in the official Church prayers, when the question arose which of the two empresses should be named first in the Liturgy, Marie Feodorovna declared that, the order of precedence of a dowager having been determined by a family ukase of Paul I, which granted her the first place before the reigning Empress, the same thing ought to apply to the public prayers said in church. To this Alexandra objected, and at last the Synod was consulted, deciding against her mother-in-law, to the irritation of all those who were trying to relegate the young wife of the Tsar to a secondary position. Nicholas was between two fires, but nothing his mother could say had any effect upon him or induced him to disavow his wife. The Synod had decided, and in accordance with its commands, the name of Alexandra followed immediately that of Nicholas II on the books of the Church.

It was a triumph, the first Alexandra had obtained since she had arrived in Russia. Immediately afterwards another matter cropped up, concerning the crown jewels. These had always been kept in the strong room of the "Winter Palace until the accession of Alexander III, when, in deference to the wishes of his wife, he had allowed them to be removed to the Anitchkoff Palace, where he resided, and put side by side with the private ornaments of the Empress Marie, who was thus spared the annoyance of applying to the State Treasurer whenever she wanted to adorn herself with the diamonds and pearls which were the patrimony of the Romanoffs. Upon her widowhood, the Minister of the Imperial Household drew Nicholas II's attention to this anomaly, and suggested that the crown jewels had better be returned to their old place in the strong room of the Winter Palace, to be taken out whenever the reigning Empress cared to wear them. To this Marie Feodorovna objected, saying that her daughter-in-law had no right to put on these ornaments until she had been crowned, and that, besides, her husband in his will had left her the guardianship of these treasures, which was partly true, although not quite. Scenes without end followed, and at last the young Empress, goaded into exasperation, exclaimed that the jewels could remain with her mother-in-law or go back to the Treasury; she did not mind, because she would never wear any of them for anything in the world, having enough diamonds and pearls to satisfy her.

This, however, could not be, so after stormy scenes the Empress Dowager had to yield to necessity, and the famous necklace of diamonds that had adorned Catherine II, and the great tiara with the pink brilliant which was one of the finest in existence, were returned to their old strong boxes, out of which they were very seldom taken, because Alexandra Feodorovna kept to her decision not to wear them except on very rare and official occasions, when she really could not refuse. But the incident did not tend to promote harmony between the two Imperial ladies who had been concerned in it.

All this, nevertheless, blew away, as such things generally do, and the next matter to occupy public attention was the expected accouchement of the young Empress; the hoped-for birth of an heir to all the pomp and the glory of the Romanoffs. By that time the palace of Tsarskoye Selo, as well as a suite of rooms in the Winter Palace in St. Petersburg, had been got ready for the Imperial couple, and the public expected that the happy event which was so eagerly looked forward to would take place in the capital. But this was not to be, because Alexandra Feodorovna had expressed the wish to remain in the country for it. This decision of hers was not received very enthusiastically by the nation, but of course it was not to be disputed and the Empress Mother herself, although she would have preferred to have the expected birth take place in St. Petersburg, reconciled herself to the inevitable, and took up her residence at the Tsarskoye Selo palace, to be in immediate attendance on her daughter-in-law, as soon as the latter needed her.

Needless to relate, there was much anxiety in Court circles as the time for the great event drew near. People began to speculate on the consequences which the birth of an heir to the Imperial throne might have, because it was assuredly going to be an heir; the idea that such might be the case never crossed the mind of anyone. Girls were rarities in the Romanoff family, in which as a rule the foirstborn had always been a son, so that all preparations were made to welcome a baby Tsarevich.

The Empress herself looked forward with great anxiety to her first step in the career of motherhood. She had by that time become aware that she had not obtained the firm hold upon the affections of the Russian nation which she had hoped to win, and she believed that she would do so, once she had a son. The birth of this boy, moreover, would increase her importance in the eyes of her husband, as well as of his family, so that she also never admitted the possibility that her expected baby might prove to be a girl. One may therefore imagine the disappointment she experienced, a disappointment that was shared by the nation at large, when a little daughter, the Grand Duchess Olga, opened her eyes upon a world that was not to show itself kind.

The cannons which had been about to thunder a salute of three hundred shots, as a welcome toi the birth of an heir to the throne, were silent, and the population of St. Petersburg learned that the hopes of its sovereigns had not been fulfilled. The Empress herself grieved, far more than her husband, at this frustration of her dearest ambitions. But she was a woman with a deep sense of duty, imbued with a keen maternal instinct; she took her baby to her heart, and nursed it with the tenderest care. Half her time was spent in the nursery, and she seemed so wrapped up in her child that people began to grumble, and declared that she might very well have trusted more to the experienced nurses and attendants whose task it was to watch over the Imperial children. Alexandra, however, was not one to listen to such reproaches, and she gave herself up entirely to the care of her little daughter, whom she scarcely let out of her sight.

In the meanwhile the period of mourning for the late Emperor had come to an end, and the Court returned to St. Petersburg for the usual New Year's reception, which was also the time when the Empress took possession of her new apartments in the Winter Palace.

Before this, however, there had taken place another of those small incidents that added to the already acknowledged unpopularity of the Empress. It was the custom at the Russian Court for the debutantes of the season to be presented before the New Year to the consort of the sovereign. The Dowager Empress, always considerate of the comfort of others, usually held a reception in honour of these young girls on a day when she happened to come to town, rather than to compel them to take, in company with their mothers, the long journey to Gatschina, where she resided with the Emperor until the eve of the New Year, and this was always very much appreciated. But her daughter-in-law chose to change this custom, and insisted on presentations being made to her at Tsarskoye Selo, whither, on a bitter, cold day, the unfortunate victims had to repair. Of course they grumbled, and of course people said that this lack of consideration on the part of Alexandra Feodorovna was unpardonable. If at least she had been amiable to all the ladies whom she had compelled to take a long journey in order to be admitted to the honour of kissing her hand, one would have tried to forgive her. But this was precisely what she was not; anything stiffer than her attitude could hardly be imagined. The result was that the discontent against her grew apace, and when, for the first time, she presided at the New Year's reception in the Winter Palace, it was noticed that a much smaller number of ladies attended it than had generally done so.

Still, all this might have been accident, and the world awaited with impatience the first great ball of the season, during which it was supposed that the Empress would reveal for the first time her qualities as a hostess, as she would have an absolutely free hand, because her mother-in-law was still in her widow's weeds and lived in absolute seclusion, not attending any festivities whatever. The ball took place, but it proved a failure. The world missed the graceful, slight figure of the Empress Marie, her lovely smile and beautiful, expressive eyes, and that irresistible charm which no one had ever been able to resist. A Court ball without her lost its attraction and animation, and the awkward, shy, and silent young woman who stood in her place did not seem to possess the talent of drawing people to her. The young Empress was at a disadvantage in a ball gown. Her complexion left much to be desired, and she had red arms, red shoulders, and a red face which always gave one the impression that she was about to burst into tears. She knew no one, and she did not seem to wish to know anyone; she danced badly, not caring for dancing; and she certainly was not a brilliant conversationalist. Nothing seemed to interest her, nothing aroused her attention, and her whole appearance suggested one of those Byzantine empresses, stately and solemn, who slowly and with measured tread walked from their palace in Constantinople to the Cathedral of St. Sophia. Everything about her was hieratic, to the very way she dressed in the heavy brocades of which she was so fond, and with diamonds scattered all over her, in defiance of good taste and common sense. She made a splendid figure, hut the world would have preferred less magnificence and a little more heart and charm of manner. The remembrance of the Empress Dowager, and of her kindness and affability, added to the dissatisfaction, and the Court balls which were such a feature of the St. Petersburg season, to which so many people had year after year been looking forward with impatience and eagerness, became dull and uninteresting. Those who attended them felt surrounded by a new atmosphere, deadly dull most of the time, and without that animation which in former days had been such a distinctive feature of these festivities.

St. Petersburg was slowly transforming itself under the influence of the young Empress. At this early period of her married life, there were still to be found persons ready to swallow any kind of insult or studied impoliteness, provided that in the long run it secured for them an invitation to the Winter Palace ; so that the Empress's rudeness was at first passed over, without comment being made, except that it was a pity, a great pity indeed.

The season dragged wearily along, and the Empress made no effort to enliven it. She was at this time going out into society, only on compulsion, as it were, and made no secret of the fact that it bored her immensely to have to be gracious to people for whom she did not care a fig. Even with ambassadors, to whom she was supposed to be particularly polite and attentive, she scarcely exchanged two words, and her thoughts seemed always to be far away. Of course people accused her of having prejudices against them and of being too proud and haughty, but they were wrong, because at that time the Empress really would have liked to please her subjects, but she did not feel sure of her position. However strange it may appear, she felt that people considered her a nonentity, and, besides, outside the care of her baby, she had absolutely nothing to do, except her social duties, which were unfortunately very distasteful to her. Hers was not a nature that could be satisfied with fine dresses, beautiful jewels, and an endless variety and round of gaieties. She neither danced nor rode well; hence, inevitably, comparisons were made between her and her mother-in-law, who had been so passionately devoted to sport and to the ball-room.

In a certain sense the undoing of Alexandra Feodorovna in those early days proved to be her aversion to society. The gay world of St. Petersburg, which at that time had a great deal to do with the moulding of public opinion in Russia, reproached her for refusing to provide it with the pleasures which, until her arrival as its mistress in the Winter Palace, it had enjoyed. Russian society, and especially that of the capital, had always been proud of the wonderful balls which in bygone times had dazzled the foreigners invited to them, and it believed that the sovereign had no right to deprive it of this enjoyment. Then again, these balls and festivities had been some criteria of the social position of those invited to attend them. Some people were bidden to all of them, others to a few, others again to only one, and, according to that, one's place in the gay world of the city of Peter the Great was fixed. A certain looseness in deportment and manners was bound to follow upon their abandonment.

They did not, however, come to an end all at once, but were curtailed and subjected to modifications which did not please those who happened to be the concerned parties. Private theatricals were substituted for balls during this first winter season when Alexandra

Feodorovna did the honours of her husband's Court, theatricals that took place in the private theatre of the Hermitage Palace, and they proved so utterly boring that many people, having sat through the first performance, declared nothing in the world would ever induce them to repeat the torture, so sent their excuses the next time they were bidden to a like entertainment.

Up to that day, no one had ever dreamt of excusing oneself from an Imperial invitation, and a precedent was established which, trivial as it appeared, was nevertheless to lead to far more serious things, because it created the idea in the minds of the public that a command from the sovereign could be disregarded, The first symptom of the carelessness with which Russian society came at last to treat its monarch and his consort was appearing, and of course was to go on increasing until the final catastrophe.

The Empress had no taste in dress, and this also was brought up against her. She liked to array herself most splendidly, but there was no daintiness about her, and the fact that she always designed her own gowns, and insisted on their being made according to her personal directions, was ridiculed everywhere. People recalled the lovely garments with which the Empress Marie had been in the habit of dazzling her friends, and wondered why her daughter-in-law could not have consulted her, or at least appealed to the art of the dressmakers whom her mother-in-law had patronized in the days when she had occupied the Russian throne. It was a curious thing, but the wonderful beauty of the Empress came to be forgotten so quickly that it was hardly mentioned as time went on, while a certain hard expression which set on her classic features was always pointed out as a blemish that nothing could diminish, much less efface. She lost her slight, elegant figure after the birth of her first child, and her complexion also suffered from the ordeal, so that, as a witty though unkind dowager remarked, she always had her colour in the wrong place, which was also true, because the pinkest parts of her person were her arms and neck, a defect about which the world never ceased talking.

As may be imagined from these remarks, the first season of the young Empress did not pass very pleasantly, and could hardly have been termed a success. To make matters worse, she contracted measles before the season was over, and to the wrath of society the last two balls scheduled to take place at Court before its close were cancelled. This caused quite an uproar, as it was remembered that on a like occasion, when the Empress Marie had been ailing with influenza, an entertainment planned before she had fallen ill had nevertheless been held with the Grand Duchess Marie Pavlovna taking the place of the hostess. But Alexandra seemed to be of the opinion that when she was ill the whole world had to do penance for it, repeating thus unconsciously the old saying, at one time current in Warsaw, that when "Augustus II, King of Poland, had drunk too much, all his subjects had perforce to become intoxicated."

It was in this way that the days and months dragged on without adding to the popularity of the consort of Nicholas II. Recalling those early times, one can but regret that there was no one by the side of this young wife and mother who could have tendered her some good advice by inducing her to look upon life and upon the world with more kindly eyes. A few smiles would have cost her so little and brought her so much. But hers was a nature foreign to dissimulation, and she forgot that, being a sovereign, she had no right to air her likes and dislikes, but was condemned by the very loftiness of her position to show herself equally gracious to all who were presented to her, or with whom she came into contact.

She had from the outset expressed her desire to reform St. Petersburg society by introducing some of the earnestness of her own nature. This, of course, had antagonized a good many people, who thought it an arrogance on the part of a Princess who had not had time to become acquainted with the country over which she reigned, to try to dictate to them. But Alexandra, then as always, had an exaggerated idea of her power and importance, and finding the whole atmosphere of Russia distasteful to her, she determined to bring into it some of her German customs. One of her early ideas was to organize a society of handwork, composed of ladies of the Court and society circles, each of whom should make with her own hands three garments a year, to be distributed to the poor. Of course such a society could not exist for any length of time. For one thing, all the independent great ladies, of whom there were many in St. Petersburg, declared that by joining it, it would appear as if they wanted to flatter a sovereign who had not even been polite to them, while others, not perhaps so important, but belonging to the ultra-smart set, said they had no time for such rubbish, so that finally the Empress's society died a natural death, a thing which she resented bitterly, declaring that Russian women cared for nothing but balls and frivolities, and were not interested in the welfare of the masses.

One day when she happened to express herself on the subject to the wife of a high official whom she was receiving in a private audience, the latter, hurt by some remarks of Alexandra, began to give her a lecture. She said it was much to be regretted that Her Majesty had not taken the trouble to inform herself of the work performed by Russian ladies on their country estates, where they looked after hospitals and schools and had induced the peasants to interest themselves in various handicrafts. The Empress looked surprised as well as hurt, and replied that probably they were exceptions, because she did not see how women who danced every night during the winter could think of anything serious in summer, and that, besides, they spent most of it abroad buying dresses for the coming season. The remark was one of those unfortunate utterances which, going from mouth to mouth, made so many enemies, and of these the consort of Nicholas II soon came to have more than she suspected. She knew very well that she was not popular, but attributed the fact to Court intrigues and also to the affection which she was aware her mother-in-law had retained, and probably would always retain. This made her look upon the Dowager Empress as an obstacle in her path, and she would have liked nothing better than to see the latter take up her residence in Denmark, which was suggested by her at one time. But though Marie Feodorovna took to spending several months of each year in her native land, she was bound by too many ties to Russia ever to wish to leave it entirely. And, as time went on, St. Petersburg society came naturally to be divided into two sections, those who surrounded the Empress Dowager and looked up to her for social direction, and a small, very small group composed of people who certainly did not belong to the old Russian aristocracy, and who, in spite of Alexandra Feodorovna's lack of courtesy, clung to her, in the hope that she would further their social **advancement. These toadied to her by means of the most abject Flatteries, the worthlessness** of which she failed to Grasp, so delighted was she to find that they were being at last showered upon her.

In the midst of these intrigues and all this gossip, the first winter season that had found the consort of Nicholas II doing the honours of his Court slowly passed away, and St. Petersburg and Moscow began to prepare themselves for the approaching coronation, which was to take place during the coming month of May.

NOTES

1 Appendix II.
2 Appendix III.

PART TWO

CHAPTER III

SIGNS OF AN APPROACHING STORM

THE coronation of a Tsar of Russia, being the most important event in his existence, invariably took place in circumstances of almost Asiatic pomp and splendour. It was eagerly being looked forward to, and the whole of St. Petersburg society, or at least as many members of it as could afford to, repaired to Moscow to be present at this ceremony. When Alexander III had assumed the diadem of his ancestors, the occasion had been seized as a pretext for a manifestation of loyalty such as few sovereigns had ever had offered to them. But somehow, this time, people affected a curious indifference to the festival, and there was a palpable lack of interest in it, despite the numerous discussions to which it gave rise. To tell the truth, in official circles a certain uneasiness was noticeable, and although no one would have dared to give it voice, there existed a fear that the admitted unpopularity of the Empress might meet with some public rebuff which, to say the least, would have been awkward, especially as representatives of almost every country in the world were expected in Moscow for the festivities. The police took extraordinary precautions to prevent any outbreak of opinion, but of course did so in a guarded manner, so as not to excite suspicion.

A stupendous programme of balls, concerts, dinners, and other entertainments was prepared, and people hoped that nothing would occur to mar the success of the event. How little then did anyone suspect the terrible catastrophe which was to leave upon it a bloody stain!

According to custom, the Emperor and Empress, with all the members of the Imperial family and the foreign guests, were to make a solemn entry into the ancient capital of Russia, and drive in procession through its streets to the Kremlin, stopping on their way to pray at the shrine of the Iversky Virgin, the patroness of Moscow. This procession was one of the most marvellous sights in the world.

Nothing can give an idea of the magnificence of the golden carriages in which rode the Empress and princesses, nor of the dazzling splendour of the uniforms of the various Court officials and military dignitaries taking part in the pageant. The streets were crowded, and every window was alive with people. After a long line of soldiers, followed by chamberlains, masters of ceremonies, and other officials, who all preceded the sovereign, Nicholas II appeared, riding a white horse, surrounded by his family, the royal and Imperial guests, and the members of his household. Hurrahs without number greeted him, whether sincere or not it would have been difficult to say just then, but hurrahs and acclamations that at least sounded as if they were genuine. Then came a squadron of cavalry followed by the immense golden carriage of the Empress Elizabeth Petrovna, the daughter of Peter the Great, a gorgeous thing surmounted by the Imperial Crown, with diamonds glittering on its panels and the handles of its doors: in it rode, all alone, dressed in white, with rows upon rows of pearls around her neck, the Empress Dowager, Marie Feodorovna.

Then occurred the one memorable incident of this memorable day. As soon as the crowds caught a glimpse of the slight figure of the mother of Nicholas II, they burst into one loud cheer, the sounds of which followed her all along her route, a cheer that had something extraordinarily sincere and pathetic, as well as enthusiastic about it; a cheer as of a nation acclaiming its mother as well as its queen. The Empress was visibly moved, and great tears fell on her lap from her beautiful, expressive eyes. The ordeal must have been more than painful to her, with all the remembrances which it could not fail to awaken, because it was just thirteen years since she had driven along that same route, also in a golden carriage, on her way to receive from the hands of her husband the crown of Peter and of Catherine. Now she was about to see it handed to another, one whom she had reason to distrust and to fear, and in whom most probably her motherly heart had scented the greatest danger that had ever threatened the Romanoff dynasty.

Wild were the acclamations, and they seemed as if they would never come to an end, when suddenly they were stopped as if by command. People looked round and wondered what had happened, the more so because the roaring cheers were caught up a little farther ahead as the Empress Mother's carriage proceeded on its way. Their curiosity had not long to wait before it was gratified, because after another squadron of cavalry there appeared another golden chariot, without an Imperial crown surmounting it, the woman it contained not yet having the right to use it, and in that chariot was sitting, also dressed in white, and also covered with jewels, the tall, commanding figure of the young Empress Alexandra, who with drawn lips and red eyes was making her entry into the ancient capital of the Tsars of Muscovy. A solemn, ominous silence followed her on her way. Not a voice was raised, not a hurrah was heard, not a sound was uttered; she might have been a doll being driven to a show, so still were the crowds who a few minutes before had so vociferously hailed her mother-in-law. There was something terrifying in this stoical absence of emotion on the part of a multitude whom one would have expected to show itself enthusiastic over the queenly beauty of the consort of their sovereign. I remember that a man, since dead, who was standing beside me, whispered in my ear: "Look at her; she is beginning to climb the road of her future Calvary!"

Of course the incident was hushed up so far as such things can be. It had been so strangely significant that no one cared to mention it, far less to discuss it. The Empress herself must have felt it acutely, though of course she was too proud to allow herself to talk about it. But the memory of it must have rankled, and she would have been less than human if she had not been embittered against her mother-in-law by this public manifestation of the latter's hold on the affections of the Russian nation, standing in such sharp contrast to her own unpopularity.

Three days later the Tsar and the Tsarina crossed the golden gates of the Cathedral of the Assumption, to be crowned there according to the old ceremonial. And here again the assistants had for the second time the feeling that everything was unreal in this religious festival. One remembered the coronation of Alexander III, and that sovereign coming out of that same church where his son was about to be anointed, with the immense crown of the Russian emperors on his head, with its big diamonds shining and glistening in the sun, the Imperial mantle of cloth of gold lined with ermine falling from his shoulders, and the sceptre firmly grasped in his right hand while the orb lay in the palm of his left. He had been indeed a splendid figure, that Russian monarch, whose gigantic frame seemed a perfect incarnation of the strength and might of the empire at whose head he stood. And the gentle Empress walking behind him, also garbed in her Imperial robes, with her hands clasped as if in prayer, and her eyes lovingly fastened upon him — what a picture those two had made! what an unforgettable picture! It was something more than a monarch one had looked at; it was Russia itself that had appeared before one's eyes, one's dazzled eyes, a great, a wonderful Russia, the Russia of Peter and of Catherine, and of a long, unbroken line of Tsars, all of them mighty, and a few among them great, but certainly none so imposing as the man walking there slowly but with such infinite majesty, such consciousness of his power, and of the duties it carried with it; the man proceeding on his path with that firmness which was never to forsake him — not even during his last hours, when, stricken in the full strength of his manhood, he was told that he must die.

And now his son was standing in his place. Everything seemed the same; one could recognize the same faces and the same people who played a part in the pageant of thirteen years before. Only the central figure had changed. There, where a mighty monarch had presented himself to the cheers and acclamations of his subjects, one saw a frail, small, almost insignificant youth, whose Imperial crown seemed to crush him to the ground, and whose helplessness gave an appearance of unreality to the whole scene ; such unreality, indeed, that when, worn out by fatigue and the weight of his regal appointments, the newly anointed Nicholas II allowed the sceptre to drop from his hand, those who saw it were not surprised at the incident ; only later did they realize the significance it might assume in the eyes of the superstitious, the bad omen they would assume it signified.

And the Empress. What was she doing all through the trying ceremony? What thoughts crowded in her brain while she was kneeling at the feet of her husband, and accepting from him that diadem which in her case was to prove such a crown of thorns? She never spoke of her feelings during that momentous hour in her life; whatever she had felt she kept to herself, and she went through her part of the trying ordeal with great dignity, but also with that bored expression which seldom was absent. Opposite her, standing also on a throne, was the Empress Dowager, whose head was also surmounted by the crown of the Romanoffs. The two ladies appeared as the personification of two different epochs, and the onlooker instinctively felt that behind all this magnificent pageant there lurked danger, an insidious danger, which was slowly creeping along towards those whom it was to engulf in one catastrophe, the like of which the world had never yet witnessed.

Then suddenly the silence was broken by the peals from the belfry of Ivan Veliki which mingled with the roar of the cannons and the shouts of the crowds as the whole world was told that Nicholas II had at last assumed the old diadem of the Romanoffs. Simultaneously with this joyous message, the people who had waited for long hours to catch a glimpse of the young sovereign saw him come out of the Cathedral of the Assumption to start on his tour of the ancient shrines and churches of the Kremlin. They had not seen or noticed the incident of the dropped sceptre; they did not pay any attention to his faltering steps; they only fried to look at him, but whether with love or with fear or with hatred, it was impossible to tell.

The long procession went on its leisurely way, the Emperor and Empress walking under a heavy canopy of golden cloth with ostrich feathers surmounting it and fluttering in the breeze. They ascended the famous Red Staircase leading to the private apartments of the Kremlin, and, turning round, proceeded to salute the crowds according to the ancient ceremonial. But at that moment the sky, which had been cloudy all that day, suddenly darkened, so that one could hardly distinguish the figures of Nicholas II and his consort as they bowed to their assembled subjects, gathered in the interior courtyard of the old fortress, and in a mist these two disappeared, like shadows in a world of shadows, the images of something that had to pass into oblivion.

"What is your impression of all this?" I asked that same evening of a man in whose judgment I had great confidence.

"What impression can I have had? It is the beginning of the end," was the unexpected reply.

And so it was with everybody; a feeling, distinct and clear, that this was the beginning of the end, that we had been looking at something neither we nor anyone else in the world would ever see again. Why did this impression exist? No one could have explained why, but there it was, and one could not get rid of it, it could not be shaken off. Nations as well as men sometimes experience a premonition of what is about to happen to them.

The sadness which, from the very beginning, had hovered over the coronation festivities, persisted in spite of all the gaiety that to the outside world seemed to attend it. Ball followed ball, and there was hardly a moment of interruption amid all these entertainments. Then one morning we were told that the reception which was to take place two days hence at the Austrian Embassy, for which the Ambassador, Prince Liechtenstein, had made huge preparations, had been abandoned owing to the sudden death of the brother of the Emperor Francis Joseph, the Archduke Charles Louis. This caused the first break in the round of festivities that filled the days and nights of delirious Moscow. Some old crones shook their heads and said that it was another bad omen, but they were laughed at for their silly fears, and no one seemed to attach any importance to their words. The French Ambassador, Count de Montebello, was to give an entertainment on the evening before the cancelled Austrian festivity, and no doubt it would make up for the loss of the one with which Prince Liechtenstein had intended to dazzle the world.

This French entertainment was to close another day of strenuous exertion, as the popular festival to which peasants from all parts of

Moscow had been bidden, was to take place in the afternoon. It was to be attended by the Emperor and Empress and all the Imperial family with the exception of the Empress Mother, who did not yet take part in any social entertainments, being still in her widow's weeds, which she had only taken off for the ceremony of her son's coronation. It had been talked about a great deal in advance, and people had been wondering whether Nicholas II would seize this occasion to say some kind words to the numerous deputations of peasants sent by their communities to be present at the gathering.

Suddenly a tale of horror startled the whole town out of its summer stillness. There had been an accident, a sad accident, a panic which had caused a sudden stampede of the vast multitude gathered together on the Khodinka Field near Moscow, and it had been attended by considerable loss of life.

At first the whole thing was treated as an insignificant incident; then gradually the tragedy that had taken place was revealed. Two thousand men, women and children had perished, crushed to death under the feet of frightened people flying from an imaginary danger. It had been something too awful for words, too terrible to relate, the more so because the authorities were trying their best to keep from the sovereign all knowledge of the extent of the calamity. But it could not be suppressed when one saw cart after cart bringing back to the town the bodies of the victims. The outcry against the incompetence of the police was loud and general, and the Moscow authorities were accused of not having taken due precautions to prevent a panic such as that which had taken place. Everybody expected that the French ball would be countermanded as a sign of mourning for the calamity.

This, however, was not so. The Emperor had proceeded in the afternoon to the Khodinka Field as if nothing had happened, and stayed a few minutes there, watching the distribution of presents made in his name to the people who had remained on the scene. To the disaster he did not even allude. The same night he attended with his consort the ball at the French Embassy, much to the surprise of Count de Montebello, who had fully expected to see it cancelled, and he chatted and danced as if nothing had occurred. One may imagine the impression which this indifference produced, an impression which was strengthened when it became known that in their haste to clear the Khodinka Field of the bodies of those who had perished there, the police had thrust some of them under the very pavilion that had been erected for the use of the sovereign and his guests, so that he had actually been standing over the corpses of those who had died, as it were, in honour of him. If the ignorance of the peasants had prevented them from uttering, before they were crushed to death, the words of greeting of the Roman gladiators to the Caesars who were sending them to their doom, the historic *"Ave Caesar, morituri te salutamus,"* it was not because they would not have been appropriate.

The Khodinka catastrophe, apart from the veil of gloom which it threw over the coronation and its rejoicings, had very grave political consequences, one of which was to accentuate the discord which already existed between the Tsar and those of his enlightened subjects who, loving their fatherland and desirous of seeing it prosper, would have liked to find that their sovereign had a true appreciation of the situation and of the needs of the country, and intended to see what he could do to meet them, as well as to cope with difficulties to which in time it would become impossible to close one's eyes. But the conduct of Nicholas II at Moscow, after the calamity which had thrown so many families into mourning, was so heartless that it could not fail to strike a most unpleasant discord in the hearts of his people.

His mother, as soon as the terrible news reached her, hurried to the different hospitals where the bodies and the injured had been brought, and spoke words of consolation to the bereaved and to the injured. Nicholas and his wife went to the French Ambassador's ball, and, in appearance at least, behaved as if nothing untoward had happened on that day. His impassivity, which later became quite notorious, manifested itself for the first time on this sad and memorable occasion. Subsequently it was said that he had been afraid if he countermanded the ball of Count de Montebello, the government of the French Republic would consider it an affront; a groundless fear, if ever there was one, because the festivity might, without inconveniencing anybody, have been put off for twenty-four hours, especially since, as it happened, the following evening was free, having been the one on which Prince Liechtenstein's reception ought to have taken place. But neither the Emperor nor anyone else bethought himself of such a simple solution, with the result that a deplorable impression was created everywhere, even among the peasantry, and many years later it was remembered by them as well as by other witnesses of the catastrophe with its attendant ghastly consequences.

Yet one must be just; Nicholas II was perhaps not so much to blame as those who did not know him may have thought. His was essentially a slow as well as a selfish nature, and it always took him a great deal of time to grasp things another person would have seen at once. Very likely he did not imagine the immensity of the disaster that had overtaken his faithful subjects; very likely, too, he was kept in ignorance of its extent, and it is certain that later on he ordered an inquest to fix the responsibility for it, and sent generous gifts to the surviving victims. But this was done much later, and came at a time when the first impression produced by his behaviour had already done its work and dug a little deeper the abyss which already separated him from Russia and the Russian people.

The few friends he had, indeed, realized this so well that they did their best to try to excuse him, but, unhappily, did it in a most awkward manner. Thus, for instance, in her book of memoirs of the Russian Court, Madame Viroubova, the friend of the Empress, relates that the Emperor, when speaking to her of the Khodinka disaster, told her that at the very time it was taking place, he and the Empress, despite their grief and horror, were obliged to take part in the coronation banquet which had been fixed for that day, and that it was only with difficulty that they had concealed their emotion, having often to hold their napkins to their faces to hide their tears; a fantastic story, because there was no coronation banquet on that day, and because even if there had been one, it would not have been possible for the sovereign to guess that while it was going on, thousands of his subjects were being crushed to death. The excuse does not hold water, and as for any display of emotion by Nicholas II and his consort, every one who was present at the ball of the French Ambassador can testify that they never exhibited the slightest sign.

The fact of the matter is that neither the Tsar nor his wife was capable of grasping the consequences of their actions. More than that, they both suffered from a heartlessness born of the profound egotism which was perhaps one of the strongest links between them, and which deprived them of the faculty of lamenting sorrows that did not touch them personally.

Later on, the Empress became more human, but it was too late, and she could no longer overcome the prejudices which existed against her, prejudices that dated from those early days of her marriage when, having the whole of Russia at her feet, she had disdained it, and herself built the wall which was to divide her from it for ever.

My readers will think that perhaps I am laying too much stress on those first months which followed upon Alexandra Teodorovna's marriage, and on her first mistake s and follies. But in every catastrophe, if one wants to explain it and to understand the circumstances that have brought it about, one must retrace one's steps until one sees the first signs of the storm, as they appeared on the horizon, stand clear before one's eyes and mind ; then, and only then, does it become possible to see whether the misfortune could have been prevented. Nothing is insignificant in those great historical earthquakes which change the fate of nations, and it is impossible to grasp the force of the circumstances which finally drove the Romanoffs from their throne if one has not followed every step of the woman of destiny who was to play such an important part in the downfall. Autocracy would sooner or later have collapsed in Russia, but it might have done so without the torrents of blood which have flowed before and after its destruction; it might have crumbled with dignity, have succumbed with courage, a courage befitting the great thing which, after all, it had really been.

One week after the Khodinka disaster, the sovereigns left Moscow. Somehow no one felt inclined to shout "Hurrah" when bidding them good-bye, and they drove to the railway station amid a profound though respectful silence. Contrary to the general expectation, instead of returning to Tsarskoye Selo or St. Petersburg, they went to the country estate of the Grand Duke and Grand Duchess Serge in the neighbourhood of Moscow, and remained there about a fortnight, to the surprise of everybody. Public rumour had attributed to the Grand Duke, who was Governor-General of Moscow, a large share of the blame for the catastrophe which had marred the coronation of his Imperial nephew and brother-in-law, and which had been compared to the one that had saddened the marriage of Louis XVI and Marie Antoinette; and people expected that he would be taken to task for it, and for the lack of foresight which had made the police neglect the most elementary measures of precaution generally adopted where large crowds are expected to gather together. And most certainly no one had believed that the Emperor, instead of showing his displeasure to the Grand Duke, would honour him with a prolonged visit at his country place. Later on, it was said that this visit had been advised by the Minister of the Interior, who did not wish the country to think that a member of the Imperial family had been made the object of blame by the sovereign. Then again, others said that the Empress, who was supposed to be in a delicate condition, had had an accident which had necessitated a few days' complete rest. All this, however, was mere guesswork, and it is certain that though an inquest was started as to who ought to be blamed for the Khodinka disaster, nothing whatever came of it, except that the general at the head of the Moscow police was told to resign his post, and then, very shortly afterwards, was reinstated in favour, receiving another appointment just as important, if not more so.

The coronation, far from being the beginning of a new epoch, marked the end of a period in Russian history. The real reign of Nicholas II can be said to have beg un after it had taken place, because the old friends and servants of his father left him then, and retired from active service, leaving him free to choose his own councillors and ministers. It was a settled thing in the public mind that his rule was to be an autocratic one, the only doubt about it being whether he really understood what autocracy meant.

But a general discontent was slowly arising, and criticisms no one would have dreamt of uttering under Alexander III were being heard on all sides. The Emperor and Empress went on a tour of visits to Foreign Courts, visits which included one to Paris, where the Parisian population hailed their arrival with unparalleled enthusiasm. But this coquetting with a Republic did not please a certain section of Russian society, who thought it beneath the dignity of a Tsar of Russia to treat as an equal the President of a government which was the antithesis of his own. On the other hand, immense capital was made by the French Press of this journey and of its possible consequences, and the idea of a war of revanche began to take hold of the public mind in France. For the first time since the fall of the Third Empire, the streets of Paris resounded with cries of *"Vive l'Empereur!"* and *"Vive l'Imperatrice!"* and every possible attention was paid to the Russian sovereigns. But when M. Mohrenheim, their Ambassador, gave a lunch in their honour to which he had invited the most distinguished men and women of France, among them the bearers of some of the proudest names of the old regime, the Empress scarcely said a word to any of them, and showed herself as ungracious as ever, so much so that later the unfortunate Ambassador had to listen to the remark, *"Votre Impératrice n'est vraiment pas amiable!"*

And yet Alexandra Feodorovna had enjoyed her visit to Paris, where for the first time in her life she found herself the central figure in one long, continuous ovation. She had felt, while in the French capital, that she was an Empress, before whom everybody bent down, to whom everybody's homage was addressed, and who was the one object of interest wherever she appeared. This tickled her vanity and pleased her sense of superiority by ministering to her natural egotism. But in spite of this, she could not bring herself to be amiable or pleasant, and her face often showed the boredom which she felt when compelled to go out of her way to show some attention to the people by whom she was surrounded.

Before coming to Paris, the Tsar and Tsarina had spent a few days at Balmoral with Queen Victoria, whom her granddaughter had not seen since her marriage. There also frictions had occurred and things had not gone so smoothly as they ought to have done. The Queen, although immensely proud of the marriage which had made the youngest child of her favourite daughter the consort of one of the most powerful monarchs in Europe, had become aware of Alexandra's lack of graciousness and of her growing unpopularity among her subjects. She had taken her to task for it, and had tried to instil into her mind the advisability of changing her demeanour and of showing herself kinder and pleasanter to a society whose idiosyncrasies she ought to respect if she wanted to be liked by it. The old Queen knew human nature, and how to propitiate it, and she could not help feeling apprehensive as to the young Empress's future unless the latter made up her mind to apply herself to the task of effacing the bad impression she had created. But her remarks were very badly received. Alexandra considered herself the equal, if not the superior, of her grandmother, and she resented the latter's interference, going so far as to let her perceive that such was the case.

Queen Victoria was so much surprised that she found herself for once nonplussed, and, discovering that she could not do anything with the spoiled child whom she could not help loving in spite of her stubbornness, she kept silent, but later on spoke to the Emperor, and attempted to open his eyes to the growing unpopularity of his wife. Nicholas was more polite than the Empress had shown herself, and, after thanking the Queen for her kind interest, assured her that the rumours which had reached her ears were very much exaggerated; that, on the contrary, people in Russia were very fond of the Tsarina, and greatly appreciated her remarkable qualities. Queen Victoria thus saw that she had made no impression, and the Imperial visit, begun with great cordiality, came to an end under a cloud.

When she returned to St. Petersburg, Alexandra Feodorovna took up the trend of her existence in the old way, hut did not seem to get on any better with her family or her surroundings. She was not at that time interested in public affairs, and her knowledge of Russia was not yet sufficient to permit her to become acquainted with the literature of her new country. Afterwards she became a very proficient Russian scholar and affected to speak Russian in preference to any other language, but at the time of which I am writing she was shy of expressing herself in it. Society did not appeal to her, she detested balls and parties, and would have liked to spend the

whole of her time in her nursery or out of doors. In short, she was intensely bored with what might be called Imperial representation, though most exacting in regard to Imperial rights and privileges. But she was not above being interested in gossip, a proclivity which was to prove her bane and her undoing, because some friends whom she chose later on, in defiance of the warnings she had received concerning them, ministered to this weakness of hers, and often repeated to her malicious things concerning people she ought to have tried to propitiate, with the result that she showed them her displeasure in such an unmistakable maimer that they shook the dust of St. Petersburg and of the Winter Palace from their feet, and began to spend most of their time abroad, where at least they were left alone and not compelled to submit to snubs which they felt they had not deserved.

The one great wish of the Empress was to have a son, and she constantly prayed to God to give her one. She keenly felt the humiliation of not having given an heir to the throne, and she instinctively knew that she was blamed for it by the world, though this was no fault of hers. She was also aware that her own position would be ever so much more secure if she became the mother of the future Emperor. But one daughter after another was born to her in quick succession, and as each one saw the light of day, Alexandra's cry was, "What will the nation say? What will the nation say?" She did not realize, happily for her perhaps, that the nation had ceased to be interested in her, and that, as time passed, the idea became so firmly implanted in the minds of the public that she would never have a boy, that it would have been almost disappointed if this had happened.

She would have liked to become interested in some charitable public institution where she could have worked for the welfare of the people, but these were all, or nearly all, placed under the patronage of the Empress Dowager, and the latter did not care to delegate any of her functions to her daughter-in-law. The relationship between the two ladies, although cordial in appearance, was in reality as cold as it could be. They exchanged a few official visits, and sometimes, on the occasion of a family festival, Marie Feodorovna repaired to Tsarskoye Selo and stayed a day or two with her children, but the atmosphere of their home did not agree with her, and she was always glad to return to Gats china or to the Anitchkoff Palace, which she had continued to occupy. The Dowager Empress, at this period of her son's reign, was beginning to gather about her a small circle of friends, with whom she very freely discussed the politics of the hour. There were many things of which she did not approve in the conduct of public affairs, but she was tactful, so she forbore to give the Tsar any advice unless he asked for it, and this did not happen often.

It would be well, perhaps, to make a digression here and say a few words concerning the Dowager Empress. The friends of her daughter-in-law have attempted to represent her as harsh and lacking in affection, and have tried to place upon her shoulders the responsibility for the undeniably bad relations which at last established themselves between the Empress Alexandra and the whole Imperial family. In reality there was nothing of the kind. Marie Feodorovna was a most tactful woman, and one who had thoroughly mastered the meaning of the word dignity. During the years she had been married to Alexander III, she had exercised a far greater influence over public affairs than the world had ever suspected, but she had done so in the most discreet, unobtrusive manner possible, and had never boasted of the confidence which her husband had reposed in her. As wife, mother, friend, and sovereign she had been perfection itself, and her hold on the affections of the Russian people, and of Court society, had been complete and unlimited. Band, sweet, amiable, condescending, eager to share the joys and sorrows of those with whom she came into contact, always full of sympathy, she had made herself loved wherever her lovely person had appeared. Her husband had once called her the guardian angel of Russia, and he had spoken the truth, because she had really shown herself the guardian angel of her family and of her people all through the years when with such dignify she had occupied the throne to which she had been raised. Neither time nor the vicissitudes of life had deprived her of any of the affections she had won, and in her exile, loneliness and poverty, bereft of all that made existence dear to her in the past, she still was beloved by those who, like her, found refuge in foreign lands.

But Alexandra Feodorovna was the last person capable of understanding the noble, frank, and generous nature of her mother-in-law, of whom she was intensely jealous. She would have liked her to live somewhere far away, and she never felt happier than when the Dowager Empress went to Denmark, where she generally used to spend the summer months, because somehow she felt freer when not within reach of Marie Feodorovna's rare criticisms, the sting of which was not lost upon her. On the other hand, she absolutely refused to permit the latter to take her place on official occasions, and when told that if she did not care for balls she could easily ask her mother-in-law to replace her as hostess, she fell into a rage, asking what she had done that people wanted to eliminate her entirely; a totally unfounded accusation, because there is nothing that Russian society would have liked better than to see her assume the position which by right belonged to her.

This strange attitude of the young Empress of course had its influence on her temper. She would not have been human if she had not tired of the lonely existence she found herself compelled to lead. Her babies took up a lot of her time, but could not fill it entirely, nor could reading, in which she indulged whenever she found the opportunity. Her literary tastes were just as earnest as her whole nature, and she would not have thought of taking up a novel, no matter how interesting it might be. She was fond of music and sang pretty well, she could draw, and she was very expert with her needle, but all this was not sufficient to keep her interested. She required friends, and these she could not obtain — I mean disinterested friends — on account of the exalted position in which she stood.

Is it to be wondered, then, that sometimes she found existence wellnigh unbearable?

CHAPTER IV

ALEXANDRA'S INTERESTS AND VAGARIES

WHEN her second child, the Grand Duchess Tatiana, was born in May, 1897, the Empress had just reached that state of mind when the longing for disinterested friends endangers the moral balance. She believed that the country was reproaching her for her inability to give her husband an heir, and she resented it deeply, perhaps even more deeply than she cared to admit. She accused the world of being unkind to her, forgetting that it was her own fault if her people, who had been ready to fall at her feet, did not worship her. She was never able to understand the intricacies of the Russian character, with its suppleness, its Slavic charm, and its languid indifference to what the morrow might bring. She classed St. Petersburg society as frivolous, vain, immoral and depraved. The many flirtations and love affairs going on around always shocked her profoundly as she had not enough discrimination to realize that half the time they were but superficial, and, where this was not the case, so deep and so true that their irregular character was overlooked.

She had expressed her intention of reforming what it had taken centuries to build up, centuries of hard work and social transformations. The value of the reforms of Peter the Great had totally escaped her, nor had she been able to grasp the slow march of civilization tempered by a wide indulgence in every kind of caprice, which, from the old Russia of the Boyars, the Streltsis, and the Opritchnikis[1] of Ivan the Terrible, had evolved the charming, intelligent, refined, amiable, and brilliant St. Petersburg society of her day. She had not tried to probe the slow-moving factors of this development; nor did she appreciate the passionate desire of modern Russia to be regarded by Europe as an equal. The charm of the country, with its vast plains, its dark forests, its silent, quiet rivers, and its infinite steppes, had been lost upon her, partly because she had not sought the opportunity of becoming acquainted with it. Passionate in many things, including her likes and dislikes, she rarely changed in her valuation of people or of facts, and it was this inflexibility of temperament, combined with her egotism, that finally brought about her undoing.

Then again, the Empress had not realized the peculiarity of the Russian system of government, which was founded entirely upon bureaucracy, and bureaucracy was perhaps more hated by the aristocracy than by the lower or the rural classes. According to the regulations issued by Peter the Great, no man who did not belong to the first four classes into which the nation was divided had the right to be received by the sovereign officially, or to be invited to official Court receptions. As a result, bureaucrats who had earned by long years of work a *tchin*, or rank, which made them second- or third-class functionaries, were *ipso facto* invited to Court on all solemn occasions of State, while a Prince Dolgorouky or a Count Scheremetieff would not be allowed to pass the gates of the Winter Palace unless he held a Court appointment. This explains the enormous number of chamberlains and gentlemen-in-waiting attached to the person of the Tsar: in reality they never attended upon him, but by virtue of their position as members of his household, could be admitted to balls and receptions of an official character. I use the term "official character" advisedly, because at all the small entertainments given by the sovereign they were invariably present, as, too, were smart society, while the bigwigs, to use familiar language, were left at home.

This abnormal state of things had the disadvantage of creating a gulf between the servants and the friends of the monarch and of his wife. The old Russian aristocracy looked with disdain upon the bureaucracy, which it execrated as much as did the *intelligentsia*; while the bureaucracy was always glad to show those proud and disdainful nobles that, after all, it was they who were ruling the country, and had in some cases unlimited power over their persons in spite of their ancient lineage and historic names.

Now, the aristocracy kept very much to itself, and there were houses in St. Petersburg where a bureaucrat, however important his position, was never received unless he happened to belong by birth to the old nobility. It enjoyed free speech everywhere, and generally headed the Liberal movement of the country. But it was essentially faithful and devoted to the sovereign in spite of the fact that it did not tolerate any snub the latter might choose to inflict. If the Empress had been wise, she would have tried to propitiate these elements of Russian society, which, after all, were the best it contained, instead of antagonizing them and causing them finally to ignore her. She might have known that she was far more likely to hear and learn the truth from a Count Vorontzoff or a Prince Volkonski than from these others.

She was not wise, however. When she saw that people gradually retired from her and became indifferent to her praise or blame, she sought her friends among those who, always ready to accept anything she chose to give them, tried to manage and influence her by shameless flattery. Not that this took place all at once, because before the small circle that finally was the only kind of society Alexandra Feodorovna tolerated surrounded her in the mesh of its intrigues, she had sought, far and wide, friends in whom she could confide, and with whom she might talk of the various things that worried her. The poor woman was hungering after affection, after love, after the companionship of persons who did not mistrust her motives or attribute to her intentions she never had. But such persons were not easy to find, owing to the solitude into which she was gradually retiring. If she had made an effort to see more people, to try to enliven St. Petersburg society by giving balls and receptions such as it had been used to in the past, she could perhaps have met men and women with whom she would have found herself in sympathy. But she never even made the experiment; indeed, she gave everybody the impression that she was perfectly content to be left alone, with her husband and her babies, to whom she seemed to give up all her time.

With the Imperial family she had never been able to get on. I have spoken already of her relations with the Empress Dowager, and as for the old grand duchesses, such as Marie Pavlovna, or the widow of the Grand Duke Constantine, she kept them carefully at arm's length. The Queen of Greece, Olga Constantinovna, was about the only one whom she welcomed, because that lady had such a charming, amiable, and flexible character that it would have been almost impossible not to like her. But towards her other relatives the Empress remained distant, and, in contrast to the Empress Dowager, who had always encouraged visits from her sister-in-law, aunts, and cousins, invariably receiving them with the greatest affability, Alexandra instituted the rule that whenever they wanted to see her, they had to ask her permission through a lady-in-waiting to call upon her. Naturally, this change did not meet with approval, and as time went on even the Romanoffs turned their backs on the wife of the head of their dynasty, and confined their relations with her to matters only of the strictest necessity.

There was, however, one Imperial lady who had managed to ingratiate herself into the good graces of the Empress, and this was the Duchess Stana of Leuchtenberg, a daughter of King Nicholas of Montenegro. She was a handsome woman past thirty, who had been so excessively unhappy in her marriage that she finally divorced her husband. The Duchess Stana succeeded in winning the sympathies of Alexandra Feodorovna, who pitied her for the manner in which she had been treated by the Duke, and who conceived the idea of marrying her to one of her favourites, for he was that at the time, the Grand Duke Nicholas N icholaievitch. His brother, the Grand Duke Peter, had wedded the Princess Militsa of Montenegro, Stana's sister. Both were in the Empress's good graces and were supposed to have spoken to her first of the unfortunate position of the Duchess of Leuchtenberg. For some reason which has never been fathomed, but which may have had its origin in the fact that the Empress Marie, after being very kind to the Montenegrin girls, had found them ungrateful and withdrawn her friendship. Alexandra Feodorovna became more than friendly with the two sisters, and soon they were almost inseparable, the Grand Duke Nicholas and his wife spending a good deal of their time in the Palace of Tsarskoye Selo as guests of its Imperial owners. And here begins the first chapter in the sordid story of superstition, stupidity, credulity, and lack of common sense which was in time to assume such gigantic proportions.

The Empress had always been inclined to mysticism, and so was the Emperor. Indeed, it ran in the family, and few of its members were entirely free from it. Ever since the accession of Nicholas II, there had been so many bad omens tending to prove that his reign was bound to be both unhappy and unlucky, that he had ended by being affected himself by the dread of some impending calamities kept in reserve for him by fate, and began to ask himself if they could be averted. At this juncture, and while he was in that frame of mind, the Grand Duke Nicholas spoke to him of a medium called Philippe, a Frenchman who was supposed to possess an extraordinary faculty in being able to read the future. The Tsar became curious ; the Empress even more so, and they asked their cousin to bring this wonderful man to Tsarskoye Selo.

Then began a series of sittings during which the spirit of the late Alexander III was invoked and implored by his son for advice. It seems that the spirit was quite successful in what he said, because Nicholas II became absolutely convinced that he had really been in communication with his dead parent, and from that day on M. Philippe became a great personage indeed, and came to Tsarskoye Selo whenever he liked. The Empress began to confide in him the various disillusionments and unpleasantnesses of her married life. Among other things, she spoke to him of her sorrow at not having become the mother of a son, and begged him to tell her whether she could still hope to give an heir to the Romanoffs. Philippe comforted her, and assured her that her wishes would be granted and that before twelve months had elapsed the long-desired heir would have made his appearance. He added another thing which was rather remarkable, considering what took place later : he told Alexandra that although he would not remain with her long, yet there would come after him another man, a man of God, who would guide her and bless her, and to whom she ought to listen, in order to avoid terrible calamities which otherwise would overtake her and her family. Philippe — this much may be said in his favour — did not take part in any intrigues, and was not even extraordinarily well remunerated for his services, but he acquired over the credulous minds of Nicholas II and his consort an influence which became absolutely unhealthy, and which began to interfere with the Emperor's work because it drove him to spend most of his time turning tables together with the medium and consulting the spirits of the dead in regard to matters much too important to the living to be treated in such a way. Ministers and Court officials became aware that Philippe was the person who ought to be propitiated, and to whom they must turn whenever they wanted to obtain anything from their Imperial master. Without holding any official position, this former hairdresser became as powerful as had been Menschikoff under Peter the Great, or Potemkin under Catherine II.

Suddenly, while the world was wondering whither all this was leading the monarchy, the Empress announced to her husband and to her family that she expected once more to become a mother. This time it was to be a son: M. Philippe had said so! So great preparations were made everywhere to welcome the long-hoped-for heir. Alexandra was radiant, and everybody commented upon her good looks and improved manners. People counted the months, the weeks, and finally the days which separated them from the great event, the birth of a successor to Nicholas II.

Time went on; yet no child appeared. The Court, and even the Emperor, began to wonder. The Empress alone remained radiant, and with her eyes raised to Heaven with an expression of unbounded gratitude gleaming from them, she prepared herself for the expected birth. But no birth took place, and finally the Emperor decided there was something the matter with his wife. He asked her to call physicians to diagnose her case, but she obstinately refused to do so, until at last the Empress Dowager arrived one day at Peterhof, where her son was spending the summer months, and told him that such strange rumours were going the rounds that in the interest of his own prestige the truth ought to be established. For once Nicholas listened to his mother, and in spite of her resistance the Empress was compelled to see a doctor, whereupon if was established that her maternal expectations had been only the product of her imagination. There was not, then, the faintest prospect of her giving the throne an heir.

Of course the scandal was immense, in spite of the efforts that were made to hush it up. The world, which had to be told something, was informed that an unlucky accident had put an end to the hopes of the Tsar and of his wife, but this explanation satisfied only the ignorant, and St. Petersburg society was extremely amused by this wholly incredible story, and of course ridiculed the Empress as much as it could. At the same time, this gave the police an opportunity to probe into the past of M. Philippe, when it was discovered that all through his life he had been an impostor, and had more than once seen the inside of a prison cell. The adventurer had to leave Russia in haste and in disgrace, but although everybody rejoiced at his departure, the Empress would not hear a word against him, lamenting bitterly the loss of the only man who had been able to bring a little rest to her troubled soul. Rightly or wrongly, she accused the Grand Duke Nicholas of having had a part in ending this diversion in the monotony of her existence. Thereafter, the affection she had felt for him and for his wife changed into real animosity, which during the Great "War turned to absolute hatred.

Philippe gone, Alexandra found herself with time again hanging heavy on her hands. Her lack of real friends had never been more apparent, and she was indeed to be pitied in every way. But in spite of the pity which her lonely position inspired, there was no one who attempted to enliven the monotony and splitude of her life ; no one, that is, except an officer who commanded her regiment of Uhlans of the guards, a certain General Orloff[2] to whom she had taken one of those sudden fancies to which she was subject. He was an attractive man, and soon he found himself continually invited to Tsarskoye Selo. Inevitably the world talked, the more so as it liked to criticize every move of the Empress, but in spite of all that has been said on the subject, it has been proved that whatever may have been her inward feelings, Alexandra never carried this friendship farther than the limits of pure and simple comradeship. The gallant officer himself may have been touched by her beauty, loneliness, and friendless position, but the romance, if romance there was, remained irreproachable in spite of the calumnies of the world. Whatever may have been her sentiments in regard to General Orloff, she had not much time to think about them, because he died in Egypt, whither he had repaired for his health, so it was officially said, but rumours without end attended his demise, which was whispered to have been a suicide under circumstances so cleverly engineered that it could never be established. His body was brought back to Russia and buried at Tsarskoye Selo, and the Empress, until the day when she was imprisoned by order of the Russian Provisional Government, used to go every afternoon to visit his grave and lay some flowers upon it, accompanied — and this is the wonderful part of this extraordinary story — accompanied sometimes by the Emperor.

Here I must make a digression. It is absolutely certain to-day that the warmest affection existed between Nicholas II and his wife, and that the latter was absolutely devoted to him. But there was nevertheless something strange in their relation to each other. The Empress ruled her husband absolutely, and occasionally could be jealous of him, or rather of her influence over him. Yet, in the case of Madame Viroubova and her friendship with Nicholas, she showed herself singularly lenient at times and very angry at others.

Madame Viroubova deserves a chapter to herself in any attempt to sketch the life of the Empress Alexandra. M. Alexander Tanieieff, the father of Madame Viroubova, was the perfect type of those bureaucrats whom I have already described, a man whose entire career had been an administrative one; a painstaking official, an honest man in his actions, but one given to intrigues, as were, indeed, all the members of his family. For this reason he was not looked upon with favourable eyes in official spheres, and St. Petersburg society practically ignored him and his wife and children. This may have had a certain influence over the disposition of his daughter, and have inspired her with resentment against certain high-born ladies. This predisposition influenced the Empress, who already disliked the real Russian nobility, a dislike that so thoroughly alienated from the Emperor and Empress the men and women who might in the hour of danger have proved a support to their throne, that they had actually driven them out of St. Petersburg long before the World War.

Formerly the Court had been the centre of society, which entirely gravitated around it, but when it became evident that this Court no longer existed, and that the monarch and his consort only wanted to lead a quiet family life and not to mingle with their subjects, the latter in their turn lost every interest in their sovereign, finding it infinitely pleasanter to live on the Riviera or in Italy or in Paris, leaving their estates at the mercy of incompetent and rapacious stewards who did nothing but embitter the peasantry against the landlords, thus paving the way for the Bolshevik upheaval. During the lifetime of Alexander III, people knew very well that he hated to see them go abroad, and consequently most of the owners of large country estates had made a point of spending several months of the year on them, returning to the capital for the winter season, when generally they were asked for news of what was going on in their province by the Emperor. The aristocracy did not go abroad much, and mostly only in autumn, when ladies used to order their gowns for the coming Court festivities, but this was always for a short time, and as a rule the New Year saw the leaders of society settled in their town houses, planning the various hospitalities they intended to offer to their friends.

But with the advent of Alexandra Feodorovna in the Winter Palace things changed, and even that palace came to be abandoned as a residence by the sovereigns. They lived at Tsarskoye Selo, where the Emperor could indulge in his liking for long walks, and where his wife could spend her time in the most bourgeois manner possible, watching her children, doing some needlework, gossiping with Madame Viroubova or one or two other obscure friends of hers, entirely forgetting that as an Empress of Russia she also had social duties to perform. Society, seeing this, thought it useless to restrain itself in any way, and the annual exodus took place much earlier than of old. Gay ladies declared that life in Nice or Cannes was infinitely more enjoyable than on the banks of the Neva or on some country estates far from the comforts of civilization.

As a consequence the aristocracy lost touch with the Imperial family, as well as with the nation, and its desire to teach the peasants, and to get them out of their state of semi-barbarity, which had been so fashionable during the preceding reign, died a natural death, with the result we have seen, when the Revolution found the rural classes solidly aligned against the aristocratic landowners. No one, I believe, has yet brought this fact to the notice of the world, though it is an important one, and in considering the work of destruction performed by Alexandra Feodorovna, it ought to receive a due place.

But in spite of all this she does not deserve to be blamed as she has been. Most of her sins were sins of ignorance. It would have been so easy to explain, so easy to amend faults born of failure to comprehend a difficult and delicate political situation. When one remembers all this, one also cannot help thinking of the old Greek fatalism which in ancient times was supposed to hover over certain people and to drive them to an inexorable doom. The least superstitious person cannot help being struck with the various bad omens that had haunted the unfortunate Empress from the first day she had set foot upon Russian soil.

But this has led me very far from Madame Viroubova and the manner in which she worked her way into the confidence of Alexandra Feodorovna and Nicholas II. She was brought to their notice thanks to a clever intrigue of her father, M. Tanieieff, who once showed the Empress some copybooks of his daughter, after having discussed with her his views about the education of girls, a hobby of Alexandra. The latter was very much interested in these copybooks, and expressed her warm approval of their contents, adding, so at least Madame Viroubova tells us: "Most Russian girls seem to have nothing in their heads but officers."

Now, this was one of those unfortunate remarks which too often escaped the lips of the Tsarina, and which certainly ought never to have been repeated, because first of all it was untrue, and then it was calculated to wound deeply those who were the objects of it, as well as their fathers and mothers. But M. Tanieieff did not possess discretion among his many virtues, and he hastened to spread right and left the words of the sovereign, thus adding to the number of her enemies. This again shows how the poor Empress misplaced ter confidence.

The incident of the copybooks, however, had borne fruit, for Alexandra kept it in mind, and a few months later sent the award of maid of honour to Anna Tanieieff, and later on had her designated for a few weeks' duties at the Tsarskoye Selo palace.

NOTES

1 Appendix VI.
2 Appendix IV.

CHAPTER V

THE EMPRESS IN POLITICS AND AT HOME

DURING the first years of her marriage, the Empress kept entirely aloof from politics. Maybe she was not interested, or was too timid, or realized that in those early days she had no influence. It would have been well if she had remained aloof. As time went on, however, when she thought her position more secure, and especially after she had borne a son, she seemed suddenly to want to have something to say in regard to public matters. She was not altogether unintelligent, and had taken measure of the character of her husband, with its many weaknesses, indecisions, and lack of initiative, and when she saw opened before her the possibility of ruling in his name, she did not allow it to escape her.

She had very definite ideas as to what was the best form of government for Russia, and repudiated the thought of any reform bringing the country to the verge of demanding a Constitution. Here again, her motives were purely personal, founded on personal experiences, likes, and dislikes. She had discovered that in aristocratic circles the question of a change in the system of government was the one most eagerly discussed, and this had added to her distrust of the Russian nobility, whom she could not forgive for their independence of character and their indifference to her approval or disapproval of their conduct. She fully believed that autocracy ought to be maintained for the welfare of Russia, and whenever the idea of curtailing some of its privileges was mooted, Alexandra rose up in arms immediately, and repeated over and over again to her husband that it was his duty to maintain things just as his father had left them; to repel any attempt to initiate reforms tending to diminish his prerogatives as an absolute sovereign. Unfortunately her words found but too willing an echo in his mind. Ministers used to complain that their best intentions were blocked by the obstinacy of the Empress and her refusal to uphold their views before the Tsar. This, of course, was not only before the Great War, but also before the war with Japan and the revolutionary upheaval which followed upon it.

The bureaucrats naturally sided with the Empress, and did their best to add fuel to the flames of her resentment against St. Petersburg society, which she believed was planning the overthrow of her husband and of his dynasty. As long as there was no son she kept aloof from any political intrigue, but later, as soon as she became the mother of an heir to the Russian throne, she took up the attitude of a defender of that son's interests, and kept repeating to her husband that he had no right to transmit to that son any other form of inheritance than the one which, he had himself received from his father.

The Imperial family hated her, principally because they had always found her a stumbling-block in their path whenever they had attempted to obtain some favour from the Emperor, and even her sister the Grand Duchess Elizabeth and the latter's husband, who, when she married, had been her best friends, had discovered that she was trying to undermine the Tsar's confidence in them. The Grand Duke, a very ambitious man, had done his best to acquire some sort of importance in the eyes of his Imperial nephew, and to persuade the latter to consult him about all grave questions of State. In this design he had found a rival in his cousin the Grand Duke Alexander Michailovitch, married to the Grand Duchess Xenia, the sister of Nicholas.

It can be conjectured, therefore, what a hotbed of intrigue, scandal, and gossip the Russian Court had become, divided as it was by the two grand-ducal factions, each arrayed against the other, each seeking absolute control over the mind of the monarch. Between them stood the Empress, very well aware that the frantic efforts of her two relatives would end in smoke, and that it was she who would have the last word to say in the most important questions of the day.

This state of things went on with but slight variations, until at last Russia stood on the brink of the war with Japan, after having passed through a period of discontent the like of which she had never experienced. The work of trying to overthrow the existing regime, which had been hinted at in the famous letter of the Geneva Committee to Nicholas II, had systematically proceeded, and the country was slowly but surely getting ready for a struggle which no longer frightened nor distressed it. The time when the people fell on their knees whenever they happened to see the Tsar walking in the streets had passed. It had been replaced by a firm determination to carry on an energetic struggle against a Government the rottenness of which was an established fact.

Whether Nicholas II and his wife were aware of this subtle work of disintegration which had been going on ever since their coronation, it would be difficult to tell. But it seems pretty certain now, judging by various documents which since the Great War have seen the light of day, that the Emperor looked upon the possibility of a war without disfavour, but, on the contrary, had the idea that a victorious campaign would strengthen the hands of the Government and thus prove a blessing in disguise. Certain it is that he refused to utter the one word which would have stopped the aggressive intentions of Japan.

The war broke out, and, as everybody knows, was not exactly a triumph for the Russian arms; instead it revealed all the weaknesses of War Office administration, as well as the insufficiency of the Navy. Mukden and Chusima ought to have opened the eyes of a great many people, as perhaps they did, and Nicholas II was urged to show himself firm in punishing severely those whose lack of conscience had brought the country to the very verge of ruin and absolute disaster.

But the Emperor did not like to change his Ministers, at least at that time. Later on he did so without any hesitation, and, indeed, with something very akin to a sense of pleasure. But even after the Japanese men-of-war had made havoc of his fleet, he still remained under the delusion that the Russian arms were absolutely invincible; that the winning of the war was but a matter of time and a test of endurance, and that its ultimate result was not to be doubted for a single moment.

Strange to relate, the Empress did not share this point of view. She was again about to become a mother, a fact that gave her more assurance than she would otherwise have had, and in the presence of the unprecedented disaster which had overtaken Russia she very quickly made up her mind to assert herself. Of course this was not the time to do so, but then what does an angry woman care when she finds her influence jeopardized? Alexandra Feodorovna, seeing what she considered mistakes without number being made at each step, asserted herself, and boldly claimed the right to be kept informed as to what was taking place at the seat of war.

And so, what with one thing and another, the ambitions nursed by the Empress gradually began to take shape. She was one who could, when she liked, make herself extremely disagreeable to those whom she did not like or had reason to distrust, and she imagined that some people, among them members of her own family, were attempting to curtail the share she wanted to fake in the conduct of public affairs. She had, as I have said already, been very fond at one time of her brother-in-law, the Grand Duke Serge, and of the Grand Duchess Elizabeth, his consort, and during the inquiry into the causes of the

Khodinka disaster, had done her best to prevent him from being blamed for it. But later on, when she saw that the Grand Duke was not completely in accord with all she did, especially in regard to the long spiritualistic *séances* with which her time was occupied in company with Philippe and other mediums, she turned against him, and when he was assassinated they were on very cool terms, so cool, indeed, that it was without emotion that Alexandra Feodorovna heard of his dastardly murder and of her beloved sister's tragic widowhood.

This crime was one of the startling incidents of the struggle which, ever since the accession of Nicholas II to the throne of all the Russias, had been going on against his rule, quietly at first, more openly later on, and which was never to stop until at last the dynasty was overthrown. The event had been startling by reason of its horrible details, some of which do not bear repeating, and also because of the determination which accompanied it. The Grand Duke had been known as a staunch reactionary and a man of inflexible character, and it is certain that during the years he occupied the position of Governor-General of Moscow, he had shown himself harsh to an unusual degree. But at the same time he was an intelligent man, and though most likely he would never have owned to it, it is known to-day that he did his very best to open the eyes of his sister-in-law to the danger of her position and to the necessity of showing herself more amiable towards St. Petersburg and Moscow society.

The Empress always replied that surely, in the exalted position she occupied, she need not be compelled to see people she did not care for, or to give up the only mode of life that pleased her. There was a stormy scene one evening when, during a visit he paid at Tsarskoye Selo, the Grand Duke had tried to persuade Alexandra that she had no right to isolate herself from the world in the manner she affected, and that former Tsars and Tsarinas had always done their best to share the interests of their subjects. "We are not living in Japan," Serge had said, "where the Mikado remains for his people a kind of divinity they never see but only hear about. Russia expects something else of its sovereigns. After all, even an absolute monarch must be able to rely on some one in case the hour of danger strikes, and on whom will you and the Emperor be able to rely should you find yourselves in peril? You know no one, you have no friends, and sometimes bayonets alone, with no reliable soldiers to use them, become not only useless but even dangerous."

The Empress was mortally offended and replied that she had some friends, but had not chosen them among the Russian aristocrats who thought themselves the equals of their Tsars, and she forthwith dismissed the Grand Duke with the request never again to refer to the subject. He never had the opportunity, being killed a few weeks later.

His murder had been planned with great care, and the man who finally threw the fatal bomb showed extreme courage in his dastardly crime. The widow of the victim, the Grand Duchess Elizabeth, tried to have him pardoned by the Emperor and went to see him in his cell to tell him that she forgave him and prayed for him. Of course her efforts were useless, because Nicholas II would not be moved to exercise his prerogative of mercy, and certainly could hardly have been expected to do so to spare the life of the assassin of a member of his own family. Nevertheless, he was bitterly reproached for having denied the Grand Duchess's request, as indeed he was reproached for everything he did. His unpopularity had already become so great that whatever he tried to perform was immediately seized upon as a pretext for upbraiding him.

Few sovereigns and few men have been so little trusted as this mighty autocrat whose life was spent in such serene unconsciousness of the responsibilities he had to carry, and of the good or evil which he could perform. His Ministers never felt safe with him and, as Count Witte tells us in his memoirs, never could get him to tell them his real wishes. He was vindictive, unreliable, and often not truthful, but he had great charm of manner and a courtesy reminding one of the knights of old, who were without fear and without reproach. Nicholas II could hardly lay claim to the second qualification, and, though brave in certain respects, was more than pusillanimous in others, especially in matters in which his wife was concerned.

The latter at last became all-powerful in everything that concerned their domestic life, partly because the Emperor did not think it worth while to arouse her anger by opposing her in what, after all, seemed to him to be trifling matters. He also did not care for the pomp of regal state, much preferring to live quietly, at Tsarskoye Selo, the life of a country gentleman of large means. Nothing simpler than the daily routine of this Imperial palace could be imagined, and one would never have thought that it was the home of one of the mightiest potentates on earth. If we are to believe the memoirs of Anna Viroubova and the reminiscences of other people who had occasion to approach Alexandra, an almost monastic existence was lived within this old residence of Catherine II, where in her time such revelries had taken place; an existence in which mystic practices, fasts, prayers without end, and everlasting church services, played the principal part.

The Emperor at times used to go and dine with the officers of the different regiments of the guards quartered at Tsarskoye Selo or in St. Petersburg, and this constituted one of his greatest pleasures. There, among his soldiers, he felt at ease, and could enjoy a quiet cigarette and a glass of champagne in company with men whom he called familiarly his "comrades." But even this more or less innocent enjoyment did not receive the approval of the public, and it began to be whispered that the sovereign liked these parties because he could get drunk at his ease, which it was hardly possible for him to do in the bosom of his family. Of course this was an outrageous lie, because Nicholas was a sober man, and not at all addicted to swallowing numberless glasses of wine or vodka. But here again was a case of giving a dog a bad name and hanging him.

The Empress, always fond of doing the opposite of what was expected of her, sometimes relaxed from her habits of isolation, particularly when she went to Livadia, in the Crimea, which was her favourite residence, and where she had built herself a palace which was a fairy dwelling all of white marble, with roses and flowers creeping everywhere around the doors and windows, and a magnificent view of the Black Sea stretching in front of it. It was at Livadia that she gave, from time to time, balls for her daughters, when the latter were grown up, to which the society of Yalta and surrounding places was bidden. But it was noticed that if some prominent person from St. Petersburg happened to be in the Crimea, he or she was conveniently forgotten, and not included among those asked to attend these entertainments. The Empress had boycotted the capital and its inhabitants, and nothing would induce her to relent in this decision.

Then again, when the Imperial family went for its annual cruise along the coast of Finland, in the Imperial yacht *Standard*, Alexandra showed herself extremely pleasant to the officers of that vessel, and always included them among those who were bidden to her table, encouraging them also to show themselves attentive to the young grand duchesses, who, being cut off from the society of their equals, were naturally only too glad to be able to see and speak with other people than their governesses, tutors, and the ever-present Anna Viroubova. This also gave offence to St. Petersburg, who reproached the Empress for not caring for any other society than that of people ready and willing to cater to all her caprices and to submit to all her snubs.

And while this was going on, while the Imperial family was speeding blindly towards its doom and a catastrophe which was in the air, which every serious man or woman could see approaching, the Anarchist parties were quietly organizing themselves for the day when they would be able to seize the supreme power which Nicholas II did not know how to keep. Of course the police were very active, and whenever a centre of revolutionary activity was discovered, it was suppressed with the greatest energy. But this only added to the unpopularity of the Government and did no good. Discontent was in the air, and it was bound to culminate in catastrophe at the first opportunity.

It was the Japanese war which brought on this opportunity. Its reverses could not fail to arouse public opinion and to add to the general wave of antagonism which existed against the administration. Its humiliations were the more felt as the Russians still remembered the old days of the Tartar yoke, when the descendants of Rurik had paid tribute to a Mongol Khan, and the idea of being once more subjugated by the yellow race, so much detested, was a bitter one for every Slavic heart. People began to say quite loudly that it was time to bring about a change, and to instal another government in place of the one that had shown itself so incompetent. When a nation begins to think and to say such things, it stands very close to the brink of a revolution.

The diary of the Emperor at this period of his reign is particularly interesting and very significant. Never has his indifference to what was going on around him appeared more completely than during those anxious months when the Russian armies were being defeated by the troops of the Mikado. His remarks when war was finally declared are characteristic:

"January 26th, Monday.— This morning a conference in regard to the Japanese question took place in my study. It was decided that we would not begin hostilities. I received several governors, and was very nervous all day. At eight o'clock in the evening we went to the theatre. They played the 'Roussalka' very well. When I came home I found a telegram from Alexeieff, with the news that last night Japanese monitors attacked our fleet in its harbour and succeeded in injuring the *Cesarevitch*, *Relwisan*, and *Palladou*; this without war being declared. May the Lord help us!"

"January 27th, Tuesday. — This morning another telegram came, with the news that fifteen Japanese men- of-war attacked Port Arthur and had a fight with our squadron. The *Pollava*, *Diana*, *Askold*, and *Novik* were slightly injured. Our losses were insignificant. At four o'clock we had Divine Service in the big church, and all the rooms leading to it were filled with people, who, when we left it, received us with numerous cries of 'Hurrah!' In general it is touching to see the universal indignation against the insolence of the Japanese. Mamma stayed with us for tea, and after dinner we had a visit from Nikolacha and Stana."

"February 22nd, Sunday. — It was foggy this morning; then the weather cleared up. At eleven o'clock we went to church with the children. The ladies [on duty], Meyendorff and Kira Narichkin, lunched with us. I received a telegram that the Japanese, with seven large ships, have shelled Vladivostok without any results. I walked in the garden for a long time. We dined earlier than usual, and at half-past eight went to a concert of several religious choirs under the guidance of Arkhangelsk. The singing was wonderful. We returned home at half-past ten o'clock."

As may be seen, the defeats which, one after another, overwhelmed the Russian arms did not affect the Emperor at all, nor pierce his marvellous indifference. Even the loss of the big cruiser *Petropavlovsk* did not succeed in shaking his equanimity to any great extent.

"March 31st, Wednesday. — This morning I received the inexpressibly sad news that on the return of our squadron to Port Arthur our Admiral ship, the *Petropavlovsk*, struck a mine and went down in an explosion, in which perished Admiral Makaroff and most of the officers and men. Cyril, slightly wounded, Jakovleff, the commander, a few officers and sailors, all of them wounded, escaped. I could not forget this terrible misfortune all day. After lunch Alix, who had a cold, went to bed. At two o'clock I went to a funeral service for Countess A. A. Tolstoy, who died this morning, after which I called on Aunt Michen and Uncle Vladimir. I had dinner alone. May the will of God always be accomplished, and we ought to pray for His mercy, sinners that we are."

Disaster followed upon disaster, but they did not seem to awake any special sorrow in the heart of this extraordinary monarch. Port Arthur fell, and the following curious incident is related in regard to this culminating defeat: The telegram in which General Stossel announced the capitulation of the fortress reached the Emperor during lunch. He read it, then put it in his pocket, and after a while said : "I wonder how long Stössel will be able to hold out." Not a sign did he give, other than this remark, that he knew all was over.

In the meanwhile the country was beginning to feel that something ought to be done to put an end to a state of things wellnigh insufferable. The old autocracy of Peter, Catherine, and their successors had had its day, and had to be replaced by a more enlightened form of administration. The nation had to be given a share in the government, or else a revolutionary movement sweeping everything before it in its impetuosity was bound to take place.

At Tsarskoye Selo, however, no one seemed to see it. Although terrorist crimes were increasing, although the Minister of the Interior, M. Plehve, had been blown to pieces in the streets of the capital, although the Emperor himself was continually receiving letters telling him to beware, neither he nor the Empress would recognize the signs of the coming storm. They had other things to occupy their thoughts. Alexandra was about to become a mother for the fifth time, and of course was all eagerness, anxiety, and terrified impatience at the thought that perhaps she would at last give birth to the longed-for son. And then one August morning, the Court and the nation were told that God had granted the prayers of the Imperial pair — an heir had been born to the throne of all the Russias.

Emperor, Empress, Court, all were mad with joy; Alexandra herself told that she required nothing more on earth to be supremely happy. After this proof of the mercy of Providence, she imagined that she had attained the possibility of making herself heard at last, and of being able to defy the remonstrances of the Dowager Empress, the enmity of the Imperial family, and the dislike of that hated St. Petersburg society which had so systematically repulsed her good intentions. Now she could speak at last with authority, speak in the name of the son she had given to Russia, that son over whose inheritance it became her duty to watch.

At the same time her mystic tendencies increased as she remembered the promises and predictions made to her by the too notorious M. Philippe. They had been fulfilled; consequently she had done right to trust him, to believe in him, right in all her appreciations of his merits. In the exultation of her joy the Empress effected a reconciliation with the Grand Duke Nicholas, resuming her old friendship with him and with his wife, brother, and sister-in-law. Once more the two Montenegrin princesses, who had already exercised such a baneful influence over the morbid mind of Alexandra Feodorovna, came to the front, and were given a free hand to encourage her in those religious ecstasies to which she was becoming more and more addicted.

It was also at that time, when the little Tsarevitch was a few months old, that Anna Viroubova entered into her intimacy with the Tsarina and started on that career of flattery, abject submission, and humble adoration which was to contribute so much to the undoing of the unfortunate woman, who sincerely believed in the genuineness of feelings which were feigned in order to obtain supreme control of the mind of Alexandra.

Mademoiselle Tanieieff, as she was still at the time, had, at the suggestion of her father, been invited to attend upon the Empress during the illness of another maid of honour. As has been explained already, the singular temper and difficulty of temperament of Alexandra had by that time become such an acknowledged fact that no one cared to obtain a position dependent on her caprices. Several young ladies had been approached by the Mistress of the Robes, the Princess Golitsin, and asked to come to Tsarskoye Selo for a three months' term of attendance on the consort of the Tsar, and they had all refused the offer with significant unanimity.

Consequently, when M. Tanieieff, who, as head of the Emperor's private chancery, was constantly at the palace, proposed that his daughter should undertake the duties, his suggestion was accepted, and Anna invited to take them up, which she of course hastened to do.

She tells us, in her book of reminiscences, of her arrival at the palace, and of the dreariness of the early days she spent there. And here we can find the first traces of the manner in which she influenced the mind of her Imperial mistress against all those in whom she might eventually have found adversaries capable of ousting her from the royal favour. She knew from her father that Alexandra's pet idea was her conviction that no one could be sincere in Russia, and she played on that weakness by expatiating on the cold manner in which she had been received on her appearance at Tsarskoye Selo. This, of course, was bound to attract the Empress and to inspire in her a strong feeling of sympathy for a lonely girl in whom she found so many points of resemblance to herself, and at the same time it strengthened her natural repugnance for her surroundings, which she rightly guessed to be hostile to her.

One can only wonder how such an insignificant person as Mademoiselle Tanieieff could have played her part to such perfection. But then what will not flattery accomplish, and Alexandra Feodorovna's vanity was touched to the quick when she saw Anna fall on her knees before her and swear that she could not live far away from her; that her only desire was to devote her whole existence to her and die for her if need be.

The Empress had never listened to such protestations of love from anybody in St. Petersburg, and, indeed, the proud Russian aristocracy would have considered itself absolutely disgraced had it indulged in any such silly manifestations. But people heard about it, and of course coupled it with the well-known propensity for intrigue of the whole Tanieieff family. It set them against this intruder into Imperial favour, who, by means of a devotion she could not possibly have felt, in the opinion of the world, was trying to ingratiate herself with the sovereign and most likely, through her insinuations and harmful gossip, add to Alexandra's already too clearly shown antipathy to those Russians who, though devoted servants of her husband, yet were far too independent to play the part of lackeys, and humbly to lick the boots of a woman who, though an Empress, had perhaps not so much noble blood in her veins as those haughty descendants of Rurik and the old Muscovite Boyars, whose acclamations had called the Romanoffs to the throne of Russia.

Considering the circumstances under which life was going on in the Tsarskoye Selo palace, it is not surprising that Anna succeeded very rapidly in inspiring the Empress with deep affection. She played her cards with great skill, and knew very well how to strike at the right place in the heart of Alexandra. For instance, the latter, having become a religious zealot, had special services celebrated during Lent in the private chapel of the palace; services which were interminable, and to which the Imperial household avoided going if at all possible. Anna, on the contrary, begged as a special favour to be permitted to attend them, and of course this was warmly approved as a sign of her religious fervour. The poor Empress was unable to differentiate between sincerity and hypocrisy. To the end of her tragic existence, she persisted in believing in what she was told by adventurers who had no other aim than their personal advantage, and she refused to listen to the disinterested advice of people who asked nothing for themselves but wanted to save her from the fate towards which she was speeding in utter unconsciousness of its perils.

The entire care of Alexandra at that time was concentrated on her little boy. Whether she knew at once of the terrible ailment with which he was afflicted, or discovered it later on, it is difficult to say. One thing, however, can be affirmed: once she realized it, the whole current of her life was changed, and she acquired that fixed expression of sadness and despair which never left her. But here again the mistake was made that the public was not taken into the secret of the sorrow that had fallen on the sovereigns. If it had been known, people probably would have shown themselves more indulgent towards the Empress, realizing the mental torture she was undergoing. But her persistence in shutting herself off from the world, and keeping not only herself but her husband and her daughters in complete seclusion, being absolutely incomprehensible, aroused against her animosities which, subsequently, became impossible to destroy, even when the infirmity of the heir to the throne could no longer be concealed.

The Empress became more morbid still, and it surprised no one that she once more reverted to mystical practices and sought, in their solace, a remedy for her state of mind. She was also fearful that the Imperial family might take steps to have Alexis deprived of the succession as a sufferer from an incurable disease; an absurd idea because no one had ever given a thought to such a possibility. The grand dukes and grand duchesses, however much they may have disliked the Empress, were yet too faithful adherents to the principles of their dynasty to try to shatter its prestige. Alexis, sick or well, was the heir, and his rights could never be disputed, even though it was improbable that he would ever reach the age of manhood.

What Alexandra desired most of all during those years was to have another boy, a healthy boy who could take the place of her sickly little one in case some untoward fate carried him away. But there never was any sign of such a possibility after his birth, and she had to resign herself to the decrees of Providence, however hard. Yet what wonder that every look she cast on Alexis was an agony, and that she never had one quiet moment after she realized that his was a doomed life!

No one, however, seemed to give the unfortunate woman credit for all her mental sufferings. She was only thought to be queer, odd, disagreeable, and prejudiced against Russia and everything that was Russian, and it is quite certain that all the unjust, untrue accusations that were launched against her during the War had their cause in that aloofness in which she had kept herself from all the people of whom her predecessors had made friends.

From saying that she did not care for her own subjects to being convinced that she was ready to betray them in favour of the land of her birth, there was but one step, and this step was taken with alacrity and— must I say so? — with exceeding eagerness. The pity of it all was that this arose from misunderstandings on both sides, misunderstandings one can only deplore, but which it is impossible to pass by in silence if one washes to examine the motives underlying the ultimate catastrophe. Put her mother-in-law, the Empress Marie, in the same position in which she had found herself when the War broke out, and it is absolutely certain that the whole of Russia would have rallied round her and — who knows? — perhaps have been able to build a wall between her and the rising tide of murder and anarchy. But the only thing Alexandra had been able to do was to shut herself up with her sorrows, far away not so much from the madding crowd as from all those in whom she might have found sympathy in her trials, and whose loyalty would have helped her to bear them.

Madame Viroubova, in whose book is explained the curious character and attitude of the Empress, tells us, in describing her, that she was always "inclined to be a bit suspicious, especially of the weak and self-indulgent aristocracy." This remark gives us the key to many things which otherwise would appear inexplicable. She was always suspicious of all in whom she did not find abject submission to her caprices, always imputing unworthy motives to them. She, who was so proud, could not admit that others had the right to be equally so; she did not want any real friends about her, only slaves.

Now, if Anna Viroubova had been her friend, she would have endeavoured to remove all those wrong ideas of her Imperial mistress, and to bring to her notice the splendid qualities of the aristocracy which she so entirely misjudged and despised, instead of retailing vulgar gossip tending to discredit if. She would have pointed out to her the great services which this aristocracy had rendered to Russia and to its Tsars, and finally she would have tried to persuade Alexandra to try to do away with the Bureaucracy, which alone had been the cause of the alienation of the Tsar from his people, and which was to succeed so thoroughly in bringing it about. But then Anna herself had been born and bred in a bureaucratic family, and it was but natural that she should work in their interests.

Can it be wondered, then, that people looked upon Anna and all those of her class as natural enemies of the aristocracy and old Russian nobility, as well as of the *intelligentsia*, whom they had persecuted, and of the peasants, whom they were supposed to hold at bay? The first March revolution was entirely directed against this bureaucracy, and if, at the time it broke out, there had existed a single man among the Romanoff family possessed of sufficient energy to fake the leadership of the movement, it is quite possible that the dynasty would not have been overturned, although Nicholas II himself might have fallen from his throne.

It is conceded that all these things could not have been foreseen in those short, eventful years which followed upon the birth of the little Tsarevitch, the precursors of so much that was to follow. Very likely, when time has done its work, it will be discovered that responsibility is shared by several persons and also is partly traceable to the circumstances under which this historical earthquake occurred. That the Empress had nothing to do with it, it is impossible to say, because everything points to the part she played, but this part was not confined to her person, and in many things she was more sinned against than a sinner herself. Whatever may have been her errors, she at least was sincere — sincere in her love for her husband and family; sincere in her love for Russia, in spite of her dislike for certain Russians; sincere in her efforts to maintain an autocracy in which she believed, and of which she thought herself the guardian; sincere even in her visions of things that never existed, in her faith in adventurers in whom her unbalanced mind saw the saviours of her people and her children; sincere in her absolute belief that she was being betrayed where this was not the case; sincere at last in her sufferings, when from her prison at Tobolsk she wrote the pitiful words, "O God, save Russia, save it!"

But the others, those who had misunderstood her, who had slandered her, who had accused her of things she would never have done, she never could have done, were they as sincere? This is the terrible question which it is impossible not to put to oneself when one tries to estimate the immensity of this Russian tragedy. "Were they sincere or were they simply giving way to old animosities, to ancient grievances, and doing so without realizing whither all their idle talk might lead? I have often put to myself this formidable question, and always feared to seek a reply.

CHAPTER VI

RASPUTIN AND OTHERS BEHIND THE SCENES

MADEMOISELLE Tanieieff's entry into the intimacy of the palace of Tsarskoye Selo was an event of far greater import than people imagined, and perhaps even to-day, in spite of all that has taken place, there are some persons who fail to grasp all that it brought along with it, or the victory which it constituted for those bureaucrats against the power and abuses of whom intelligent, honest, and sincere Russia was rising. The letter which the Revolutionary Committee of Geneva had addressed to Nicholas II, in reply to his famous speech concerning the "senseless dreams" that had angered him so much, gives the key to the Russian situation and to the Russian Revolution. It had been directed not so much against the dynasty, but against those who dishonoured its good intentions and kept it in bondage.

The Russian bureaucrats were the direct descendants of the Opritchnikis of Ivan the Terrible under a different name ; they ruled the country, they had built the high wall which at last divided the sovereign from his people so entirely that when he found himself in peril he could not appeal to anyone to defend him. The predecessors of Nicholas II, who had understood the dangers of Bureaucracy while not knowing how to get rid of its tyrannical power, had applied themselves to the task of minimizing the harm being done by keeping in touch with other classes of the nation and by gathering about them descendants of the old nobility, from whom they more than once sought information as to what was going on in Russia.

Thus, at the time of the great famine of 1891, it was a lady belonging to select Court circles who was the first to apprise Alexander III of the disastrous condition of the crops in the Volga region, and to draw his attention to the necessity of taking measures to relieve the distress which was sure to follow. She even sent him some specimens of the bread the peasants were eating, and this in direct defiance of the Minister of the Interior. Alexander thanked her warmly when he saw her later on, and immediately started an investigation, which disclosed that all the lady had written to him was more than true.

With Nicholas II it would have been impossible to do such a thing, because he would simply have refused to take any notice of the facts reported to him, and the Empress would have been sure to say that this again was the invention of one of those great ladies of St. Petersburg desirous of drawing the attention of the monarch to their person. No one had a chance to make himself heard with the last Tsar of Russia except a member of the bureaucracy, the nefarious work of which was so ably sketched in the letter the Geneva Committee addressed to the young Emperor; indeed, this letter held the key to the future; it explains why the Romanoffs fell so quickly, at the first blow struck at them and their dynasty.

For centuries a struggle had been going on between the bureaucracy and all the other classes of Russian society, and this struggle was finally to engulf one of the parties fighting it. Unfortunately for the country, those who won it were too weak themselves, and perhaps too much demoralized by years of oppression and bondage, to be able to hold the power they had snatched, with the result that they were themselves to fall under the attacks of a new and savage force which had been organizing itself in silence and which was to sweep them away just as they thought they had suppressed the hated bureaucrats who had separated them from the throne and annihilated all their efforts to support it.

At the time of the first March revolution, there was not a single person near Nicholas II and his consort who could be said to represent old and loyal Russia. There were only bureaucrats of the type of M. Tanieieff, the father of Anna Viroubova, men like Protopopoff, Sturmer, and others like them, with a sprinkling of shameless adventurers, of whom Rasputin, though the most famous, was by no means the most dangerous. On the contrary, he was himself led by them, and converted into a tool, not only of their ambition, but of their love of lucre. The saddest thing, in the turmoil of intrigue amid which the Emperor and Empress were living, was that they all had in the background some financial quest. While Russia was bleeding to death, vultures were disputing among themselves who should snatch the biggest morsel out of the quarry that lay before them.

This is the blackest spot in the reign of Nicholas II, one that has not been sufficiently brought to the notice of the world. All the disasters that attended his rule were in some way connected with money: financial integrity, which had stood so high under his father's government, had absolutely disappeared. Everybody who could do so was plunging into speculations of some kind or other, and if it had not been for the famous mistake **of the Yalu concessions** granted by the Tsar to a small group of adventurers, with nothing to recommend them but impudence, the Japanese War, with its disasters and loss of prestige, might easily have been avoided. It is sufficient to read the memoirs of Count Witte to realize that such was the case.

During the Great War, this daring exploitation of everything that could be laid hold of by groups of speculators, such as those who surrounded Rasputin, reached gigantic proportions. All those speculators either belonged to the bureaucracy or were closely connected with it, for by that time no one but bureaucrats had the chance to approach the sovereign or to be honoured with the attention of his consort.

With the Imperial family the relations of the Empress were more than cool, except in two or three cases. Her great misfortune was that she had not undergone the experience of being for a while the second lady in the land. If Alexander III had not died so unexpectedly, it is likely that his daughter-in-law would have turned out a different woman from what she became. She would have been compelled to obey, to submit to dictation, to being told what she could or could not do. She would also have learnt to know and to appreciate St. Petersburg society, from which she would not have held herself aloof as she did when she became Empress. But coming at once into a position of unlimited power, where she had to give an account of her actions to no one except a weak and adoring husband, she conceived an exaggerated idea of her own importance, and really came to consider herself above everybody else in the world.

Withal, she had in her character a vein of German sentimentality, a craving for affection, especially for flattery, and she felt angry that it was not at once showered upon her. Can one wonder, then, that when she found herself in the presence of Anna Viroubova, who used to go into hysterics if she thought herself ignored by her Imperial mistress, and who continually repeated to her that she adored her while the rest of the world disliked and condemned her, or of men like Protopopoff, who always assured her that she was another Catherine II, and that no one had ever equalled her in intelligence, kindness, and virtue — can one wonder that her head was turned, and that her very superficial intelligence, not grasping all that was untrue in those exaggerations of language, made her think that these were the people whom, she ought to trust and endeavour to keep in power, in spite of the fact that the whole country spurned and despised them?

The Empress Dowager had tried more than once to open the eyes of her son to what was going on under his roof, but with no result whatever, except to estrange him from her. Alexandra had always shown herself deferential towards her mother-in-law, but among her personal friends she had made fun of her and criticized her. It had become the custom among the entourage of the young Court, as it was called, to speak of the Empress Marie as of a frivolous woman, who all through her reign had done nothing but dance, amuse herself, and run heavy bills with Paris dressmakers, but who had suddenly been seized with the ambition to rule in the name of her son. At the Anitchkoff Palace the same sort of thing went on, only that it was Alexandra Feodorovna who was said to nurse exaggerated ideas of her ability to govern a country like Russia; and, the Dowager having far more friends than her daughter-in-law, her opinions and those of the persons who surrounded her counted far more than anything that that daughter-in-law could have said or done. This appreciation of her person and her activity, having been repeated to the young Empress, naturally incensed her, and she came to regard her mother-in-law as her natural enemy.

The same feelings interfered with her relations with the Grand Duke Michael, the Emperor's brother, who, until the birth of little Alexis, stood in the position of heir to the throne, and she detested him in particular. When the Grand Duke, against Nicholas II's wishes, contracted a morganatic marriage with a lady whom the fact of having been twice divorced before she became his wife had made persona non grata at Court, Alexandra thought it advisable to excite the Emperor's anger instead of trying to smooth matters, with the result that the Grand Duke was deprived of his commands, of what money he had not had the wisdom to invest abroad before his marriage, and exiled from Russia for ever, as was said at the time, a "for ever" which did not last long, as ultimately he was restored to his brother's favour and received an important military command during the War.

At the time of Nicholas II's accession to the throne, the most important member of his family was his uncle, the Grand Duke Vladimir, who, with his wife, a clever, ambitious, and scheming woman, had won for themselves a privileged position in St. Petersburg society, exercising a considerable influence over it. The Grand Duchess, a German by birth, had done what she could to insinuate herself into the good graces of her new niece and had tried to explain to her some of the inevitable difficulties with which she could not help being confronted. But the Empress had coolly turned down these sincere efforts, and antagonized her aunt so completely that the latter put herself at the head of a party the aim of which was to look out for every peccadillo of the Empress, exaggerate it, and do its best to discredit her in the eyes of Russian society.

This deplorable situation became even more acute when the eldest son of the grand-ducal pair, the Grand Duke Cyril, without asking anyone's advice or permission, married his cousin, the divorced Grand Duchess of Hesse-Darmstadt, whom Alexandra in her girlish days had so much disliked, and whose separation from the Grand Duke she had done so much to bring about. The Empress was absolutely frantic when she found that this hated sister-in-law was to arrive in Russia and take her place at Court as the wife of a Russian grand duke standing in the direct line of succession to the throne. She seized the pretext that marriages between first cousins are forbidden by the Greek Church, to entreat the Emperor to make an example of his cousin and to banish him from St. Petersburg and deprive him of his income and military rank; she succeeded, indeed, in persuading Nicholas to publish a manifesto on the subject.

This proved too much for the Grand Duke Vladimir, who went to the Tsar and told his Imperial nephew that he had exceeded his powers, and that he would have liked to see what his father, Alexander II, would have said had he known that his granddaughter was banished from the Winter Palace. The Grand Duke was noted for his violent temper, and the extreme bluntness, not to say rudeness, of his language, and he completely overawed the unfortunate Nicholas, who hastened to say that he had been misinformed and would retract some of the harsh measures he had ordered. Cyril was told that he might return to Russia with his wife after a while, which he did, and Alexandra consented to receive her cousin and former sister-in-law more or less graciously. But the incident rankled in the minds of all the parties concerned, and when the revolution of 1917 took place Cyril Vladimirovitch was among the first to go to the Duma, taking with him the troops he commanded, and to recognize the new Government.

Then again, there was the Grand Duke Paul. The latter had also contracted a morganatic marriage, and under circumstances which in his case fully justified the indignation of the Empress. He also was sent abroad but later allowed to return, when his wife began to try to play a leading part in St. Petersburg society and to induce it to recognize her, if not as a grand duchess of Russia, at least as a very important personage. This lady, who during the War was created Princess Paley and played a very conspicuous part all through that tragedy, afterwards claimed to be a friend of Alexandra, who, however, to judge by her letters, did not respond.

The Grand Duke Nicholas and his wife and brother were about the only members of the Imperial family who at one time were really intimate with Alexandra. She warmly upheld the Grand Duke when the latter tried to bring some high military officials to trial for their part in the disasters which had attended the Russo-Japanese War, but a note of discord arose between them when the Grand Duke, together with Count Witte and one or two other people, urged upon the Emperor the necessity of calling together some kind of representative assembly, so as to give the people at least a semblance of constitutional government. The whole idea was absolutely abhorrent to Alexandra, who tried her utmost to influence the sovereign against it. Some people, Anna Viroubova among others, have said that Nicholas hesitated because he thought the Russian nation was not yet ready for such a reform, and was also afraid of a conflict between the dense ignorance of the masses and the fanatical and badly digested Socialism of the intelligentsia; and that, besides, he had very serious misgivings as to the wisdom of any radical change in the Russian system of government. The poor Emperor's doubts had more to do with his apprehensions as to the possibility of his own rights and prerogatives being curtailed than with misgivings as to how the country might react to what ought to have been an invitation to it to take its share in the work of the government. No love for his people was at the root of his at last consenting to grant them the shadow of a constitution; there was only apprehension as to how the event might affect him personally in its development.

His diary of those days is curious. Speaking of the first meeting of the Duma, he writes:

"April 27th, Thursday. — Remarkable day of the reception of the Council of State and of the Duma of the Empire, and the beginning of the official existence of the latter. Mamma arrived at eight o'clock from Gatschina, and together with her we travelled by sea to Petersburg. The weather was quite summery and warm. On the cutter *Peterhof* we went first to the fortress and then to the Winter Palace. We lunched at eleven o'clock. At one began the march to the hall of St. George. After prayers had been said, I greeted the Assembly with a speech. The Council of State was placed on the right side of the throne, and the Duma on the left. We returned to the Malachite room in the same order. At three o'clock we boarded the cutter again, and later the yacht *Alexandra*, and were at home [at Peterhof] at four-thirty. I worked for a long time but felt relieved at the peaceful manner in which the ceremony took place. We drove out in the evening."

In this quiet way Nicholas II took the beginning of what was expected to be the first chapter of a new era of prosperity for Russia. In an even quieter way he notes, three months later, the closing and dissolution of this same Duma he had opened with such pomp, a measure which was resented all over Russia as a violation of the pledges he had voluntarily taken when he had decided to grant the country a semi-constitutional form of government, and which, to say the least, ought not to have been resorted to in such a hurry.

This is what the Tsar writes on the subject:

"July 9th, Sunday. — It has taken place. The Duma has been dissolved to-day. At lunch-time, after mass I could see that many people had very long faces. The manifesto for to-morrow was composed during the day. I signed it at about six o'clock. The weather was lovely."

An amusing passage in the memoirs of Madame Viroubova, which tends to show how very little she understood what was going on around her, or of the true state of public opinion in Russia, especially in St. Petersburg, is a paragraph in which she assures her readers "that few men and fewer women of her class attached any particular importance to the Duma."

When one remembers the agitation in St. Petersburg at that time, and the eagerness with which the deliberations of this assembly was discussed, **as well** as the various comments made as to its fate in the leading salon of the capital, one realizes how wide a gulf existed between the bureaucratic circles to which the Empress's friends belonged and the really intelligent, well-meaning elements of Russian society, among whom existed real love of country and ardent desire for its welfare. It was those Russians who had all along urged upon Nicholas II the necessity for reforms, the indispensable necessity of putting Russia on a level with other great European powers. But they had never been understood, their disinterestedness had never been appreciated, and it was the voice of Bureaucracy which, in the words of the Geneva manifesto, "kept the monarch removed from free communion with the representatives of the nation." That voice alone was listened to, probably because what it said was in such thorough accord with the despotic feelings of the Emperor, and especially of his consort, who never would admit the possibility of any curtailment of autocracy.

In the meanwhile the whole land was rising in agitation against the Government, and mutinies broke out everywhere and were repressed in the most cruel and ruthless manner possible. I will mention only the incident of that Bloody Sunday when, led by the priest Gapone, the workmen from the many factories in St. Petersburg walked towards the Winter Palace to lay their grievances before the Tsar.

They had no intention of being disrespectful; they only wanted to talk to him as to their "Little Father," little thinking that they would be met with loaded guns and sharpened bayonets. For the third time in his life the Emperor had had the opportunity of having a heart-to-heart talk with his subjects, and for the third time he bad repulsed them, little thinking that a few years later it would be their turn to repulse him.

The Empress, it seems, was asked a few weeks after this Bloody Sunday whether she did not regret that such a terrible thing had taken place, and replied that she did not, because rebellious people must be taught a lesson. The importance of what had occurred did not strike her in the least.

It was at about the time when the whole of Russian society was in a state of ebullition, that Alexandra Feodorovna began to interest herself seriously in politics. She had a trump in her hands, the existence of her son, and the necessity of preserving intact for him the vast inheritance of the Romanoffs, and whenever she saw that her husband was hesitating in regard to some reform or other she immediately told him that he had no right to do anything that might endanger this inheritance. Unfortunately, she was always listened to, because Nicholas loved their boy even more ardently than she did, and was constantly thinking of him and of his future. The great sorrow of the Imperial couple was the state of health of this child of promise. They knew, of course, the nature of the ailment with which he was attacked, and it was a source of poignant self-reproach to Alexandra to think that this incurable disease, which made the life of little Alexis one long torture, had been transmitted to him through her, was in fact hereditary in her family, so that every attack the boy suffered wrung the heart of his mother with a grief which was the more passionate because she concealed it from the world.

And here comes the very natural question, why was the fact of this infirmity so studiously concealed? It would have been so much better, from every point of view, if a clean breast had been made of the whole affair, and the Russian people been told that their future Emperor was doomed all his life to be an invalid. Such a confession would have won for the troubled parents the sympathy of the nation, and perhaps made the latter more indulgent in regard to the extraordinary conduct of the Empress. But neither she nor Nicholas II would consent to own to the misfortune which had befallen them, with the result that all kinds of impossible and untrue tales found vogue. Whenever Alexis suffered an attack of his chronic disease, gossip went wild, so that at last even the Foreign Press followed suit, and when the Tsarevitch was at death's door at Spala in Poland, about two years before the War, British papers printed lengthy articles in which it was strongly inferred that the illness of the Heir to the Throne was the result of an attack of Nihilists on his person, of which all kinds of gruesome details were given. Thus is history written.

The Empress meanwhile used to spend hours in prayer before sacred icons, imploring the Virgin and all the saints to cure her son. Always inclined to religious fanaticism, she had allowed herself to be absolutely carried away by the agony of her soul, and had no other idea than to subject herself to every sort of penance in the hope that the Almighty might be moved to restore Alexis.

It was just at that time, when like a drowning person she was ready to catch at any plank of salvation in sight, that one of the great events of her life took place and Rasputin was brought to the palace of Tsarskoye Selo by the Grand Duchess Militsa Nicholaievna, one of the Montenegrin princesses of whom Alexandra had always been so fond.

The Grand Duchess Militsa was another mystic and believer in all kinds of supernatural things. She had made the acquaintance of Rasputin through a Bishop Feofan, who was his first protector, and she really believed him to be a holy man able to get into communication with the Deity Himself. She spoke to the Empress about him, saying that he was a being evidently in possession of some kind of supernatural power that enabled him to raise the dead from their graves, cure the sick, and bring rest and peace to troubled souls. The very idea of meeting someone who might give her some hope of a cure for her beloved child filled the Empress with eager and almost painful anticipation. She allowed the Grand Duchess to bring Rasputin to the palace, and fell under his influence from the very first moment she set her eyes upon him.

Rasputin was already known to a few superstitious ladies in St. Petersburg, mostly the wives and daughters of bureaucrats, but it is difficult to explain or to understand the secret of the undoubted ascendancy which he gained over the minds of so many of them. He was an absolutely uncouth peasant, a man who could hardly read or write, and yet he obtained the confidence of highly educated women, who became his tools and blindly followed every instruction he chose to give them; and this from the very first day he arrived in St. Petersburg. Later on, and especially during the last two years of his life, he had fallen into the hands of a clique of greedy and unscrupulous adventurers, former secret police agents, speculators in quest of money or influence, and then it became quite comprehensible that these same people who wanted, through him, to obtain some favour or other from the Government should do their best to boast of his extraordinary powers and try to represent him as a real "Prophet of God," to use the words dear to Alexandra Feodorovna. But when she first met him, nothing of the kind was the case and Rasputin was known to but very few people, while the rest of the world had not heard a word about him. 'What had made the Grand Duchess Militsa so enthusiastic it is difficult to say, unless she thought that through Rasputin she might secure some advantage and enshrine herself even more than she had done already in the favour of the Empress.

In view of all that was to follow, it is well to lay stress on the circumstances under which Rasputin was brought into the presence of Alexandra. People have said, far and wide, that it was Madame Viroubova who brought him to Tsarskoye Selo, but this statement is absolutely incorrect, because, though she had been very much struck by certain things he had told her in regard to her future marriage, 'which caused her some misgivings that circumstances later on were to justify, it was not she who introduced him to the Court.

Anna also did not realize at that time the importance of having near the Empress, and in close touch with her, a man more or less dependent upon her to maintain himself in the position which he had attained, and so perhaps she did not attach any great meaning to her acquaintance with him. But she was herself so superstitious that she firmly believed he was gifted with certain powers enabling him to know the future. And it was principally for this reason that she perhaps played into the hands of those who wanted to use Rasputin for their own ends, by casually mentioning his name to the Empress as that of a holy man, a man of God, as she termed him, capable, with the help of his prayers, of curing little Alexis in spite of what the best doctors had prophesied in regard to him.

By a strange coincidence, he had no sooner been introduced into the room of the Tsarevitch and prayed by his bedside, than the latter's health showed signs of improvement, and soon he was able to sit up and read. The Empress became quite persuaded that this recovery had been the work of Rasputin, and she made up her mind that she would try to keep him always near her, so that he could pray for the child every minute, day and night.

If everything connected with the little Tsarevitch had not been so inexpressibly sad, one might feel tempted, when speaking about him, to recall the old saying that "granted wishes are often self-sown curses." For years his parents had been ardently longing for the birth of an heir to all their might and splendour. When that heir was at last granted to them, they nearly went mad for joy, and forgot, in their exuberance, the brave Russian soldiers fighting and dying by thousands in distant Manchuria, as well as the loss of prestige and the growing discontent which was slowly rising in the country. They only saw the succession assured at last in the direct line, and for the Empress this meant even more than for her husband, because she realized very well what her position would have been had she become a widow without having a son to protect her. The health of the Emperor had never been over-strong, and he had several times been seriously ill, once in the Crimea, when the Imperial family had gathered together in council and decided that, should anything befall the sovereign, the Grand Duke Michael would be proclaimed Tsar, without taking into account any possibility of Alexandra being with child, which was suspected at that moment.

Alexandra felt that exile from Russia would probably be her portion if she ever lived to see her brother-in-law upon the throne, and perhaps this was one of the reasons why she always behaved so bitterly in regard to him. Suddenly everything changed, and she brought into the world the much-wished-for and long-awaited heir. Hers was a passionate nature, and she concentrated on her boy all the affection of her soul, all the love of her heart. There was everything in the almost superhuman tenderness with which she viewed him — joy, gratitude, pride, hope for a brighter future, all the sentiments that can move a human being to ecstasy, combined with a mother's anxiety and a mother's affection.

Alexis was but a few weeks old when the affliction with which he had been born was discovered, and it is easy to imagine into what state of consternation and despair his parents were thrown. For the Empress the blow was so crushing that it was said her hair began to turn grey from the agony of the knowledge imparted to her. She swore to herself that she would cure her son, cure him in spite of what the doctors said, in spite of the decrees of science and the futility of human help. Doctors were very well in their way, but it was not to them that she looked for succour. Above them there was God, the God in whom she trusted, and who would never be so cruel as to rob her of the happiness for which she had been waiting for ten long years. God could perform miracles; saints could perform them, prayers could obtain them. And she began passionately, fervently, ardently, to pray as one does when human help seems to fade into dim space. She would not believe her child was doomed. In a certain sense she hurled a challenge at the Almighty by her refusal to admit He could inflict such agony upon her. All her energy was henceforward to be devoted to her baby, and more than ever did she think herself obliged to watch over the inheritance to which he had been born, and to safeguard the autocracy of which he was in the course of time to become the representative.

This was the great tragedy of the life of the last Russian Tsarina. Had she been the mother of a healthy son, it is likely that she would not have allowed herself to fall so completely under the dominion of quacks and rogues, that she would have shown herself more human in her appreciation of people and of facts, and that she would not have admitted into her intimacy the persons who towards the end formed the only society she would consent to see, the only companionship she sought.

After Alexis was born, the future of Alexandra's daughters became a subject of everlasting gossip in St. Petersburg, which only increased as time went on and they grew up. The Empress was reproached for not giving them the enjoyments and pleasures which all other girls had, and for preventing them from mingling and becoming acquainted with the best elements of the society of the two Russian capitals. But the prejudices entertained ever since her arrival in Russia by Alexandra Feodorovna against the nobility had only increased with years. She made no secret of them; on the contrary, she never missed an opportunity to say that she considered her daughters would be contaminated if she allowed them to have friends among girls whose parents belonged to the smart society. It is easy to imagine how such utterances, which of course were immediately repeated, wounded those whom they concerned, and the enmities against the Empress they aroused. It cannot be gainsaid that she neglected her daughters. There were times when she hardly saw them during the day, but at others she insisted on their following her in her religious ecstasies and joining in her prayers and her veneration for Rasputin, whose influence was already becoming very serious.

It was at about this time — that is, two or three years before the War — that a painful incident occurred which was the cause of more indignation and anger against the Empress. The education of the young grand duchesses was supervised, as far as possible, in view of her constant interference with it, by a lady of great intelligence, impeccable integrity, and absolute devotion to her duties, Mademoiselle Sophie Tutscheff, whose family was one of the oldest and best-known in Moscow. Mademoiselle Tutscheff was dissatisfied with certain liberties taken by Rasputin in regard to her pupils, and objected to his visiting them in their apartments. Finding that the Empress did not agree with her on that subject, she boldly went to the Tsar and told him that she could no longer remain responsible for the rearing of his daughters, and that unless he gave her a free hand in regard to certain delicate matters, she would resign. In other memoirs this incident has been distorted, but in truth, this devoted servant of the Imperial family preferred to give up a position so many would have submitted to anything to retain, rather than witness passively things which she felt in her heart were tending to discredit the dynasty in the eyes of the world, but which she was powerless to alter.

Towards the last the young grand duchesses kept apart from girls of their own age, concentrating their sympathies on their mother's friends, such as Anna Viroubova, with whom they were evidently on the most intimate terms, — Madame Lili Dehn, the wife of an officer of the Imperial yacht *Standard*, a pretty, inoffensive, and simple little thing, whom her admiration for Rasputin had caused to be taken into the good graces of Alexandra Feodorovna; and one or two others. They were allowed to flirt as much as they liked with the officers of the Imperial yacht, and to treat them with familiarity, which also caused much scandal and added to the unpopularity of their mother.

And in the meanwhile the little Tsarevitch was passing from one attack to another, and each time his distracted parents became more and more convinced that the only person who could help him was Rasputin. The crafty peasant had told them that with time the child would outgrow his infirmity and that meanwhile they had better let him lead a simple life, be as much as possible in the open air, and not worry him too much with lessons.

The boy was charming, affectionate, and attractive, but he had his mother's imperious disposition, and in consequence was not easy to handle, especially as there was always the fear that any undue exertion or emotion or even fit of anger might bring about another haemorrhage. M. Gilliard, his tutor, tells us, in his interesting book, that it was a problem to him how to bring him to study as he ought, and it is certain that in consequence of his physical condition, his education came to be sadly neglected. But during the War, and especially during the time his father had him at the front with him, the boy's character began to improve, as he realized the seriousness of life and of the times, as well as the enormity of the struggle under which Russia was succumbing slowly, and it is likely that if he had survived he might have attained to a clear understanding of the gravity of the days in which he was living.

In the meanwhile the poor little fellow was having a hard time of it, and he hardly ever was entirely free from pain. Active and lively as he was, one may imagine how disagreeable it must have been for him to be always reminded of his infirmity and told he must not play in the same way other boys of his age were allowed to, or exert himself in any way. At such times he used to cry, and his tears wrung his mother's heart, with the consequence that she became increasingly morbid under the strain, and her own health came to be affected. She developed heart disease, which furnished her with another pretext for continuing her secluded existence, and St. Petersburg society another reason for criticizing her. "We don't want to see her," was said at the time everywhere. " She can shut herself up as much as she likes, but why does she insist on her daughters being kept prisoners, and on her husband refusing to meet people from whom he could obtain useful information as to what is going on in the country?"

It is certain that the seclusion in which the Imperial family persisted in living, ended by destroying that respect for the person of the monarch which had formerly been so strong a feature in the Russian character. It also had an influence on the general morals of society, which became more and more lax as society realized that there was no one above it whose praise or blame could make or mar its standing. Formerly it would have been considered a dreadful thing to have incurred Imperial displeasure for an infraction of the moral code, especially since it would have involved the loss of invitations to Court balls or festivities. Now no one bothered about such things: Court balls were no longer given, the Winter Palace had been converted into a lumber room; society had turned its back upon the sovereign and his consort and, sad to say, had discovered that not only could it exist very well without them., but that it was infinitely more comfortable and agreeable to feel sure that nothing one might ever do would be censured by people having the right to do so.

Slowly but surely, Imperial prestige was disappearing, and autocracy was losing its hold upon the public mind, and this came but too vividly to light during the celebration in St. Petersburg of the three-hundredth year of the accession of the Romanoffs to the throne of the Ruriks. The Imperial family came from Tsarskoye Selo to the capital to be present, and remained three days in the Winter Palace, the last time they ever slept under its roof, and a solemn service of thanksgiving was celebrated in the Kazan Cathedral. The streets were crowded with people eager to **catch a glimpse of the Imperial** *cortège*, **but in spite of the hurrahs, most of which** came from the troops massed on its route, there was absolutely none of the enthusiasm such an occasion usually evokes. The nation had ceased to care for anything connected with its ruler; had become indifferent. The nobility of St, Petersburg, however, gave a ball to which the Emperor and Empress were invited, and which they consented to grace with their presence. But Alexandra remained absolutely impassive, and hardly exchanged a word with the hosts. She looked very pretty, and for the last time appeared covered with the most splendid of the crown jewels. But there was something quite unreal about the entire festival, something exceedingly forced and sad, although no one suspected that this jubilee was to mark the end of an epoch in Russian history; the prophecy uttered by a beggar woman at the time of the election of Michael Romanoff to the throne of Moscow, that "it would be for three hundred years, and no more," was going to be tragically fulfilled.

In regard to this lack of amiability of the Empress, Prince Volkonski, in his memoirs, describes it accurately:

"The Empress Alexandra," he writes, "was not amiable, and affability did not belong to her character. Moreover, she was painfully reserved, though not shy, as some imagined. She spoke only with great hesitation, and every word she uttered seemed to be wrung from her by force, while large red spots appeared upon her face as a result of the effort she made in opening her mouth. The one outstanding feature of her nature was hatred of mankind and distrust of individuals, and of course this had deprived her of every vestige of popularity. She was only a name, a walking image, and her whole conduct and manner seemed to be only the performance of an official duty, deprived of every trace of spontaneity, . . . She was not only cold but icy. All her movements, whether she entered or left a room, were nothing but a pantomime. She never made any remark of her own accord, never expressed an opinion or a judgment in public. In the course of the two years during which I occupied the position of a director of the Imperial theatres, I heard her voice only once, and that was when somehow my conversation with the Emperor turned upon the subject of the skirts of our ballet dancers, which she thought, and very justly so, much too short."

After the jubilee, the Court returned to Tsarskoye Selo, and resumed its usual existence, varied by a journey to Moscow and to the old town of Kostroma, where they visited the monastery where Michael Romanoff, the founder of the Russian dynasty, had lived; a monastery called Ipatieff, which by a curious coincidence happened to be the same name as that of the house where Nicholas II and his family were to be so brutally murdered in the city of Ekaterinburg. For a while all seemed to be quiet in the Russian Empire.

About this time a powerful camarilla, composed of a handful of adventurers eager and greedy for gain and riches, hit upon the idea of trying to obtain material profits and advantages by means of the influence exercised by Rasputin over the Empress, an influence which was no longer denied or disputed, but acknowledged everywhere and by all.

Among those who remained devoted to the dynasty was M. Rodzianko, the president of the Imperial Duma. In the very interesting memoirs he wrote, which unfortunately stop at the most critical moment of his political career, the first March revolution and the abdication of the Emperor, he tells us of the efforts he made to open the eyes of Nicholas II to the identity of the peasant who had become a power at his Court and in his household. Rodzianko was an honest man whose integrity has never been disputed, nor his attachment to the monarchy. The conversations he had with the Tsar on the subject of Rasputin make curious reading. Unfortunately he also was led to believe the many false reports which at that time were circulating all over St. Petersburg, and he did not check sufficiently the information given to him. The fact that some of the things he told the Emperor proved to be either exaggerated or not quite true obviously weakened his case, and allowed the Empress to represent him to her Imperial husband as a libeller. Rodzianko was anything but that. What he said, he believed to be the truth, but the difficulty was to know what was really the truth during the eventful years which preceded the War.

After the Revolution the first Provisional Government had the entire question of Rasputin and his relations with the Empress investigated by a magistrate of undoubted integrity, who received instructions to do all that lay in his power to ascertain how trustworthy were the different reports circulating in Russian society concerning Rasputin. He himself acknowledges, in the report he presented, that he had been prejudiced against the Empress before he even began the task he had been commanded to undertake. But he was compelled to own that much of what had been believed in regard to Rasputin was not true, resting in fact only upon gossip of a most malicious nature. I will not here try either to refute or to support his view, as I have not before me any official documents enabling me to form an independent judgment on such an important matter. I will therefore allow the reader to think what he prefers, taking into consideration, however, the fact that both M. Rodzianko and Judge Rudneff were people in whom one could have complete confidence.

The question therefore arises whether there were any persons before the War who were trying to bring about a revolution with the help of false reports destined to influence even the men known to be entirely devoted to the monarchy. Kerensky, in his book, tells us that the War delayed the Revolution instead of hastening it, and unfortunately there cannot be any doubt in the minds of those who were watching the course of public events and home politics in Russia during the last three or four years which preceded the outbreak of the Great War, that Kerensky speaks the truth. Revolution was in the air, and there existed a general idea that it was going to break out in terrible form and sweep away the Romanoff dynasty with all its adherents, when the assassinations of Sarajevo settled the fate of Europe, and of Nicholas II as well, though for a while the event delayed the climax.

And now I am going to make a digression, and try to tell the reader something of the real Rasputin. For one thing, he was neither a priest nor a monk, but one of those wandering pilgrims such as one used to meet before the War at the gates of every Russian monastery. He had visited Jerusalem, the convent of .Mount Athos, the famous sanctuary of Solovetsk on the White Sea, that on Troytskaia Lavra near Moscow, and the holy shrines of Kieff. He succeeded, with the help of some people whose names so far have remained unknown, in worming himself into the intimacy of two bishops, Hermogene and Feofan, who were the first to believe in his supernatural powers, which, they bitterly regretted afterwards. They introduced him to the Grand Duchess Militsa and finally to the Empress herself, always seeking prayers for her little sick boy. We know that, as chance would have it, the child grew better after Rasputin had visited him for the first time, and as he was the first and only person who gave hopes of his recovery to his distracted mother, there was nothing wonderful in the fact that a woman who, like Alexandra, had for years been absorbed in religious practices, with a strong tendency to mysticism, should have really come to consider him a sort of saint. She imagined in all sincerity that he was a kind of guardian angel sent by God to watch over her son, her family, and Russia. The presence of Rasputin was a comfort to her, just as the conversations of M. Philippe had been, and she found in that common peasant the second sympathetic soul she had ever met. Rasputin himself did not at first attach any undue importance to the favouritism which was extended to him. But others saw all the advantages that could be drawn from it, and began to lecture and advise him, to urge him to make use of the exceptional opportunities which were being granted to him.

Among those who played a leading part in the bolstering up of Rasputin was Maniuloff, a former detective who was very well known, and who by some mystery no one was ever able to fathom, had contrived to win the confidence of several Ministers, and finally to become editor of the *Evening Times*, a gossipy little newspaper which every inhabitant of St. Petersburg religiously read every afternoon, to enjoy Maniuloff's latest spicy bit. He must have required a great deal of money to live in the luxurious style to which he had become accustomed, and being extremely clever, was the first to recognize the immense advantages that might be derived from a close acquaintanceship with Rasputin. With him were other persons, all more or less compromised, and it is a fact that during the Great War some German agents joined their group. But although, as the recently published letters of the Empress make clear, Rasputin eventually gave her political advice and had a finger in the appointment or dismissal of Ministers and other important functionaries, yet the aim of those of whom he became the tool was not political but financial.

The best proof of this may be found in the numerous letters addressed by him to people in high position in the Russian capital, asking them to do this or that for him. The demands always had something to do with money, the granting of some concession or contract to those in whom he was interested, and naturally this had a great deal to do with the discredit into which the dynasty fell towards the end, and in a certain sense justified some of the reproaches addressed to the Empress. Rasputin was always in need of money, though when he died he left no fortune to speak of, because what he earned he immediately spent, and those who were constantly at his side to urge him to obtain some favour or other for them needed money even more than he did and were not scrupulous as to the methods of obtaining it. This soon became known, until at last the whole of Russia became aware that there was, at the side of the Tsarina, a man who, at a time when the country was fighting for its very existence, was always ready to appropriate for his own use, or that of his friends, as much as possible of its wealth.

That he never hesitated to serve these friends is proved without doubt by letters of his which were found in the official archives of several Ministries, and it was never denied by any of his followers and devotees. Even Anna Viroubova admits it, and in view of this fact it is interesting to quote from her book the following passage:

"The wave of popular opposition against Rasputin began in the last two and a half years of his life. Long before it started, long before his name was reviled and execrated in the Press and in society, his lodgings in Petrograd, where he began to spend longer and longer periods, were constantly crowded with beggars and petitioners. These were people of all stations who believed that, whether he was good or evil, his influence at Court was limitless. Every kind of petty official, every sort of poverty-stricken aspirant and grafting politician, revolutionary agents, spies, and secret police haunted the place, pressing on Rasputin papers and petitions to be presented to the Emperor. To do Rasputin strict justice, he was for ever telling the petitioners that it would do no good at all for him to present their papers, but he did not seem to have the strength of mind to refuse point-blank to receive them. Often in pity for those who were sick and poor, or, as he thought, deserving, he would send them to one or another of his rich and influential acquaintances, with a note reading: 'Please, dear friend, receive him.'"

Madame Viroubova naturally attempts to excuse a man whom in all sincerity she considered a holy creature; but not even she could deny the fact that the house of this common, uncouth peasant had become a meeting-place for every kind of adventurer eager to obtain, through him and with the help of his influence, some favour or other from the Emperor or the Empress of Russia, and that the manner in which he boasted that he could make them do whatever he wished had become a public scandal.

There is in existence another document, far more important than the reminiscences of a woman whom, without slandering her, one may say was as much the tool of clever intriguers as Rasputin himself. It is the report, to which I have already alluded, of M. Rudneff, the judge who had been appointed by the Government to examine what truth there was in the various rumours connected with Rasputin. It is such an important document that it is given in extenso[1] and it certainly disposes with finality of the various lies which had been put into circulation in regard to the Empress, clearing her entirely of the accusation of immorality, or of having been during the World War a German agent.

But after having read this extraordinary document, one can hardly credit that the facts related in it refer to things which actually happened in our own day: they read like the intrigues of the ancient Byzantine Court.

But at the same time this report of a judge of excellent reputation, proves conclusively that the reproaches addressed to Alexandra Feodorovna, both as to her private and her political activity, were founded principally upon gossip of the worst kind. The Tsarina was an exceedingly foolish, vain woman, but she was no traitor and remained until the end a faithful wife and almost too devoted mother, because it was her misguided, morbid, and exaggerated love for her son that partly caused the ultimate disaster in which she ended by being involved. What further proof can one want of the inanity of those accusations which charged her with being a shameless woman?

The Empress, in a certain sense, always remained seated in that ivory chair from which she viewed so wrongly the people who surrounded her, and the events which were to overpower her. She was misjudged, she was slandered, and an ocean of hatred was let loose against her. But at the same time it would be useless to deny that this woman of destiny was the principal cause of the ruin of Russia; of the fall of the dynasty that had ruled the country for three hundred years and had made it the great thing which it appeared to be until the feet of clay gave way. Anna Viroubova is right when she says that "the soil in Russia had been very well prepared for Bolshevism, and that it was the Russians themselves who were responsible for the catastrophe in which the country perished," but she is wrong when pretending that it was the privileged classes who were principally guilty.

The culpable ones were the bureaucracy, that bureaucracy which, from the time of Peter the Great, had kept the sovereign in its clutches, shamelessly enriching itself through the toils of the nation, and which had steadfastly stood between that nation and the road to progress and to freedom of thought and speech; that bureaucracy which had maintained itself in power only through the help and force wielded by an unscrupulous, rotten police system which had dishonoured and contaminated everything it had touched. The aristocracy had fought it, the intelligentsia had fought it, the peasantry had tried to fight it; but they had all failed ; the peasants had fallen back into a state of complete apathy, the intelligentsia had joined extremist parties to which it would never have allied itself had it not been persecuted and driven into this mistake, while the aristocracy, weary of an unequal struggle, had given up, and was waiting for an opportune moment to get rid of a sovereign whom it had grown to hate just as, a century and a half before, if had hated his ancestor Paul I. Unfortunately — and I use the word advisedly — it had lacked the energy to strike a decisive blow and allowed the Revolution to come from below instead of from above, forgetting the famous words of Nesselrode, who, when asked by a foreigner what sort of government it was that presided over the destinies of Russia, had replied that it was "an autocracy mitigated by political assassination."

None among that gay, frivolous St. Petersburg society which, even during the agony of the War, had continued to lead its merry, happy-go-lucky existence of selfish indulgence, shutting its eyes to the signs of the approaching storm, had the courage of the men who removed Paul I from the path of his and their country. But they hurled every kind of odious accusation and slander on the Emperor and on his wife, which in the long run discredited them both at home and abroad, until the whole world felt that for the general welfare of Russia, as well as of her allies, a change of government had become inevitable.

Alexandra Feodorovna was well aware of the campaign that had been started against her, and this knowledge had added to her personal feeling s of bitterness. Although, as I have said, she was a silly woman, yet she was sufficiently clear-minded to realize that the nobility, while clamouring so loudly for a constitution, wanted it for itself alone, while the **intelligentsia** claimed it because it imagined that it would put those of their way of thought in the place of those who were ruling the country in such a misguided fashion. But she lacked the calm judgment which would have enabled her to fight her way through all those difficulties, and she was hampered by that excessive tendency to mysticism which was to prove her bane.

Perhaps the man who has judged her most clearly, and best understood Alexandra's mysterious character, is Sir George Buchanan, who during the War was British Ambassador in St. Petersburg, and who had known the Empress since her girlhood days, when he had been Great Britain's Minister at Darmstadt. Speaking of her, he writes that:

"despite her many good qualities — her warm heart, her devotion to husband and children, her well-meant but ill-advised endeavours to inspire the former with the firmness and decision which his character lacked — the Empress Alexandra was not a fitting helpmate for a sovereign in his difficult position. Of a shy and retiring disposition, though a born autocrat, she failed to win the affection of her subjects. She misjudged the situation from the very first, encouraging him, when the political waters were already running dangerously high, to steer a course fraught with danger to the ship of state. The tragic element is already discernible in the first act of the drama. A good woman bent on serving her husband's interests, she is to prove the chosen instrument of his ruin. Diffident and irresolute, the Emperor was bound to fall under the influence of a will stronger than his. It was her blind faith in an unbridled autocracy that was to be his undoing. Had he had as consort a woman with broader views and better insight who would have grasped the fact that such a regime was an anachronism in the twentieth century, the history of his reign would have been different, and he might still be Emperor of Russia."

There is nothing to add to this appreciation by a man who, better than most, was able to come to a conclusion as to the complex character and strange nature of the Empress. Her destiny developed itself according to an inexorable plan in which one calamity follows upon another. She was imprudent, often selfish, always imperious, sometimes cruel, and never happy. But this should be said in her favour, and this justice must be rendered to her: she never was a traitor, and her mistakes were always sincere.

The report of Judge Rudneff is partly confirmed and partly

contradicted by the investigating magistrate whom Admiral Kolchak entrusted with the inquiry into the murder of the Imperial family after his army had combined with that of the Czechoslovaks and taken Ekaterinburg three days after the tragedy. This magistrate, Sokoloff by name, was one of those great judicial figures of whom there were not many in Russia, and whose conduct reminds us of the judges described by Balzac in his "Comedie Humaine." He went deeply into the psychology of both the Emperor and Empress in the investigation which he made of their murder, and condensed it into a volume he was about to publish when death suddenly overtook him in Salbris, in France. His friends brought it out a few months later. Sokoloff tries to fix the responsibility for the crime and at the same time to reconstruct its details, and especially to discover its origin and the causes that brought it about. He frankly admits that, having been born into a quite different sphere, he finds it hard, if not impossible, to enter into the temperamental make-up of the murdered sovereigns, but this is what he writes about the Empress:

"She was absolutely sincere in thought, and most deeply convinced that the masses of the Russian nation understood her as well as she understood them, and that her religious proclivities had an echo in theirs. One could not offend her more than by saying that she did not know and did not understand the Russian soul. She lived, as it were, with closed eyes, and never noticed the storm that was slowly arising on the horizon.

"All her existence was clouded by one fact, and this was the illness of her beloved son, and the necessity for her to control her feelings in regard to this crushing sorrow turned her into a religious fanatic and completely upset her nerves. In a word, she was hysterical and not normal. Her aversion to people, her seclusion, the loneliness of her soul and heart, had all of them one cause and one reason: they proceeded from the state of her health, from her hysterical condition. This explains her feelings with reference to Rasputin, in whom she firmly believed she had found the saviour of her child, and who at last became absolutely powerful in the palace and the only being except Anna Viroubova who could influence the Empress; and the latter's maid, Madeleine Zanotti, whom I had the opportunity of questioning in Paris, said in regard to this that 'little by little Rasputin entered into the family existence of the sovereigns. For the Empress he was a saint and nothing else. His influence over her in the last years was absolutely colossal. Every word of his became a law for her. Rasputin often came to the palace, certainly several times a month. Her Majesty received him alone, and she became his tool and his slave. I am convinced, from what I have observed, that towards the end the Emperor fell completely under the influence of his wife, and, in consequence, of Rasputin. In the beginning he was not so religious as he subsequently became. The Empress towards the last liked to mix herself in the affairs of the government and to interfere wherever she could. But in reality she did so because Rasputin had told her it was her duty.'"

To this Magistrate Sokoloff adds mournfully:
"The curse of Rasputin was to follow the Imperial family to the last."

NOTES

1 Appendix V.

Queen Victoria with the children of her second daughter Alice, Grand Duchess of Hesse and the Rhine, 1879, shortly after Alice's death, with Princess Alexandra seated bottom right

Emperor Alexander III

Empress Marie Feodorovna

Princess Alexandra and Grand Duke Nicholas, the Tsarevich,
during their engagement, 1894

Nicholas and Alexandra with their eldest child Olga, Queen Victoria and the Prince of Wales, later King Edward VII, at Balmoral, 1896

Alexandra, a signed photograph, 1899

Tsar Nicholas and Alexis, the Tsarevich, c.1912

Empress Alexandra and Grand Duchess Tatiana, c.1908

Rasputin

The opening of the first Duma, 1905

The Tsar and Tsarina with their children

The British and Russian royal families at Cowes, 1909

Grand Duchesses Marie, Olga, Anastasia Tatiana and Tatiana in captivity, 1917

The former Tsar Nicholas II in captivity, surrounded by guards, 1917

PART THREE

CHAPTER VII

THE WOMAN OF DESTINY

THE reader will perhaps feel that I have dwelt too much on the different causes that brought about the unpopularity of Alexandra Feodorovna, or have given too much space to the story of her early years in Russia; but it was the only way in which I could hope to draw an exact picture of the Empress. It is her first steps at the Court of St. Petersburg that give the key to the development of her character, and to the subsequent errors into which she was drawn. A few judicious friends might have saved her. But such friends she did not have, she could not have, because she would not endure near her independent people capable of telling her the truth.

Then again, she had a special genius for wounding those whom she disliked or in whom she suspected opponents, if not enemies. Her snubbing of Prince Orloff, whom she had always detested, perhaps because the Emperor liked him, and who was head of his military cabinet, delighted St. Petersburg society, only too glad to repeat it on every possible occasion.

The Prince generally accompanied the Imperial family on its annual cruise in the Finnish waters, on board their yacht. Now, the Empress did not want him there, but was afraid to say so openly. She therefore resorted to a roundabout way of getting rid of her *bête noire*, as she called him. When she was on the point of embarking, and the suite waited at the landing-place, together with the authorities and some friends who had come to bid the Imperial pair good-bye, she went straight up to Prince Orloff, and in the blandest manner possible asked him where he intended to go for his vacation while the Emperor and she were cruising. The Prince was so taken aback, that at first he did not know what to say, his luggage being already on board, and also his valet. He recovered himself, however, and coldly replied that he would go where the orders of His Majesty could reach him most rapidly. Alexandra smiled. "Oh, but you know he won't have any orders to give you while we are on the yacht," she said, and then turned her back upon him. The Prince could do nothing but remain on shore, and (so at least the busybodies declared) three days passed before he could recover his luggage and his valet could be landed. Such incidents certainly did not help to make friends for the Empress.

It should here be added that the Prince, who must not be confused with General Orloff,[1] the friend of Alexandra Feodorovna, as some people do, later proved one of the bitterest opponents of Rasputin and more than once implored the Tsar to get rid of that adventurer, with the result that Orloff finally lost his position, and when the Grand Duke Nicholas was appointed Viceroy of the Caucasus, was also sent there as chief of his household, an honorary exile if ever there was one. It was related that when Nicholas II was stopped at Pskoff and detained there on his return to the capital, in order to be compelled to sign his abdication, he exclaimed, "If Orloff had been here, this would not have happened!" and very likely it would not, because the Prince, in some way or other, would have contrived to bring the sovereign back to Tsarskoye Selo, or in any case would not have forsaken him, as all the other members of his household, with only one or two exceptions, hastened to do.

In spite, however, of all these incidents, it is probable that the storm of calumnies which was launched against the Empress would not have been so terrible if the War had not taken place. It was the War that gave the signal for the loosing of passions, it was the War that destroyed the last remnants of prestige left to the Romanoffs, and it was also during the War that Alexandra Feodorovna began to take an active part in politics and, as her correspondence shows, really ruled Russia, or at least tried to do so.

This correspondence, to which I will constantly refer while continuing my study of the personality of this woman of destiny, and to which Judge Rudneff, by the way, had no access, because the Emperor took it with him to Siberia, where it was discovered after his assassination, gives the clue to the whole tragedy, and while it utterly and absolutely clears Alexandra of any suspicion of having ever been in sympathy with the Germans, it proves that she tried by every possible means to influence her husband, to rule him, and to impose her will upon him. It also exposes her lack of political acumen, her complete unfamiliarity with public affairs, and her blind faith in Rasputin's knowledge and competence to give advice, not only to her, but also to the Tsar and to his generals. Little wonder that she became so unpopular at Headquarters whenever she visited there, and that the staff and suite of the Emperor dreaded her arrival. If she was convinced of the necessity of obeying and cheerfully allowing Rasputin to direct the war operations as well as choose her husband's Ministers, it could hardly have been expected that experienced commanders and statesmen would share her sentiments on the subject.

In regard to the War, the Empress showed herself all through the sincere friend of the Allies. She remarked once to Sir George Buchanan, "I am English, not German," and her affection for her mother's land never shone to more advantage than during that dreadful period. But, at the same time, she opposed the War before it was declared, and tried sincerely to persuade Nicholas II that it was his duty to do everything in his power to avoid it breaking out.

Rasputin also inspired her in her conduct during those days of anguish and suspense before the world was turned into Armageddon. He was not in St. Petersburg, but in his native village of Pokrovski in Siberia, recovering from an attempt upon his life made by a woman named Gussieva, who pretended that she had been sent to stab him by Iliodor. But from his sick-bed he wired to the Emperor, begging him not to go to war and predicting that it would result in the destruction of the Empire. This was supposed by his followers to have been a miraculous inkling of the future, but no one knowing the state of ferment in which the country was plunged, and its utter unpreparedness for the struggle, could have helped seeing that this time it would not be as it had been after the Russo-Japanese War, but that the nation, exasperated by inevitable disasters, would rise against its rulers and overthrow them, because the army this time would side with the adversaries of the Government, which it had not previously done.

Madame Viroubova tells us that the Empress hoped against hope, until the last minute, that Rasputin's advice would be followed and war averted, and that when she had to resign herself to the inevitable, she gave way to a passion of weeping, exclaiming: "This is the end of everything!" The next day, when the Imperial pair came to St. Petersburg to be present at the reading of the manifesto in the Winter Palace, Alexandra's emotion was noticed by everybody and harshly attributed to her German sympathies. She had already, however, a complete plan of action prepared in her mind, and took up at once the organization of medical relief and of suitable trains to convey the wounded from the front to base hospitals. The Red Cross was placed under the patronage of the Dowager Empress, but her daughter-in-law, instead of trying to work in conjunction with her, organized independent evacuation hospitals over which she alone had control.

She enrolled herself and her two elder daughters as student nurses, and spent several hours every day learning the duties she had to fake up. But here again she offended many people, because the only person whom she asked to share her work was Madame Viroubova, while St. Petersburg had expected that she would appeal to ladies of the highest society to help her in her labours of mercy, and not engage in them under the same system of secrecy that seemed to characterize ail her actions. Not unnaturally this added to the irritation which already existed in regard to the Empress's making a constant companion of a person whom no one liked, many feared, and all viewed as not belonging to the social sphere in which the consort of the sovereign ought to have looked for her friends.

Alexandra devoted all her energy to her self-imposed task of transforming herself into a sister of charity. But in spite of what her flatterers said, her conduct, admirable though it was — for it is certain that she devoted herself entirely to her sick and wounded, and performed the most repugnant duties of a sick-nurse without flinching — neither pleased nor appealed to the masses. The soldiers themselves, though they professed much enthusiasm when they saw her enter their sick wards, infinitely preferred to be attended by professional nurses. Somehow the idea of a Russian Tsarina taking upon herself the most menial work, instead of appealing to those for whom she performed it as something sublime, deprived them of the awe with which the Empress as Empress inspired them, and placed her on a level with other women, which shook all their notions as to what was right or wrong.

Russians had always found their empresses seated on an ivory chair, receiving the homage of their faithful subjects, and they could not understand how it could come that they should suddenly see her by their bedside, talking familiarly with them, washing their wounds, or giving them their medicine. It lowered her in the estimation of these men, who, strange as it may seem, would have preferred to see her come and speak to them surrounded with all the pomp of Imperial power, dressed in gold brocade and blazing with jewels. They would then have realized and felt that it was the Tsarina interesting herself in them and talking to them. Seeing a woman dressed as a sick-nurse, assisting a doctor, somehow destroyed all their inborn ideas of what an Empress should be, and consequently took away her prestige.

Happily for her, Alexandra did not guess what was going on in the minds of these men on whom she lavished such loving and tender care, and perhaps it was just as well. But even she must have felt that in spite of her endeavours to show herself a ministering angel to her suffering subjects, she was getting more and more unpopular. This became particularly evident during a short stay she made in Moscow without the Emperor on her return to Tsarskoye Selo from a tour of inspection of different base hospitals, when the population of the ancient capital received her most coldly, not to say insultingly, and when even her sister, the Grand Duchess Elizabeth, plainly showed that she disapproved of her conduct, and treated Anna Viroubova more than coolly. The latter tells us that it was during this Moscow journey that she realized there existed a plot to strike at the Empress through her friends, but it was nothing of the kind; it was simply the public's disapproval of things which distressed and wounded it, slowly coming to the surface, together with the bottled-up resentment of years which at last was able to manifest itself publicly.

But the Tsarina herself seems to have remained unconscious of the approaching upheaval almost to the last minute. One of her first letters to her husband shows her state of mind:

"Looking after the wounded," she writes, "is my consolation, and that is why the last morning I even wanted to get there while you were receiving, so as to keep my spirits up and not break down before you. To lessen their sufferings even in a small way helps the aching heart."

And later we find the characteristic words:

" Such a war ought to cleanse the spirits and not defile them, is it not so ? . . . When I get hold of people alone who I know suffer much, I always touch on this subject, and with God's help have many a time succeeded in making them understand that it is a possible and good thing to do, and it brings relief and peace to many a weary heart. With one of our officers I also spoke and he agreed, and bore his pains far better. It seems to me this is one of the chief duties of us women — to try to bring nearer people to God, to make them realize that He is more attainable and is near to us, waiting for our love and trust to turn to Him. Shyness and false pride — therefore one must help them break this wall. . ."

But even in those early letters, dated the first year of the War, we find references to Rasputin which show the important part he was playing in the life of Alexandra Feodorovna. On October 27, 1914, she writes to the Emperor:

"I intend, if possible, to stop perhaps at Dvinsk on the way to you, if there is time. There we shall go as sisters- — our Friend likes us to — and to-morrow also. But while we are with you at Grodno we shall dress otherwise, in order not to make you shy driving with a nurse."

Beautiful thoughts and beautiful words, but who ever gave credit for them to this unfortunate woman, who, in her vain quest of a popularity for which her heart and her soul yearned, and which she was never to obtain, allowed herself to fall under the power of a handful of people whom even she suspected and at times distrusted. For Alexandra Feodorovna — and this is one of the curious incidents of the tragedy — was at times even harsh in her judgments of this same Anna Viroubova, from whom she was inseparable, and whom she would not allow to leave her side, although there was a time when she had believed that she had tried to win away from her the affections of the Emperor.

Madame Viroubova, whose conscience is evidently not at ease on this point, tells us, in her book, that Alexandra was jealous of her and suspicious of her as well as of the Emperor, and that at one time a cloud had come between them. And certainly something painful must have occurred, judging from the following passages in the Tsarina's letters to her husband:

"I only dread Ania's humour. . . . Let's hope she will keep herself in hand. I take everything much more coolly now, and don't worry about her rudeness and moods as I did formerly. A break came as a result of her behaviour and words in the Crimea. We are friends, and I am very fond of her, and always shall be, but something has gone, a link broken by her behaviour towards us both; she can never be as near to me as she was. One tries to hide one's sorrow, though not one's pride with it. After all, it is harder for me than for her, though she does not agree, as you are everything to her and I have the children; but she has me, whom she says she loves. It is not worth while to speak about this, and it is not interesting to you at all."

And a little later the Empress writes:

"I enclose a letter from Ania; I don't know whether you agree to her writing, but I can't say no, once she asks me, and better this way than through the servants. She sent for Kondratiev yesterday — so foolish to get the servants to talk to — in the hospital she already wanted to see them— only to make a fuss. It's not quite ladylike, I must honestly say. Now she will be sending for your men, and that will be quite improper; why can't she, then, rather ask after the poor wounded she knows, and with whom she won't have anything to do?"

These remarks can only add to the mystery of the link which bound the Tsarina to the woman. But in spite of her bitter remarks, and her evident conviction of the selfishness, lack of tact, and lack of intelligence of this favourite, she persisted in keeping her near her, although she would undoubtedly have recovered some popularity among the people if she had had the moral courage to free herself from this influence. Can it be that Rasputin had hypnotized her into refusing every other friendship for the sake of a woman who was not even sincerely attached to her, but from whom she accepted a familiarity she would undoubtedly have repulsed most energetically had it come from anyone else? One cannot help thinking that there may be some truth in this supposition, because there were certainly moments when Alexandra did not want Anna Viroubova near her, as shown in the following letter:

"My dear, Ania has been wheeled by Shuk as far as Woyeikoff's house. Dr. Korenev near her, and was not a bit tired; now she wants to visit me to-morrow! Oh, dear, and I was so glad that for a long time we should not have her in the house! I am selfish after nine years, and want you to myself at last; and this means she is preparing to intrude upon us when you return, or she will beg to be wheeled in the garden, as the park is closed, so as to meet you; and I won't be there to disturb. . . . I foresee lots of bother with her; all hysteria! Pretends to faint when one pushes the bed, but can be banged about the streets in a chair."

This certainly does not sound as if the Tsarina could not do without this hysterical friend, but then how does it happen that she was unable to shake her off, when everybody would have been but too glad to lend her a hand in doing so? She was the Empress, and it was easy for her to keep far from her those who bothered or annoyed her. "Why then, did she, who had snubbed so many people, never muster sufficient resolution to bar from her palace a woman whom, among other things, she suspected of having tried to win away from her her husband's heart? Verily, the whole truth concerning the inner drama of Alexandra Feodorovna's life is still to be disclosed.

It is curious to find, in this correspondence, how the Empress sometimes likes to give a little slap on the cheek to people of whose actions she does not approve. Sometimes, however, she is right, as for instance when she mentions the Countess Hohenfelsen, the morganatic wife of the Grand Duke Paul, who had written to her to ask for the favour of a Russian title, not caring to wear a German one under the circumstances:

"I send you," writes Alexandra, "an endless letter from the Countess Hohenfelsen to read through in a free moment and then return to me. Only speak to Fredericks about it. Certainly not on my name-day or birthday, as she wishes; but everything is all right in her wish except the 'Princess' part: that is vulgar to ask for. You see, it will sound well when one announces them together, almost as well as 'Grand Duchess.' Only what right to Misha later? Both had children before, while married to other men; but no, Misha's wife was already divorced. And she forgets that eldest son; if one acknowledges the marriage from the year 1904, that son, as everybody realizes, was an illegitimate child. As for them, I don't mind; let them openly carry their sin; but the boy? You talk it over with the old man — he understands such things — and tell him what your mamma said when you mentioned it to her. Now perhaps people will pay less attention."

And at the end of this same letter we find this phrase, which appears to have been written casually: "*Au fond*, our friend would have found it better had you gone after the war to the conquered country; I only mention this." This is an allusion to a journey taken by Nicholas II to Galicia, where he was dragged in the guise of a Roman conqueror, a journey which caused much hilarity among those who well knew the conquest of Galicia could be only ephemeral, and that the Russian troops would never be able to hold their positions there. Rut among them neither the Tsar nor his generals nor his advisers figured, and Rasputin seems, in this case, to have had far more foresight than the people who surrounded and flattered the sovereign.

The leitmotiv of these letters, which, in spite of the things they hint at, do not give us the key to many riddles we should like to see solved, is a profound affection and tenderness on the part of a devoted wife who has her husband constantly in her thoughts, and they awake a poignant regret that this affection was not able to lead its object towards the aim it had in view, his happiness.

"The little birdies," she writes among other things, "were singing away — all nature awakening and praising the Lord! Doubly does it make one feel the misery of war and bloodshed; but as after winter cometh summer, so after suffering and strife may peace and consolation find their place in this world and all hatred cease and our beloved country develop in beauty in every sense of the word.

"It is a new birth, a new beginning, *Läuterung* and cleansing of minds and souls, only to lead them aright and guide them straight. With so much to do, may all work bravely hand in hand, helping instead of hindering work for one great cause and not for personal success and fame."

It is very soon after this letter that one can perceive in the Tsarina's communications with her husband the first signs of an active participation by Rasputin in public affairs, and the persistence with which he was beginning to bring them to her notice. On April 10, 1915, she writes:

"Gregory is rather disturbed about the meat stories; the merchants won't lessen the price though the government wished it, and there has been a sort of meat strike, one says. One of the ministers, he thought, ought to send for a few of the chief merchants and explain to them that it is wrong at such a grave moment, during war, to raise the prices, and to make them ashamed of themselves."

Soon afterwards she begins, very cautiously at first, then, as time goes on, with more insistence, to urge upon Nicholas the necessity of showing himself the Emperor and enforcing his will:

"So sad we shall not spend your dear birthday together — the first time. Remember Wify will be praying and thinking of you, oh, so much, and miss you terribly. May God bless you richly and give you strength and wisdom, consolation, health, peace of mind to continue bravely bearing your heavy crown. Ah, it is not an easy nor light cross He has placed upon your shoulders! Would that I could help you to bear it; in my prayers and thoughts I ever do. I yearn to lessen your burden — so much have you had to suffer these twenty years, and you were born on the day of the long-suffering Job, too, my poor sweetheart. But God will help, I feel sure, but still much heartache, anxiety, and hard work have to be got through bravely, with resignation and trust in God's mercy and unfathomable wisdom. Hard not to be able to give you a tender birthday kiss and blessing! One gets at times so tired of suffering and anxiety and yearns for peace. Oh, when will it come, I wonder. How many months of bloodshed and misery? Sunshine comes after rain, and so our beloved country will see its golden days of prosperity after her earth is sodden in blood and tears. God is not unjust, and I place all my trust in Him unwaveringly, but it is such pain to see all the misery, and to know that not all work as they ought to, that petty personalities often spoil the great cause for which they ought to work in unison. Be firm. Levy mine, show your own mind, let others feel you know what you wish.

Remember you are the Emperor, and that others dare not take so much upon themselves ..."

It is heartrending to read these letters, with their loving but misguided advice, and then to remember the terrible tragedy which destroyed all these hopes. In the meanwhile the War was going on, and after the first Galician successes a series of crushing disasters drove the Russians back and liberated Galicia from their presence. The Empress went to Head-quarters at the beginning of June to see her husband, and on her return to Tsarskoye Selo she wrote him the following remarkable letter, in which is disclosed for the first time how complete was her confidence in Rasputin, and how she sought his advice and encouragement in regard to the most important political questions. Slowly, but surely, the net in which she was to be entangled was closing about her, until it held her inextricably in its meshes.

"My very own precious one, I left you this time with a heavy heart — everything is so serious, and just now particularly painful, and I long to be with you, to share your worries and anxieties. You bear all so bravely and by yourself — let me help you, my treasure. Surely there is some way in which a woman can help and be of use. I do so yearn to make it easier for you and the ministers all squabbling among themselves at a time when all ought to work together and forget their personal differences — to have as their aim the welfare of their sovereign and country — it makes me furious. In other words, it is treason, for people know it, they feel that the government is in discord, and then the Left profit by it. If you could only be severe, my love! It is so necessary that they should hear your voice and see displeasure in your eyes; they are too much accustomed to your gentle, forgiving kindness.

"Sometimes a word gently spoken goes far, but at a time such as the one we are now living through, one needs to hear your voice uplifted in protest and reprimand when they continue not to obey your orders, when they dawdle in carrying them out. They must learn to tremble before you — you remember Philippe and Gregory say the same thing too. You must simply order things to be done, not asking if they are possible; you will never ask anything unreasonable or foolish. For instance, order, as in France (a Republic), other factories to make shells, cartridges ; if guns and rifles are too complicated, let the big factories send teachers — where there's a will there's a way, and they must all realize that you insist upon your wishes being speedily carried out. It is for them to find the people, the manufacturers, to set everything in motion; let them go themselves and see that the work is done. You know how talented our people are, how gifted — only lazy and without initiative; start them going and they can do anything; only don't ask, but order straight off — be energetic for your country's sake!

"The same with the question which our friend takes so much to heart, and which is the most serious of all, for the sake of internal peace — the not calling in the second class. If the order has been given, you tell N. that you insist on its being countermanded — by your order, to wait —the kind act must come from *you* — don't listen to any excuses. I am sure it was done unintentionally through lack of knowledge of the country. Therefore our friend dreads your being at the Head-quarters, as all come round with their own explanations and involuntarily you give in to them, when your own feeling is the right one but does not fit in with theirs. Remember you have reigned long, have far more experience than they — N. has only the army to think of, and success — you carry the internal responsibility on for years — if he makes faults, after the war he is nobody, but you have to set all straight. No, hearken unto our friend, believe him. He has your interest and Russia's at heart — it is not for nothing that God sent him to us — only we must pay more attention to what he says — his words are not lightly spoken — and the gravity of having not only his prayers but his advice is great. The ministers did not think of telling you that this measure is a fatal one, but he did. How hard it is not to be with you, to talk over all quietly, and to help you to be firm!"

It was all very well to say that the calling of the second class of reserves was a fatal idea, but what else could the Government do? The ranks had to be filled, for three-quarters of the army that had started for the front when war was declared had already been annihilated. Mackensen had begun his famous drive which was to see the whole long line of fortresses on the Polish front fall into German hands. There were no rifles, no guns; there was no ammunition, and the whole position looked so desperate that it is no wonder people in Russia began to speak of the possibility of concluding a separate peace. In the meanwhile France was getting uneasy and continually insisting upon Russia's making another effort to save the situation. This can be seen from the book of M. Paleologue, who represented the French Government in Petrograd, and who makes no secret of the fact that time and time again he harried and worried the Russian Ministers for military and other steps in support of the French, which insistence it is impossible to deny was exhausting the credit of the Allies.

The British Ambassador, Sir George Buchanan, who perhaps judged most clearly the whole Russian situation, and whose advice, had the Emperor only followed it, might have saved the dynasty, saw very well whither such demands were to lead. "I wish we did not ask them to do too much," he is reported to have said to a friend in the spring of that fateful year 1916. Sir George had perhaps more at heart the interests of the unfortunate Emperor than he ever received credit for, while his French colleague was all the while haunted by baseless fears concerning the attitude of the Tsar and Tsarina, and he was most probably strengthened in those fears by his good friend the Princess Paley, the morganatic wife of the Grand Duke Paul. Very likely the Princess encouraged him in his idea of choosing the Grand Duke as his spokesman before the Empress, and of asking him to try to find out whether the latter was really so entirely pro-German that she was working for an understanding with the Kaiser, a thing which had never so much as crossed her mind. The Tsarina, in writing about it to her husband, mentions some other gossip repeated to her by the Grand Duke, which proves the excitability of public opinion in Petrograd during those sad and eventful days, and how everybody tried to poison the mind of everybody else through senseless talk.

"Paul came to tea," she says, "and remained an hour and three-quarters ; he was very nice and spoke honestly and simply, meaning well, not wishing to meddle with what does not concern him, only asking all sorts of things which I now repeat to you with his knowledge. **Well**, to begin with, Paléologue dined with him a few days ago, and then they had a long private talk, and the latter tried to find out from him, very cleverly, whether he knew if you had any idea of forming a separate peace with Germany, since he had heard such things being spoken of here as though one had got wind of it in France, where he said they intend to fight to the very end. Paul answered that he was convinced it was not true, all the more so as, at the outset of the war, we and our allies had agreed to conclude peace only together, and on no account separately. Then I told Paul that you had heard the same rumour about France; and he crossed himself when I said you were not dreaming of peace and knew it would mean revolution here, and that therefore the Germans were trying to egg it on. He said he had heard even the German mad conditions proposed to us; I warned him he would next hear that I was wishing peace to be concluded.

"Then he asked me whether it was true that Stcheglowitoff was being changed and that fellow Manukhin named in his place. I said I knew nothing, nor why Stcheglowitoff had chosen this moment to go to the Solv convent. Then he mentioned another thing to me which, though painful, it is better to warn you about — namely, that for six months there has been talk of a spy at Head-quarters, and when I asked the name, he said General Baniloff [the black one], that from many sides one has told him of this 'feeling,' and that now one speaks of it in the army. Lovy mine, Woyeikoff is sly and clever; talk to him about this and let him slyly and cleverly try to keep an eye on the man and his doings — why not have him watched? — of course, as Paul says, one has the spy mania now, but as things are at once known abroad which only very well initiated people at Head-quarters can know, this strong doubt has arisen, and Paul thought it honest to ask me whether you had ever mentioned this to me; I said no.

"Only don't mention it to Nikolasha [the Grand Duke Nicholas] before you have obtained information, as he can spoil everything by his excited manner and tell the man straight out or disbelieve all. But I think it would be only right, though the man may seem perfectly charming and honest, to have him watched. While you are there, the yellow men and others can use their eyes and ears and watch his telegrams and the people he sees. It is said that he often receives large sums. I only tell you this not knowing at all whether there is any truth in it; only it is better to warn you. Many dislike the Head-quarters and have an uncomfortable feeling there, and, alas, we have had spies and also innocent people accused by Nikolasha; now you can find out carefully, please. Forgive my bothering you so, poor, weary sweetheart, but one longs to be of help and perhaps I can be of some use by sending such messages.

"Our friend was with us at Ania's from 10 to 11.15. 1 send you a stick [fish holding a bird] which was sent to him from New Athos to give to you; he used it first and now sends it to you as a blessing; if you can, use it sometimes; it would be nice to have in your compartment near the one M. Philippe touched, which is nice too. He spoke much and beautifully on what a Russian Emperor is; though other sovereigns are anointed and crowned, only the Russian one has been a real anointed one for three hundred years. Says you will save your reign by not calling the second class now — says Shakhovskoy was delighted you spoke about it, because the ministers agreed, but had you not begun, they did not intend to speak.

"Finds you ought to order factories to make ammunition, simply you give the order, even choose whose factory, if they show you a list of them, instead of giving the order through commissions which talk for weeks, and never can make up their minds.

"Be more autocratic, my very own sweetheart; show your mind."

At that moment, when the Russian troops were experiencing disaster upon disaster, the Empress was more than ever convinced that Rasputin alone could save Russia, and she was most anxious to know exactly what was going on. The Grand Duke Nicholas was still in command of the army, and Alexandra Feodorovna knew very well that her presence at Head-quarters was not welcome to him, so she applied herself to the task of removing the Grand Duke, an attempt in which she finally succeeded. She was beginning then to feel suspicious of everybody who did not share her sentiments of admiration for Rasputin, even of her sister the Grand Duchess Elizabeth. When Samarine, a man of known integrity, was appointed Procurator of the Holy Synod, the Empress rose up in arms against it.

"Yes, lovie, about Samarine," she writes, "I am much more than sad, simply in despair; just one of Ella's [the Grand Duchess Serge's] very bigoted clique; bosom friend of Sophy Iv. Tutcheff; that Bishop Trifon I have strong reason to dislike, as he always spoke and now speaks in the army against our friend — now we shall have stories against our friend beginning, and all will go badly. I hope heart and soul he won't accept — this means Ella's influence and worries me from morning to night, and he against us, once against Gregory, and so awfully narrow-minded, a real Moscow type — head without soul.

"Have the church procession now; don't go on putting it off. Lovie, listen to me ; it's serious. Oh, why are we not together to talk over everything together and to help prevent things which I know ought not to be! It's not that my brain is clever, but I listen to my soul, and I wish you would too, my own sweetest one."

and then, a little later, she adds:

"People are afraid of my influence, Gregory said, because they know I have a strong will and sooner see through them and help you to be firm. When our friend says not to do a thing and one does not listen, one always sees one's mistake afterwards.

"I entreat you, the first time you see Samarine and have a talk with him, to speak very firmly. Do, my love, for Russia's sake : Russia will not be blessed if her sovereign lets a man of God sent to help him, be persecuted, I am sure.

"Tell him severely, in a strong decided tone, that you forbid any intrigues against our friend, or talks about him, or the slightest persecution — otherwise you will not keep him; that a true servant dare not work against a man his sovereign respects and venerates."

While the Empress was using all her influence with Nicholas II to get him to give his support to Rasputin, the whole of Russia was wondering what was going to happen if the German advance was not stopped. Soukhomlinoff, the Minister of War, had not only been dismissed, but arrested on the charge of high treason, and public opinion was demanding a change in the high command as well as an investigation of all the corruption that had interfered with the work of the War Office and finally brought about the shortage of ammunition to which were attributed all the military disasters of the campaign. People were wondering why the Duma was not called together and the country apprised of the true condition of affairs, but neither Rasputin nor the Empress — the unfortunate, misguided Empress — wanted the Duma to meet, as they feared that it might want to substitute its authority for that of the Emperor.

"So many things worry me," writes Alexandra Feodorovna. "Now the Duma is to come together in August, and our friend begged you several times to convoke it as late as possible and not now, as they ought all to be working in their own places, and here they will try to mix in and speak about things that do not concern them. Never forget that you are and must remain autocratic Emperor — we are not ready for a constitutional government; it is N.'s fault and Witte's that the Duma exists, and it has caused you more worry than pleasure. Nobody knows who is the Emperor now — you have to run to Head-quarters find assemble your ministers there as though you could not have them alone here as you did last Wednesday. It is as if N. settled everything, made the choices and changes . . . Forgive my writing all this, but I feel so utterly miserable, as though everybody were giving you wrong advice and profiting by your kindness. Hang Head-quarters! No good broods there. . ."

One can imagine the impression which such letters produced on a mind as weak and vacillating as that of Nicholas II and how difficult it would have been, in view of the Empress's perpetual entreaties to be guided by Rasputin, for the Tsar to take any measures against the "saint" even had he wished to, which was far from being the case, for in some ways he was just as superstitious as his wife. One can also imagine the deplorable impression produced by this insistence on the part of Alexandra Feodorovna putting her favourite above everybody else in the councils of her husband. The worst of the whole situation was that the advice which she was always giving him to be firm was not even Rasputin's, but that of a clique of needy money-grubbing adventurers, and the thing was fast becoming a public scandal. A few people tried to open the eyes of the Tsar as to what Rasputin really was; among others. General Dzunkovski, who, as head of the political police, knew certain facts which he imagined would have convinced the Emperor that he was being exploited by a man whom no one respected and all despised. But the only result was the disgrace of Dzunkovski, while new and frantic efforts were made by the Tsarina to get rid of the Grand Duke Nicholas, whom she could not forgive for having threatened Rasputin, when the latter paid a visit to Head-quarters, that if he appeared there he would have him hanged on the nearest tree.

Alexandra wanted the Tsar to show himself more to his troops, and accused the Grand Duke of preventing him from doing so.

"Sweetheart," she writes, "needs pushing always, and to be reminded that he is Emperor and can do whatever pleases him ; you never profit by this; you must show you have a will of your own, and are not led by N. and his staff, who direct your movements and whose permission you have to ask before going anywhere. Now go alone, without N.; by your very own self bring the blessing of your presence to them — don't say you bring bad luck— at Lemberg and Przemysl it happened, for our friend knew and told you it was too early, but you listened to Head-quarters instead.

"Forgive my speaking so directly, but I suffer too much — I know you — and Nikolasha. Go to the troops; say not a word to N. You have false scruples when you say it is not honest not to tell him: since when has he been your mentor, and in what way do you disturb him? Let one at last see that you act with your own mind, which is worth all theirs put together. Go, Lovie, cheer up Iwanov too — such heavy battles are coming — bless the troops with your precious being; in their name I beseech you to go — raise their spirits, show them for whom they are fighting and dying — not for Nikolasha, but for you; thousands have never seen you, and yearn to look into your beautiful, pure eyes.

"Ah, my Nicky, things are not as they ought to be, and therefore N. keeps you near to have a hold over you with his ideas and false counsel. Won't you believe me, my boy?

"Can't you realize that a man who turned rank traitor to a man of God cannot be blest, nor his actions be good? Well, if he must remain at the head of the army, there is nothing to be done, and all kinds of bad luck will fall upon his head, but mistakes in the interior will be brought home to you, as who in the country can think that he reigns beside you?"

The Empress knew very well what she was saying and the impression which her words were bound to produce on one so jealous of his authority as Nicholas II. But she was encouraged in her denunciations of the Grand Duke Nicholas, not only by Rasputin and the latter's clique, but also by a certain part of the public which felt exasperated against the Grand Duke, and accused him of incapacity in his conduct of military operations. The fact of the matter was that things were already going so very badly everywhere, and in every direction, that people were spending their time looking for scapegoats upon whom to put the responsibility for their own errors. The Empress also believed that the prestige of the commander-in-chief was gradually eclipsing that of the sovereign, and she feared that he might be induced to lend himself to a palace revolution which would put him in the place of his cousin on the throne of Russia. Nothing, however, shows that Nicholas Nicholaievitch would ever have done such a thing, and whatever may have been his failings, his loyalty has never been assailed, except by Rasputin s friends and by the Empress. Madame Viroubova, in her memoirs, tries to impress us with the idea that it was the Emperor alone who had conceived the idea of taking upon himself the supreme command of the army in the field, and that the Empress, "although she approved of her husband's resolution, had no part in forming it." The correspondence from which I have just quoted some passages proves exactly the reverse and it will be impossible, after reading it, not to realize the influence of Alexandra Feodorovna in the determination of the Tsar to substitute himself for the Grand Duke as commander-in-chief.

Among the Allies the decision of Nicholas II was viewed with grave apprehension, and his own Ministers did their best to persuade him to abandon it. Sir George Buchanan, who at about that time had an audience with the Empress, was the only one who had the courage to tell her that he shared the anxiety with which the Emperor's decision was viewed by his Ministers, and he added that not only would the sovereign have to bear the entire responsibility for any fresh disaster that might befall his armies, but that " he would, by combining the duties of commander-in-chief with those of the autocratic ruler of a great empire, be undertaking a task beyond the strength of any one man." The Empress, upon hearing this, immediately protested, says Sir George, and asserted that the Emperor ought to have assumed the command from the very first, and that, now that his army had suffered so severely, his proper place was with his troops. "I have no patience," she continued, "with ministers who try to prevent him from doing his duty. The situation requires firmness. The Emperor, unfortunately, is weak; but I am not, and I intend to be firm."

And Sir George adds sadly:

"Her Majesty kept her word. The Emperor, when in residence at Head-quarters, could not keep in constant touch with his ministers, and was too absorbed by military matters to give that close attention to questions of internal policy which the growing gravity of the situation demanded. The result was that the Empress, more especially after Sturmer Became president of the Council in February, 1916, virtually governed Russia."

Nevertheless, there was a certain sense of relief among the public when it became known that the Tsar was himself going to take the leadership over his troops. Of course the immediate circle that surrounded the sovereign showed great enthusiasm, and the Tsar nursed the illusion that his people were with him in the supreme resolution he had made up his mind to take. A solemn service was celebrated in the private chapel of the palace at Tsarskoye Selo to invoke the blessing of God on the new commander-in-chief, and Nicholas II left for Head-quarters amidst great manifestations of loyalty. On his arrival at Mohilev he was received by the Grand Duke, and he immediately assumed the command over demoralized regiments that regretted the loss of their former chief and had no confidence in the new one.

Nicholas Nicholaievitch behaved with immense dignity, and in this crisis remembered only that he was a Romanoff, and as such owed complete obedience and submission to the head of his dynasty. In the order of the day he addressed his troops to bid them farewell; he urged them to go on doing their duty and never forgetting that their Tsar was henceforward to lead them to victory. Then he left for his new destination, the Caucasus, of which he had been appointed Viceroy, accompanied to the railway station by the Emperor, from whom he parted respectfully without a single murmur, and whom he was never to see again.

At Tsarskoye Selo the Empress heard and rejoiced, and betook herself to her hospital with a lighter heart than usual. She was absorbed by her work among her wounded, and never noticed how she was deceived even in regard to them. As I have indicated already, the soldiers did not care to be attended by her and neither did the officers. They all hated the fiction which had to be maintained that the Empress and her two daughters were expert nurses, when they all knew that such was not the case. As a matter of fact, the administration, which meant the Minister of the Interior together with the Minister of War, had issued orders that every day some lightly wounded fellow was to be taken to Alexandra's hospital, where his condition was represented to her as being highly dangerous. She then had the illusion of having brought him back to health through her care. It was the same thing with the grand duchesses. Two soldiers were carefully selected every day to receive their help, and before they were sent to their ward they were washed and cleansed so as to be presentable. The whole thing was a ghastly comedy, which had as its origin the basest flattery. Yet it was accepted as truth by the Empress, who in all sincerity had come to look upon herself as an angel of light ministering to the wants of her suffering subjects.

NOTES

1 Appendix IV.

CHAPTER VIII

RASPUTIN'S DEATH AND
THE TSAR'S ABDICATION

WHEN the Emperor assumed command over the army, the Empress became virtually the mistress of the situation in St. Petersburg, She received the Ministers, discussed with them the affairs of the State, and decided the most important questions without perceiving that such an infringement on the prerogatives of the Tsar would be sure to add to her own unpopularity.

Soon there was a rumour that she wanted to dethrone him and have herself proclaimed Regent until the majority of the little heir to the throne. Needless to say, this was an invention pure and simple, but Alexandra Feodorovna was so intensely disliked that people were but too glad to say and repeat anything to her disparagement. What exasperated public opinion against her was her underhand work against the Duma, about which she never could find words harsh enough to utter.

Writing to the Emperor on September 1, 1916, she says:

"There is talk of proroguing the Duma till October 15th ; pity the date is fixed so early again, but thank goodness it is now dispersed; only one must work firmly now to prevent them from doing harm — they intend to launch forth against Ania — that means me again. Our friend was for me too, so Ania sent a letter she received to Woyeikoff to-day, that he must insist that Frolov forbid the writing of any articles against our friend or Ania; they have the military power, and it is easy for them. Woyeikoff must take it upon himself; your name must not be mentioned; in his place he has to guard our lives and anything that harms us, and these articles are against us; nothing at all to be afraid of, only very energetic measures must be taken — you have shown your will and no slacking in any direction ; once begun, it is easy to continue."

Later she writes:

"Now the members of the Duma want to meet in Moscow to talk over everything when their work here is closed ; one ought energetically to forbid it: it will only bring great trouble. If they do that, one ought to say that the Duma will then not be reopened till much later — threaten them, as they try to threaten the ministers and the government. Moscow will be worse than here — one must be severe. Oh, could one not hang Gutschkoff?

"Lovie, have that assembly in Moscow forbidden; it is impossible, will be worse than the Duma, and there will be endless rows. You are lord and master of Russia, autocrat — remember that."

It is easy to imagine how the poor Emperor was distracted when he read these effusions, and how painful the conduct of the Empress and her perpetual remonstrances and reproaches must have been to him. He must have felt in his inmost heart that she was wrong, and that the time had passed when an autocratic regime could be re-established in Russia. But nevertheless he seemed to try at least to follow her advice, for very soon after she had indulged in a violent tirade against Sazonoff, he dismissed the latter, a decision which of course caused consternation among the Allies, the more so as his successor, Sturmer, did not enjoy their confidence nor that of Russia.

But the Empress was reckless, and she simply wanted to have out of her way all those who had dared oppose her or the ever-growing influence of the Rasputin clique, for, as I have said already, the man himself was but the tool of an unscrupulous gang that made use of him to further its own sinister designs and interests. She wanted, above all else, to suppress the Duma, and failed to realize that at a time of national danger it would be an advantage rather than the reverse for the dynasty to share its responsibility with the representatives of the nation.

It is here that one sees more clearly than ever the lack of judgment of the Empress, as well as her despotic, autocratic temper, which might have been that of Elizabeth or of Catherine II, but without the immense intelligence and knowledge of humanity and politics which had distinguished those two great sovereigns. Had she been allowed a free hand, it is likely that she would have summarily hanged the people who displeased her, and it is curious to note that her regret at not being able to do so appears on almost every page of her correspondence with the Tsar:

"We are not a constitutional country, and dare not be; our people are not educated for it, and, thank God, our Emperor is an autocrat, and must stick to this, as you do — only you must show more power and decision. I should have cleared out **quickly those I did not care for.**"

Reading these amazing words, one cannot help wondering what Queen Victoria would have thought, had she lived long enough to see her granddaughter thus leading her husband and her country to their ruin, without the least hesitation in a line of action which everybody having at heart the welfare of Russia told her was bound to end in disaster. Under the influence of Alexandra, one Minister after another was dismissed, with the exception of those who, like Sturmer and Protopopoff, simply bowed down before her, and told her that whatever she did was well, until at last people began to wonder whether the Emperor had not gone insane under the weight of responsibility which was daily accumulating upon his shoulders. Even if he had tried to resist his wife's perpetual complaints, he could hardly have withstood the insidious evil caused by the gossip she repeated to him, gossip which most of the time rested on nothing more tangible than the fallacies of Madame Viroubova and the latter's friends, who towards the end were the only people whom the Empress saw. She had come to hate with a ferocious hatred the few men left in Russia who had the courage to tell her the truth.

For instance, writing about Samarine, the Procurator of the Holy Synod, who had attempted to oppose the encroachments of Rasputin in the internal affairs of the Church, she says;

"I told you Samarine is a stupid, insolent fellow; remember bow impertinently be behaved to me at Peterhof last summer about the evacuation question, and his opinion of Petersburg in comparison to Moscow, and he had no right to speak to his Empress as he did. Had he desired my good, he would have done all in his power for me, taking it as I wished; he would have guided and helped me, and it would have been a big and popular thing ; but I felt that he was hostile to me, and that is why he was proposed to you, and not for the Church's good. I am inconvenient to such types, because I am energetic and stick to my friends wherever they may be."

Sometimes, in perusing this correspondence, the thought comes involuntarily whether Alexandra Feodorovna was really sane, or whether the superstitious practices in which she indulged, combined with her anxiety for her only son, had not dulled her brain, or at least destroyed her judgment. Some of the recommendations which she makes to her husband would be too funny if they were not so sad, as, for instance, when she urges him to keep "an image in his hand, and several times to comb his hair with Rasputin's comb before seeing his ministers." No woman in the Middle Ages could have expressed herself more absurdly.

She ended by estranging the Emperor from everybody, even from his own mother, whom she does not spare in her correspondence;

"The conversations at Elaguin [the residence of the Dowager Empress] are awful against our friend; old Madame Orloff has heard this — she knows ladies who go there. When you see poor, dear Mother, you must rather sharply tell her how pained you are that she listens to slander and does not stop it, as it causes mischief, and others would be delighted, I am sure, to turn her against me, people are so mean."

As time goes on, one can notice that little by little everything for the Empress resolves itself into the one important question: Who are the people devoted to Rasputin, and who are his enemies ? When she speaks of anybody, she begins by saying, "He is devoted to our friend," or "He dislikes our friend." Outside of this, there is no salvation for any, and when one follows her trend of mind, the disastrous course of conduct to which she clung, one realizes that the Revolution was absolutely inevitable, and that, moreover, owing to the enmities aroused by Alexandra Feodorovna, it was bound to be a bloody one, though how bloody it was impossible then to suspect.

In the meanwhile people were getting alarmed at the whole political situation, and the possibility of a palace revolution began to be openly discussed in the various *salons* of St. Petersburg. Unfortunately it did not take place; I deliberately say **"unfortunately," because if the upheaval had been engineered from above, it might** not have ended in the terrible way in which it did. It seems that even among the Imperial family the question of compelling the Empress to retire to a convent was raised, but rejected after its impossibility had been demonstrated. The Romanoffs may have disliked and even hated her, but she was the Empress, and therefore they naturally hesitated before having recourse to violent measures to put her aside.

It was suggested, however, and this at the instigation of the French Government, as was related at the time, that she should be invited to repair to the South of France for her health, and kept there until the end of the War. But Alexandra, of course, rejected the idea with indignation, she believed herself to be indispensable to her husband as well as to Russia. Besides, she thought herself protected by the prayers of Rasputin, in whom she so absolutely believed that at times she compared him to Christ Himself.

"During the evening reading of the Bible," she writes, "I thought so much of our friend, how the Scribes and Pharisees persecute Christ, pretending to be so perfect, and how far from perfect they really are. Yes, indeed, a prophet is never acknowledged in his own country. And how much we have to be grateful for, how many prayers of his have been heard! And where there is such a servant of God, the evil crops up around him to try to harm him and drag him away. If they but knew the harm they do! Why, he lives for his sovereign and for Russia!"

There is something touching in this blind faith of the poor Empress, and her conviction that God had sent her a prophet to watch over her and her family. Again I suggest that all through this tragedy of her mind she was sincere, absolutely sincere. It was not her fault that she was daily growing more infatuated with the intriguers who surrounded her, because she had at first shut herself up from those who might have advised her for her good. Later on they had forsaken her and given up every attempt to open her eyes to the abyss already opened before her, so that, hearing but one sound, she was bound to fall every day more and more under the influence of the persons who ultimately were to ruin her first and kill her afterwards, because it was they who became morally responsible for her horrible death and the murder of her innocent children.

In the meanwhile the War was dragging on. Russia was getting weary of it, and, what was worse, the army also was tired and on the verge of mutiny. The first enthusiasm that had followed upon the Emperor's assuming the supreme command had quickly died away, and, besides, the old soldiers who had been trained into feelings of devotion to their sovereign had all, or nearly all, disappeared during the three years of the struggle, and the new contingents were imbued with revolutionary ideas. The disorganization among the troops was complete, the demoralization of the country even more so. Everybody knew that they were heading straight for a catastrophe, and, horrible to relate, very few cared, because a catastrophe would mean the end of the Empress and of her influence, and in the wish for that consummation the whole of Russia was united.

Nevertheless, the Imperial family made an effort to save the monarch and the dynasty. A family meeting was held in St. Petersburg, in which all the grand dukes in the capital participated, and the old Grand Duke Paul was delegated to speak with the Tsar and beg him, in the name of all his kinsmen, to grant a constitution to Russia before it was too late. The Grand Duke undertook the task with great diffidence, but with the feeling that it was a solemn duty he had no right to shirk. He asked his Imperial nephew to receive him during one of the latter's short stays at Tsarskoye Selo, and tried to make clear to him the dangers of the situation; to point out the state of excitement into which the society of Moscow and Petrograd had fallen; the growing discontent of the nation, worn out as it was by the sacrifices it had been compelled to make since the War, and, finally, the continuous increase in the cost of living and the difficulty of obtaining food in the large cities of the Empire. He concluded by saying that the Imperial family had requested him respectfully to entreat His Majesty to grant a constitution, which was the only way left to save the country and the dynasty.

Nicholas II listened in silence, then slowly, after considerable hesitation, replied that this was impossible because he had sworn on his coronation day to uphold the principle of autocracy and to transmit it to his son. The Grand Duke then entreated him at least to choose Ministers enjoying the confidence of the nation and to get rid **of people like Sturmer and Protopopoff, who were accused of being the creatures of** Rasputin, whose growing influence public opinion feared and dreaded. The Emperor continued to keep silent, smoking a cigarette, but the Empress rose from her chair and began to speak with great emotion. Rasputin, for her, was a friend who was praying for her and for her children, and in regard to the Ministers, neither she nor the Tsar would ever consent to sacrifice men in possession of their confidence to the clamours of a few persons of no importance. The Grand Duke could only withdraw, without having achieved anything at all.

The Empress Dowager then intervened. She had left Petrograd to reside in Kieff, and during a visit which the Tsar paid to her there, while on a tour of inspection in the South, she tried to open his eyes to the perils of the situation as well as to the discredit into which his wife and he were falling owing to the constant presence near them of Rasputin. The only result of her attempt was, if not exactly a Quarrel, at least considerable coolness between mother and son. The Grand Duchess Victoria, wife of the Grand Duke Cyril, then spoke with the Empress, but was also told to mind her own business. The Grand Duchess Elizabeth came from Moscow to see her sister, and warn her of the danger of a revolution of which she would probably be the first victim, but was not only rudely repulsed, but told to return to her convent immediately. Other people, too, were reproved for what

Alexandra called their unwarranted interference. Finally the Grand Duke Nicholas Michailovitch, the clever man of the family, and a historian of considerable merit, wrote a letter to the sovereign in which he implored him to send Rasputin away. An order to leave Petrograd for one of his estates in the South and remain there three months in exile was the only reply vouchsafed him. In the presence of this obstinacy, one could not **help thinking of the old Latin saying.** *"Quos Deus vult perdere, prius dementat."*

Everything in the governmental machine was thrown into an indescribable state of confusion. Nobody knew, and, for that matter, nobody cared, whither one was drifting. The whole attention of the public remained concentrated upon the thought of how to get rid of the Empress, or, rather, how to deliver the country from the man under whose influence she had fallen. It was in such circumstances that the murder of Rasputin was planned and finally accomplished.

The whole conception and consummation of this assassination carries one back to the days of the Greek Empire. It was an essentially Eastern plot to which Rasputin owed his destruction, one which had recourse to the meanest of tricks in order to bring about its success. It proved beyond a doubt that Russia's pretended civilization was in reality a veneer. After all, what, also, was the Tsar but an Eastern potentate, imagining he had the right of life and death over his subjects and forgetting that times had changed, civilization advanced, and men come to realize their rights as well as their duties? The fact of the matter is that for sixty to seventy-five years before the War, a struggle had been going on between what was left of autocracy and the best elements in the country, a struggle in which both parties had had advantages in turn and shown themselves equally merciless. But had a serious attempt at reform been made by Nicholas II, the country as well as he himself and his family might have been saved.

As things stood, his fall was inevitable, because he leaned on no one and on no party except that of the few flatterers who pandered to his ideas of absolutism and those of his wife, and who hastened to abandon them when the hour of danger struck. And here again I must repeat that both sides were at fault, and that Anna Viroubova is not so wrong after all when she throws part of the blame on Petrograd society, because there is no doubt that its gossip and ill-natured talk contributed considerably to the disaster. It was by the aristocracy that long before the War all kinds of reproaches had been flung at the Empress, all sorts of calumnies launched against her. From the fashionable, smart *salons* of the capital aspersions had travelled far and wide, reached the farthest provinces of the Empire, and at last been repeatedby the people. The War was but the pretext for an upheaval against autocracy that would have taken place sooner or later, with or without it, for the nation was so exasperated against the existing regime that it would have tried to destroy it no matter what happened.

In the army, threats to refuse to obey the *commanders* were heard every day, and it was with the greatest difficulty that soldiers were kept in the trenches. The troops had the idea that the War was being prolonged and their lives sacrificed because the people who surrounded the Tsar and Tsarina, the Rasputins, Sturmers, Manassewiches, Maniuloffs, and others were making money out of it, and the fact that the Empress was continually sending to her husband petitions handed to her by one or other of her favourites, most of which had reference to war contracts, for ammunition, provisions, or war materials, strengthened this feeling, which was prevalent everywhere. When she interceded for a banker of Hebrew-German origin named Rubinstein, who had been accused of corruption by the military authorities, and had him released from prison, the indignation became even stronger. The fact of the matter is that the unfortunate woman was fighting against odds far too strong for her, and was herself groping in the dark in search of the truth, a truth which was never to be revealed to her.

Anna Viroubova and the latter's friends and sycophants kept Alexandra away from disinterested people who might have opened her eyes. And it is they who ought to be held responsible for the absurd rumour, at that time prevalent in Petrograd, that the British Ambassador, Sir George Buchanan, was in league with those who wanted to dethrone Nicholas II. Sir George, as history will show, was the best friend the Imperial family ever had, and if the Empress had been wise, or even if she had had common sense, she would have seen that as the Englishwoman she professed to be, or rather to have been, it was to the representative of her cousin in Russia that she ought to have turned for guidance. But she believed the evil-minded and evil-disposed persons who, with the intention of severing her from every tie that had bound her to her mother's country, persuaded her that Sir George Buchanan was plotting against her and wanted to place upon the throne her cousin the Grand Duke Cyril.

To this senseless accusation one can only reply, that the British Ambassador was far too clever a man to have ever tried to change the order of succession to the Russian crown. If the Emperor had been removed, his son and his brother the Grand Duke Michael, who personally was very popular in the Army, would have been his natural successors.

Sir George was accused of receiving at his home the leaders of the

Liberal parties in the Duma, among them M. Miliukoff, whom the Empress abominated in particular, but, as Sir George himself says, "it was his duty as Ambassador to keep in touch with the leaders of all parties." He further avows that he was in sympathy with their aims, as every rational being would have been, because at that time no one in the Duma, not even the most radical among the deputies, wanted to provoke a revolution while the War lasted, and " when that revolution did actually take place, the Duma sought to control if by giving it the sanction of the only legally constituted organ in the country. The majority of its leaders were monarchists, and its President, M. Rodzianko, up to the last, had hoped to save the Emperor by drafting for him a manifesto granting a constitution."

But people like Madame Viroubova told the Tsarina that Sir George was in league with, her enemies. She tells how she introduced to the Empress a Karaite Jew, named Gaham, who had made, as she assures us, the journey to Petrograd from the Crimea to warn the Tsarina that there was an organized plot against the throne which was being carried on by near relatives of Nicholas II, in the seclusion of the British Embassy in Petrograd. How the news that such a plot existed had reached Gaham, in distant Crimea, Madame Viroubova does not explain to us, and why the Imperial family had to have recourse to a foreign ambassador to concoct a plot they could just as well have carried on from the security of one of their own palaces, which would not have been half so compromising, did not seem to strike the Empress at all. In fact, she was in such a frame of mind as to give credence to any absurdity, so that if she had even been told that it was the camarilla surrounding her that had called Gaham to Petrograd in the hope that his words might strengthen her conviction that her only friends were Rasputin and his gang, which in fact was the case, she still would have had faith in him in preference to anybody else.

In regard to the attitude of the Empress, Sir George Buchanan remarks :

"Her Majesty, unfortunately, was under the impression that it was her mission to save Russia, and in advocating, as she did, a policy of 'Thorough,' she was honestly convinced that she was acting in Russia's interests. She was so obsessed with the idea that there must be no weakening of the autocracy that she was opposed to all concessions, while she encouraged the Emperor to choose his ministers more out of regard for their political opinions than for their qualifications for office."

This is judgment of a clever man, an honest man, and a man, moreover, who did all in his power to save Nicholas II. The Empress's correspondence justifies entirely the above appreciation of her character. But Sir George, like all those who had the opportunity of approaching the unfortunate woman, also says and believes that all through the tragedy she acted sincerely, and that she never for one single moment had had even the temptation to play false with the Allies, or indeed with anybody.

When she visited Head-quarters Alexandra could not but notice the dark looks which she received from every side, but this made her only the more determined to have her own way and to dominate her husband.

In many respects her letters to him are amazing, and ought to have made him see how ill-balanced she was, as, for example, when she wrote to him, "Hang these generals! Why are they so weak and good for nothing? Be severe with them!" and other things of the same kind. But the Emperor accepted everything and did not even attempt to explain to his wife that one could not hang people just because they happened not to please or to be in accord with one's ideas. Russia might be backward in its civilization, but nevertheless it had got beyond the times when rulers killed their subjects for a "yes" or a "no."

Alexandra was so determined to keep everything in her own hands that she did not even see the importance of the responsibility such a course of action would inevitably put upon the Tsar, and the terrible way in which he might have to answer for it before history.

"You cannot make concessions," she writes to him; "an answerable ministry and all the rest they wish. It must be your war and your peace, and your and our country's honour, and by no means the Duma's; they have not a word to say in such matters."

But although the Empress was urging her husband to keep firm and refuse the nation the right to interfere in matters in which it was perhaps even more interested than the Tsar, because it was not only its future but its whole historical development that was at stake, events were going to prove too strong for her, and the general discontent bring about the startling catastrophe which unfortunately was to mark the opening of the revolutionary movement.

I do not wish to expatiate on the murder of Rasputin. The details have been told and repeated *ad nauseam*, but I wish to point out some of the reasons which perhaps inspired that act of violence and, in a sense, of madness. They were not justifiable reasons, but one can understand them, especially if one takes into account the exasperated state of the public mind, the general conviction which prevailed everywhere that at a time of national danger and national crisis, he and his followers were exerting themselves to the utmost to try to get something more out of the fast-vanishing riches of the nation. Rasputin, rightly or wrongly, was, in the eyes of many, the symbol of the systematic plundering of Russia's wealth. He was supposed to be the one dark power behind the throne that alone decided questions of the utmost importance to the whole country. Moreover, in the eyes of the faithful monarchists, he was the image of the degradation of the sovereign, for "whom respect was fast disappearing, thanks to Rasputin alone, as some people imagined, though in reality this would have happened with or without him. Add to this the instinctive arrogance of the Russian nobility, the vague remembrance of the days of Peter III and of Paul, when Tsars who either had become obnoxious to their subjects or stood in the way of others coveting their throne, had been forcibly removed from it, together with the feeling that it was high time to do something, and that, after all, it was better to kill Rasputin than to murder the Emperor, and one can realize under what circumstances the crime took place.

The curious fact about this murder is that it was both planned and committed entirely by men belonging to the highest aristocracy of the land, men whom one would never have supposed capable of taking part in an assassination. By a strange irony of fate, the suspicions of the Empress and her inveterate dislike of the Russian nobility had been justified, and the noblest and bluest blood in Russia had conspired to deprive her of her favourite, of the one man on earth in whom she had confidence, confidence to such an extent that she even believed him to be infallible in military matters, as may be seen from a letter which she wrote to the Tsar on June 4, 1916:

"Ania forgot to tell you that our friend *sends his blessing to the whole Orthodox army.* He begs that we should not yet strongly advance in the north, because he says if our successes continue good in the south, they will themselves retreat from the north, or advance, and then their losses will be very heavy. He says this is his advice."

One can imagine the painful impression such messages must have produced on the generals in command of the army and on the staff who were told to be guided by the counsel of a common peasant without any education, unable even to read and write correctly, but who was taking upon himself the solution of the gravest, most important political and military questions. Is it to be wondered if, confronted with such facts, the army mutinied, and all its leaders entered into the conspiracy which finally compelled Nicholas II to abdicate his throne? We again find the hand of Rasputin in the anti-English feeling which developed among the intimate friends of the Empress towards the end of the War, a feeling which towards the last she herself shared completely: "Ania forgot to tell you that our friend says it is good for us that Kitchener died, as later on he might have done Russia harm, and that no harmful papers were lost with him. You see, he always fears England at the end of the war, when the peace negotiations begin." A Russian moujik judging of Lord Kitchener's aims and actions and commenting upon them! One wonders whether one is dreaming.

At times the Empress really acted as if she had lost her reason. She was absolutely unnerved, and no wonder, considering the persistence with which her so-called friends tormented her, and insisted on her telling this or that to her husband. The poor woman — one can read it in her letters — was looking in every direction for men capable of helping her to rule Russia according to the orders of Rasputin. There is not one letter in which she has not an unkind word to say to her husband concerning some person or other, and the way in which she attempts to set him against his Ministers is pathetic when one remembers where this was to lead her and the Tsar, who never had the courage to contradict or to resist her, and who allowed her; to bring him every kind of gossip concerning the people whom she did not like.

Nicholas II was by nature an autocrat, or rather a despot, and was only too ready to bring his authority to bear on his people; he did not require any urging to pursue a **policy of compulsion. Under the influence of his wife, he was to entrench himself in a system of *non possumus* which was to prove his undoing, but in which he persisted to the very end, until he actually found himself confronted by the people who had come to claim his abdication, and whom his father, had he found himself in the same position, would have been impossible, would have had thrown out of his presence with a gesture of Imperial rage, which might, even at that eleventh hour, have saved the situation.**

But Nicholas II, like every weak nature, was incapable of resisting anyone coming with courage and authority to require him to submit to things he had obstinately refused to perform when he had thought himself the absolute master; which reminds me of an incident mentioned by Count Witte, in his memoirs, concerning the judgment passed upon the Tsar at the time of his accession by the then Minister of the Interior, I.N. Durnovo. The latter was certainly not a man of super-intelligence, but he had considerable political experience, and was a good judge of character. In the course of a conversation with Count Witte, he used the following words, which events were sadly to justify: "I know our young Emperor, and let me tell you that his reign has many misfortunes in store for us. Mark my words: Nicholas II will prove a modernized version of Paul I."

A man like the unfortunate monarch who was to come to such a lamentable end required a wife endowed with tact, clearness of mind, and a kindly disposition, not a hysterical, restless creature subject to likes and dislikes, uncertain in their intensity, who was perpetually trying to set him against the people who had fallen into her disfavour and that of Rasputin.

"Show everybody that you are master," she writes to him, on December 4, 1916, a few days before the murder of that friend to whom she refers with such passionate devotion, "and your will shall be obeyed — the time of great indulgence and gentleness is over— now comes your reign of will and power, and they shall be made to bow down before you and listen to your orders and to work how and with whom you wish— they must be taught obedience ; they do not know the meaning of that word; you have spoilt them with your kindness and forgiveness. *Why do people hate me? Because they know I have a strong will, and that when I am convinced a thing is right (when, besides, blessed by Gregory) I do not change my mind ; and that they can't bear. But it is the bad ones. Remember M. Philippe's words when he gave me the image with the bell. As you were so kind, trusting, and gentle, I was to be your bell; those who came with wrong intentions would not be able to approach me, and I would warn you. Those who are afraid of me do not look me in the eye or are up to some wrong, and never like me. Look at the black ones— then Orloff and Drenteln — Witte — Kokovtzev — Trepoff, I feel it too — Makaroff — Kaufmann — Sofia Ivanovna — Mary — Sandra Obolensky, etc., but those who are good and devoted to you honestly and purely love me — look at the simple people and the military. The good and bad clergy — it's all so clear, and therefore no more hurts me as when I was younger. Only when people permit themselves to write you or me nasty, impertinent letters, you must punish them. Ania told me about Balashoff (I have always disliked the man); I understood why you came to bed so awfully late, and why I had such pain and anxiety waiting. Please, Lovie, tell Fredericks to write him a strong reprimand (he and Nikolay Mikhaylovitch and Vass are three of a kind); he has such a high court rank and dares to write unasked. And it's not the first time — in bygone days I remember he did so too.

Tear up the letter, but have him severely reprimanded — tell Woyeikoff to remind the old man — such a smack to a conceited member of the Council of the Empire will be very useful. We cannot now be trampled upon. Firmness above all!

"And our dear friend is praying so hard for you — a man of God near one gives the strength, faith, and hope one needs so sorely. And others cannot understand this great calm of yours, and therefore think that you don't understand, and try to weaken, frighten, and prick at you. But they will soon tire of it. Should Mother dear write, remember the Michels are behind her. Don't heed or take it to heart — thank God she is not here, but kind people find means of writing and doing harm."

: her errors were destined to be paid for so dearly; but in the presence of her obstinacy in refusing to see who were her real friends, as well as the friends of the monarchy, one need no longer wonder that every honest man in Petrograd society breathed more freely when it became known that Rasputin was dead.

One of the last things he advised the Empress to do was to insist on the dismissal of the Duma, in spite of the entreaties of the then Prime Minister, M. Trepoff, who implored the Tsar to try to rule in accord with the representatives of the nation.

"I could hang Trepoff," writes the Empress, "for his bad counsel — I hate **him**, who does everything to harm you, backed up by Makaroff. Had I but got you here again, everything would at once have been calmer, and had you returned, as Gregory wished, in five days, you would have restored order, would have rested your weary head upon your wifie's breast, and Sonny would have given you strength, and you would have listened to me and not to Trepoff. God will help, I know, but you must be firm. Dissolve the Duma at once. When you spoke of the seventeenth to Trepoff you **did not know what they were up to. I should quietly and with a clear conscience, before the whole of Russia, have sent Lvov to Siberia (one used to do so for far less grave acts), taken Samarine's rank away (he signed that paper from Moscow), and sent Miliukoff, Gutschkoff, and Polivanoff also to Siberia. It is war, and at such a time internal war is high treason.** Why don't you look at it that way? I really can't understand — I am but a woman — but my soul and brain tell me it would be the salvation of Russia: they sin far worse than the Sukhomlinoffs ever did. Forbid Brussiloff, and when they come to touch on any political subject, they are fools who want a responsible cabinet.

"Remember even M. Philippe said one dare not grant a constitution as it would be your ruin and Russia's, and all true Russians say the same. I know I worry you — ah, would I not far, far rather write only letters of love, tenderness, and caresses, of which my heart is so full? — but my duty as wife, mother, and Russia's mother, obliges me to say all to you — blessed by our friend. Be master, and all will bow down to you. We have been placed by God on a throne, and we must keep it firm and give it to our son intact. If you keep that in mind, you will remember to be the sovereign — and how much easier for an *autocratic* sovereign than for one who has sworn to support a constitution!"

A very clever man who, without taking an active part in it, was cognizant of, and to a certain extent inspired the murder of Rasputin, told me a few years later, when I happened to meet him in New York, that the greatest mistake the Liberal parties had done, was not to try to persuade the Allies to buy the co-operation of Rasputin through the latter's friends. They led him entirely, making him bear the responsibility for their doings, and they were people who for money would have done anything and everything. Had they believed that they could obtain the millions they coveted from another source than the ammunition contracts and railway and mining concessions they were after, they would have exerted all their efforts to convert Rasputin to the cause of a constitutional government, and the latter would undoubtedly' have persuaded the Empress that the only road to salvation consisted in her inducing her husband to agree to it.

Paradoxical as this assertion may appear, it is certain that it contained a good deal of truth, and that it would have been to the advantage of Russia if Rasputin had been won over to the only course of action that might — and I intentionally use the word "might" because even that is not sure — have averted the Revolution, with all that followed upon it.

But in his soul every Russian is an Asiatic, and the murder of the Empress's favourite was determined upon in a truly Asiatic spirit. Poison, dagger, and firearms were used, worthy of a melodrama by Dumas if it had not all been so serious, and also so shameful and shameless. The man was slaughtered in cold blood by people whose hospitality he had accepted, which in Russian eyes makes the crime a doubly hateful one. The only result of the atrocity was that it further exasperated the Empress against the aristocracy; her whole thoughts thereafter became concentrated on the idea of revenge.

Anna Viroubova tells us of the grief of the Empress when the dreadful news was brought to her and adds a few details which cannot possibly be true concerning the denials by the murderers of having been concerned in the crime. She also says that the whole Imperial family gave vent publicly to its joy at the disappearance of the dangerous personage who in a certain sense had ruled Russia. From the Tsarina herself we have only her first letter to the Emperor, written immediately after she had received the news, and when she did not yet believe it.

"We are sitting together," she writes; "you can imagine our feelings — thoughts — our friend has disappeared. Yesterday Ania saw him, and he said Felix asked him to come in the night— a motor would fetch him — to see Irina. A motor fetched him (a military one) with two civilians, and he went away.

"This night, big scandal at Youssoupoff's house — big meeting, Dmitri, Purischkievich, and all drunk. Police heard shots. Purischkievich ran out screaming to the police that our friend was killed.

"Police searching, and officer now entered Youssoupoff's house — did not dare to before as Dmitri there.

"Chief of police has sent for Dmitri. Felix wanted to leave to-night for Crimea, begged Kalinin to stop him.

"Our friend was in good spirits but nervous these days, and for Ania too, as Batiuschin wants to get information against Ania. Felix pretends he never came to the house and never asked him. Seems quite a paw. I still trust in God's mercy that they have only driven him off somewhere. Kalinin is doing all he can. Therefore I beg for Woyeikoff; we women are alone with our weak minds. Shall keep her to live here, as now they will get at her next.

"I cannot and will not believe he has been killed. God have mercy.

"Such utter anguish! I am calm and can't believe it.

"Thanks, dear, for your letter. Come soon — nobody will dare touch her or do anything when you are here.

"Felix came to him often of late."

The Emperor returned to Tsarskoye Solo, and was present at the funeral of the simple but cunning peasant who for a while had been all-powerful at his Comet. Whether he regretted his death or not, it is difficult to say, because on no occasion did Nicholas II's fortitude desert him. But under the influence of the Empress, hard reprisals were taken against the authors of the crime. Young Youssoupoff was exiled to one of his country estates, and the Grand Duke Dmitri sent to one of the most insalubrious spots in Persia. The Imperial family presented a very respectful petition to the Tsar, begging him to choose another place of exile for his cousin. But the only reply vouchsafed was a remark scribbled in pencil by the Tsar on the back of the document. "No one has the right to commit murder, and I am surprised that the family dares to approach me on such a subject."

The young Grand Duke had to leave Petrograd in the dead of night on New Year's Eve, and was not even allowed to take leave of his father or his sister.

The state of Petrograd was indescribable. When the news that the Empress's favourite had been killed became public there were manifestations of joy everywhere, and in the theatres especially the enthusiasm of the crowds reached unheard-of proportions; the portraits of Felix Youssoupoff and of the Grand Duke Dmitri were publicly exhibited, and cheered wherever shown. The capital seemed to feel that the dark days were at last at an end, and that now that Rasputin was gone, the military as well as the political situation would improve.

This feeling of optimism, however, did not last very long, for the spirit of revenge shown by Alexandra Feodorovna brought about a renewal of hostility against her. People were no longer guarded in their language, and a palace revolution was spoken of as a thing likely to happen any day. Sir George Buchanan tells us, in his memoirs, that a Russian friend of his who had formerly occupied a high position in the Government declared to him that it was a mere question whether both the Emperor and Empress, or only the latter, would be killed. On the other hand, the prevailing food shortage, which was daily growing more acute, had excited popular feeling to such an extent against the sovereign and his advisers that it was felt everywhere that an outbreak on the part of the population of Petrograd was but a matter of time, and might happen at any moment.

At this juncture the British Ambassador felt that he could not bear any longer the sight of the approaching catastrophe without making at least some effort to try to avert it. He applied to his Government for permission to try to save the Emperor and the dynasty. He asked to be allowed to speak in the name of King George, whose friendly feelings for his cousin were well-known to Nicholas, but could not obtain it as he was told that the King was out of town. Nevertheless Sir George insisted, and did so in terms which are entirely to his honour and credit.

"I replied," he says in his account of that eventful time, "that the crisis through which Russia was passing was fraught with such untold dangers that I must ask His Majesty's Government to reconsider their decision. We owed it, I said, to the Emperor, who had always been such a loyal friend and ally; we owed it to Russia, which had made such sacrifices to the common cause; and we owed it to ourselves, who were so directly interested, to endeavour to avert those dangers. If His Majesty's Government would not authorize me to speak in their name, I was prepared, with their permission, to speak in my own name and to assume all responsibility for doing so. This permission was eventually given me."

And this is the man who has been accused of having connived at the Revolution, the man who alone had the courage to speak out, and when everybody else was forsaking and abandoning the Tsar, took upon himself the painful and ungrateful task of warning Nicholas II of impending disaster. In this crisis and extremity, the only and best friend of the luckless Tsar proved to be the representative of his British cousin, and if Russian monarchists are sincere in their feelings of regret for their murdered sovereign, they ought to be for ever grateful to Sir George Buchanan for his courageous conduct, instead of hurling at his head senseless accusations which rest on nothing but the personal animosity of certain interested people.

Sir George's interview with the Emperor was a momentous one. The Ambassador tried to bring to the knowledge of the monarch the peril in which he stood; he tried to get him to see the necessity of relaxing the hand of autocracy in favour of a more representative government that could share with him the responsibility for bringing the War to a successful finish, and at last he asked him whether he realized all the dangers of the situation and was aware that revolutionary language was being used not only in Petrograd but throughout Russia. The Emperor replied that he was aware of it, but that it would be a mistake to fake it too seriously, whereupon the Ambassador retorted that a week before Rasputin's assassination he had heard that the attempt was about to be made on his life and had treated it as idle gossip, but that it had after all proved true. He could not, therefore, turn a deaf ear to other reports which had reached him of assassinations of certain exalted personages said to be in contemplation. If such assassinations began, there was no saying where they would stop. Sir George concluded with an eloquent appeal to the Emperor to listen to him, to listen to a friend who, seeing him walk through a wood on a dark night along a path which he knew ended in a precipice, thought it his duty to warn him of his danger; he also asked Nicholas to remember that the army was dissatisfied and that in the event of a revolution only a small part of it could be counted upon to defend the throne and the dynasty.

The Emperor was visibly moved, and he thanked the Ambassador before saying good-bye to him, but whatever momentary impression the words of the latter may have produced upon the mind of the sovereign, it was not strong enough to counterbalance the adverse influence of the Empress and her determination to compel her husband to enforce to the bitter end the principles and aims of that autocracy so dear to her heart.

In the meanwhile events were moving forward, and every day was bringing the dynasty closer to that moment which had been prophesied as being inevitable "in a not too distant future" in the letter written by the Revolutionary Committee of Geneva in answer to Nicholas II's famous speech to representatives of the *zemstvos* when they came to congratulate him upon his marriage and accession to the throne and when in reply he bade them not indulge in "senseless dreams." Recapitulating in one's mind all that had taken place since that day, it is impossible not to see in that historical letter the first warning of the inexorable fate which was to overtake the dynasty.

The Empress alone seems not to have had any forewarning as to what the future was holding in store for her. She was too much absorbed in her grief for Rasputin to be thinking of anything else except avenging him so far as lay in her power, and, besides, she was convinced that now that he was gone further misfortunes were bound to fall upon her as well as upon Russia. We know very little about her feelings during those days which preceded the great storm, but they must have been sad and dreary ones until the moment when they were to turn really tragic.

On February 19 (Russian calendar) the Emperor's only brother, the Grand Duke Michael Alexandrovitch, came to Tsarskoye Selo and told Nicholas that it was his duty to return immediately to Head-quarters, because of grave threats of mutiny in the army which the presence of its commander-in-chief alone could subdue. Most reluctantly the Tsar complied with his brother's request. He did not care to leave his wife and children at this juncture, the more so as in Petrograd, too, some disorders had broken out and Cossacks called out to stop them. The food situation in the capital was getting more and more acute, and the shortage of provisions was exasperating the population. But no one at Tsarskoye Selo seems to have had the slightest idea that the much dreaded crisis was at last at hand.

As fate would have it, the children of the Imperial pair took the measles as soon as their father had left for the front, an unlucky circumstance if ever there was one, because if they had been in a condition to be moved, it is likely that the Empress might have escaped with them to Finland or Sweden immediately after her husband's abdication. As it was, she became entirely absorbed in her duties as a sick-nurse and, mercifully perhaps, did not realize the magnitude of the disaster that was overtaking her. The Tsar had arrived at Head-quarters but, after staying there a few days, had received such disquieting messages from the capital that he decided to return to Tsarskoye Selo. His train, as is known, was stopped and compelled to return to Pskoff, where the sovereign hoped he would be in safety among loyal troops commanded by General Russki, one of the few men whose war record had been clean, and on whose devotion he believed he could rely. But Russia also had been won over to the cause of the Revolution, which was already at that moment an accomplished fact.

He, as well as most of the other generals in command of the armies on the different fronts, had come to the conclusion that their men would refuse to fight for a Tsar in whom they had lost confidence, but in response to urgent telegrams from the president of the Duma, M. Rodzianko, asking them to use their best efforts to persuade Nicholas II of the necessity of granting a constitution, they had promised to make the attempt. Then something happened which has never yet been explained to the satisfaction of the historian desirous of going to the bottom of the causes that brought about the final upheaval, and General Russki became convinced that even if the Emperor made concessions to the demands of the nation, it would be too late, and so lie took it upon himself to claim from Nicholas II his abdication pure and simple.

Here again we find ourselves in the presence of discrepancies, for some people are sure that Russia wired to Rodzianko that the army insisted on the deposition of their monarch, while others are sure that it was Rodzianko who informed the General that the Duma no longer desired any promises from the Tsar, in whom it had lost confidence, and that nothing short of his abdication would satisfy it. Where the truth lies it is almost impossible to guess. The two men who knew it have died; Rodzianko in exile at Agram, in Jugoslavia, more from a broken heart than from anything else, because he had loved his country sincerely and well, even if he had not known how to serve it, and Russki, murdered by the Bolsheviks under conditions of particular cruelty. But in regard to the latter, who had been the recipient of many favours from the unfortunate sovereign whom he helped to dethrone, it is impossible not to sympathize with the Empress, who, when speaking of him, exclaimed: "That Russki, what a Judas!"

He was not the only one to whom this name might have been applied, because nearly every member of the Emperor's staff, suite, and household basely deserted him in his misfortune. As if by a stroke of magic, the palace of Tsarskoye Selo emptied itself, and all the courtiers and officials who had filled it vanished into thin air as soon as the news of the fall of its master reached them. Of the numerous people who had been quartered there in attendance on the monarch and on his family, only a handful of old servants remained, together with the aged Count Benckendorff, a German by origin; two ladies-in-waiting, Doctor Botkine, who was to perish together with the Imperial family whom he had followed into exile, and an aide-de-camp of the Emperor, Count Adam Zamoyski, a Pole, whose conduct during those trying days was absolutely admirable. Count Zamoyski, who had never been a favourite of the Empress, nevertheless hastened to Tsarskoye Selo as soon as he heard that she might be in danger, and remained in constant attendance upon her until the new government ordered him to leave the palace. As for her former favourites. Count Apraxine, the Tanieieff family. General Ressine, the commanding officer of the Svodny Polk, a mixed regiment entrusted with the personal safety of the sovereign, the officers, as well as the men, of the Cossack escort, a corps which was particularly beloved by Nicholas II, they one and all abandoned Tsarskoye Selo and joined the Revolution.

In that vast palace there remained a woman and her sick children, a miserable, unhappy woman, forsaken by all, detested by all, with no one near her on whose heart she could have sobbed out her despair. Anna Viroubova, the ever-present Anna, had also contracted the measles, and lay in a darkened room, attended by Alexandra herself, as no one else was left to take care of her except another friend of the Empress, Madame Lili Dehn, the wife of an officer of the Imperial yacht *Standard*, who had also been one of the devotees of Rasputin, and who later wrote a book of reminiscences on her existence at Tsarskoye Selo, a book which, in spite of its insignificance, contains a few interesting details concerning the family life of the last Tsar of Russia. She who had been the Empress of that vast empire, with the world at her feet, and one hundred and eighty millions of people prostrated before her, was now almost entirely alone, and never even heard of her husband's abdication until the Grand Duke Paul came at last to acquaint her with the terrible news.

She bore the blow with immense dignity, and although great tears fell from her eyes as the Grand Duke unfolded his sad tale, she did not utter a single word of regret for the grandeur which she had lost. "I am no longer an empress," she said, "but I am still a sister of charity, and as such only do I want to be considered." She impressed the old, broken-down Grand Duke by her calm and resignation, which was far superior to his own, but when she returned to her room, where

Madame Dehn was awaiting her, her strength nearly left her, and she had to lean heavily against a writing-desk which stood between the windows. Then, taking into her own the hands of Madame Dehn, she exclaimed in a broken voice, "Abdicated!" and then, immediately afterwards, "And he all alone there, what must he have suffered!"

Did she guess what very probably was the truth, that the sovereign had been purposely kept back at Pskoff, and not allowed to resume his journey to Tsarskoye Selo, so as to be compelled to sign his abdication before he had the chance to discuss such an act with his wife? If she had been at his side, it is likely that she would have protested so energetically against his consenting to such a "degradation," as she termed it later, that the weak Nicholas would have resisted the demands of his rebellious subjects and refused to put his name to the document. And here comes the question: did he realize its importance, did he guess the tremendous consequences that would follow upon it? He, the autocrat, the absolute monarch who could have ordered to be hanged the men audacious enough to claim from him the crown he had solemnly assumed in Moscow twenty-one years before — he submitted without a murmur to demands which were not even just, and which certainly were not justified. He might have avoided the catastrophe if he had listened to the many warnings he had received, if he had accepted the disinterested advice offered to him by Sir George Buchanan and by other devoted friends. He might have saved himself and his wife and children from the terrible fate which befell them, but then destiny had to be accomplished and the curtain to fall on what would prove to be the greatest tragedy of modern times, as it later fell on one of the greatest crimes recorded in the annals of history.

The days which followed must have been days of agony for the unfortunate Empress, deprived of news from her husband, not knowing what had happened to him, fearing that perhaps he had been murdered by his soldiers, those same soldiers who a few days earlier had cheered him with their never-ending hurrahs; anxious for her desperately ill children, worried about Anna, her dearest friend, also ill in another room of that vast palace which had already assumed the aspect of a prison. It was then that she uttered the famous words for which she was so bitterly reproached later on. "If our friend had been alive, he would have helped me to destroy all this rabble," thus helping to give some show of plausibility to the theory that it was Rasputin who had inspired her in her fight for the maintenance of autocracy; that in reality he had been ruling Russia instead of the Emperor.

A few more days passed, and then she was made a prisoner in her own palace, deprived even of the liberty of communicating with the few people still faithful to her. She scarcely realized the importance of the event, scarcely understood what it meant. All her thoughts were concentrated on the absent Emperor : where was he, what was he doing, would she ever see him again ? This last question at least was to be answered soon, for not many days had passed before he was brought back to her, a prisoner like herself, a captive in the home which had seen their former happiness and power, an unfortunate man, forsaken by all, hated by many, despised by more than a few, insulted by mobs unable to realize the tragedy of this fallen grandeur; brought back a simple colonel, where he had been a Tsar!

CHAPTER IX

THE FINAL TRAGEDY

THE drama had come to an end; the tragedy had begun. For the first time in his life, the composure of Nicholas broke down when he found himself once more in the presence of his wife, and he is said to have completely collapsed under the weight of the agony he had endured. Perhaps the sight of her, standing calm and serene in that very room where he had left her an Empress, had proved too much for him, because he fell sobbing in her arms. She, the strong woman, tried to comfort him, the weak man, who, while loving her, had sacrificed her high estate and the inheritance of their son; who had allowed that mob she had always despised to dictate to him — to him, the Tsar of all the Russias! She forgot all that; she did not remind him of her entreaties to show himself firm when met with the demands of his people. She did not reproach; she, herself, had suffered so much.

The conduct of the Empress all through that terrible time was admirable in its submission to what she considered the Divine Will. She never murmured, and she did not allow others around her to murmur. The proud woman kept her head high under circumstances that would have bowed that of the majority.

It was then that the beauty of her faith appeared at its best. Others placed in her position would have been inclined to rebel; to curse, perhaps, those who had destroyed all she had cared for in life, who had cast down the throne she had wished her son to inherit. Alexandra Feodorovna rose above all her trials, all her sufferings. She expiated her follies and mistakes with amazing fortitude. Her follies had been great, her mistakes terrible, but she had been so sincere in her blindness all the time that she could afford to tell herself that at every moment of the hard, dreadful years which had preceded the catastrophe, she had desired the good of Russia, as well as that of her husband and little boy. It was not her fault that God had refused her the necessary intelligence to distinguish between friend and foe, that she had allowed her superstitious leanings to obscure her reason; but she was prepared to expiate them all; and expiate them she did, in the terrible manner which we know.

Once, however, she broke down, and that was when, by order of the new Government, Anna Viroubova was removed from Tsarskoye Selo and taken to the fortress at Petrograd. This was the last crushing blow that nearly destroyed her composure, and the proud woman who had never humbled herself to ask any favour of her gaolers, stooped now to entreat them not to separate her from the woman to. whom she was bound by so many ties, among which not the least were their remembrances of Rasputin. "What possible good will it do you to arrest one helpless woman?" she asked. "Parting from her would be like losing one of my own children." But the new commandant of the palace, Colonel Kotzebue, to whom this impassioned appeal was addressed, could only reply: "If I could, Madame — but there is nothing I can do, nothing."

So these two women who for so many years had shared joys and sorrows, hopes and fears, and even if one is to believe the hints thrown out by Madame Viroubova in her book, the love of a man they both seemed to adore — these two women, one of whom had led the other to her doom, were parted at last, and this time for ever.

There is nothing on record concerning the impressions of the Empress at that moment which severed the last link with a past when everything seemed bright and splendid around her, the time when she was an Empress, worshipped by millions of human creatures who looked upon her as a divinity. She must have suffered untold agonies of passionate regret.

Yet who knows whether at the bottom of her heart she did not feel relieved, after the first shock of her separation from her friend had assuaged, to have her husband to herself at last, without anyone trying to step between them and to distract his attention from her? Whatever had been her faults, her love for Nicholas II was always intense and sincere; maybe she did not feel sorry to be able to tell him how much she had cared and still cared for him, without anyone listening to her, criticizing her, or envying her.

Life dragged on at Tsarskoye Selo in sad and monotonous days, in which the restraints imposed ever became more galling and more severe. They were practically isolated from the world, without any means of communicating with the few friends left to them or with their family, for even the Emperor's brother, the Grand Duke Michael, was refused permission to see him. The soldiers who guarded them were becoming more and more insolent, and spared them neither mockery nor insult. Princess Paley, wife of the Grand Duke Paul, relates in her book how one afternoon, wishing to catch a glimpse of the Emperor if only from afar, she managed to get close to the railings in the park of Tsarskoye Selo, and saw the former sovereign breaking ice on a canal running close to the road, in company with Prince Basil Dolgoroukoff, his faithful aide-de-camp who was to perish together with him at Ekaterinburg. Soldiers were around them talking at the top of their voices, and jeering at the monarch:

"Ah, here you are at last, Nicoloichka, breaking ice in your turn! If you do this to-day, what will you do to-morrow? This is a change, is it not, from the war? And in summer, when there isn't any ice, what will you do? Perhaps you will be throwing sand in the alleys? Do you feel now that you have drunk enough of our blood?" . . . and so forth.

The Emperor must have heard every one of these horrible taunts. He suddenly stopped in his work and, raising his head, looked at these men sadly and tensely. Somehow this seemed to sober them, for they became silent. At that moment Nicholas II noticed Princess Paley on the other side of the railings, and his mournful glance rested on her for a moment with such an expression of distress and hopeless resignation that she burst into tears. This was the last time she ever saw him.

People's mentality was changing every minute; those who had been timid became arrogant, and seemed to be trying to justify to themselves, by means of a coarse brutality, their sudden accession to a power they had never imagined they could ever wield. There is nothing more cowardly than a mob, even in its moments of fury. Even the sailor-attendant on the poor little Tsarevitch, Derevenko, who had seemed to be quite devoted to him, and who had been the recipient of numerous kindnesses from the Emperor and Empress, became imbued with the temptation to follow the example of the shoemaker Simon during the great French Revolution, and like him to ill-treat the royal child he had in his care. Madame Viroubova relates how, a few days before her arrest, she happened to pass the open door of Alexis's room, and saw the sailor "stretched out in an easy chair, bawling insolently at the boy, whom he had formerly pretended to love so dearly, to bring him this or that, to perform any menial service of which his mean lackey's brain could think. Dazed and apparently only half-conscious of what he was being forced to do, the child moved about trying to obey." Verily, revolutions always repeat themselves in their excesses; there was little difference between the scenes which took place in the Tour du Temple in Paris and those which were happening in the Imperial palace of Tsarskoye Selo.

But through it all the royal prisoners bore themselves well; their dignity never left them for a single moment, and they proudly suffered without complaining. But it was a weary life, one that would have broken down the strongest natures, and it would have broken down those of Nicholas II and his consort if they had entirely realized whither all these insults, these affronts, would finally lead. But — and this is curious — they seemed both still to have the idea that their persons were so sacred that no rough hand would ever find the courage to raise itself against them. In their prison palace in the loneliness of their Siberian exile, and in the horror of their captivity at Ekaterinburg, they never lost their hope of a brighter future, or the idea of their own importance, as may be seen from the words of the Emperor when he was taken away from Tobolsk and told his entourage that he felt sure the Soviet wanted to bring him to Moscow in order to obtain his signature to the Brest Litovsk Treaty — an illusion so sad that it is best not to try to discuss it.

As I have said already, we have no record of what could have been the thoughts of the Empress during those weary months of waiting. She displayed enormous fortitude after the first explosion of grief which had followed upon the return of the Emperor to Tsarskoye Selo and the arrest of Anna Viroubova, but after that she retired within herself and preserved that same haughty silence for which she had been so much reproached in the days of her glory. Her disdain was absolute, and she simply ignored the insults of her gaolers, as well as the discomforts of her daily existence.

People said afterwards that she had always believed the Allies would insist that the new Government should send the Imperial family abroad, and there was really some question of it, but the Soviets were already too powerful, and they were determined to have the Emperor's blood. Sir George Buchanan relates how, after the British Government had offered an asylum to the Tsar, the Administration, headed by Prince Lvoff, did not find itself strong enough to ensure his safe arrival in England or to take him and his family to Port Romanoff on the Mourman coast, where he ought to have embarked. The workmen had threatened to pull up the rails in front of his train, so the whole plan therefore fell through, and subsequently the Imperial family was taken to Tobolsk, which proved to be the first station on the road which was to lead them to the dark cellar at Ekaterinburg, the grave of the Romanoff dynasty.

At last the new Government came to a decision in regard to the fate of the unhappy family. It had become evident that it was impossible to keep them in Tsarskoye Selo, where their lives were not safe, as every moment might see revolutionaries storming the palace to murder them without pity or mercy.

The question naturally arises, was there no spot on earth where one could have sent them other than Tobolsk, one of the dreariest towns in dreary Siberia? The Emperor had begged permission to go to Livadia and end his days there in the lovely white marble palace he had built on the shores of the Black Sea, but the new Government would not hear of it. Again, one asks whether some members of the new regime, such as Kerensky, who knew what Siberia was, and who had seen many of his friends sent there into exile, did not try to satisfy their revenge by sentencing the Tsar to the same punishment that, in his name, had been inflicted upon so many innocent people. A Romanoff sent to that distant land whither the haughty dynasty had dispatched so many noble souls, so many honest men and women, guilty of no other crime than a passionate aspiration after a liberty which had been denied to their native land! If ever the Biblical saying that children have to expiate the crimes of their parents was fulfilled, it was in the case of Nicholas II and his family.

Magistrate Sokoloff, in his book, declares that there really was no reason to send the Imperial family to Siberia except malice on the part of the Government, and he bitterly reproaches Prince Lvoff for having given his assent to such a measure. When, later, he had occasion to question Kerensky on the subject in Paris, the latter declared that the reason for the decision to remove the Tsar with his wife and children from Tsarskoye Selo had been fears for their safety if they remained there. But Sokoloff denies that such was the case, and calls the explanation a very lame one. He treats with equal incredulity the statement of Prince Lvoff that Siberia had been chosen because it was a quiet place and the Governor's home at Tobolsk a comfortable residence!

Kerensky explained to Sokoloff that at first he had thought of sending the family to some place in the centre of Russia, either to the country estate of Grand Duke Michael Alexandrovitch or to that of Grand Duke Nicholas Michailovitch, but that it had been found impossible to do so after investigation. It could not be thought of to take the Tsar to either of these places, which would have meant travelling through the whole of peasant and industrial Russia. Just as little could one have taken them to the South or to the Crimea, where there lived several members of the Imperial family and the Dowager Empress Marie, whose presence on the Crimean coast had already given rise to some disturbances and misunderstandings. "At last," added Kerensky, "I myself decided in favour of Tobolsk. Its loneliness and geographical position put the town almost out of reach of dangerous revolutionary elements. Moreover, I knew that the home of the Governor would be a decent residence for the family. But in order to be quite sure of it, I sent a commission to examine conditions in Tobolsk, and after I had received its report I decided it was the best place to send our prisoners."

"I fail to understand," writes Sokoloff, "why it would have been so bad for the Tsar to travel through peasant and industrial Russia when going elsewhere than to Tobolsk. Of course conditions of life were at that time such that disturbances might break out anywhere, but it is a fact that all the members of the Imperial family who were in the Crimea contrived to escape abroad, while those sent into exile to Siberia or the Urals perished."

No one in Petrograd knew or suspected the intentions of the Government in regard to the dethroned sovereigns, and everything connected with their departure from Tsarskoye Selo was surrounded with the greatest secrecy; such secrecy, indeed, that even the engineers in charge of the train were not advised until the evening before of the hour fixed for its departure, with the result that they could not get it ready in time and the Emperor and Empress, with their children and attendants, had to wait all night, until at last Kerensky advised them that they could start. What this night must have been for them one can imagine. It seems that Nicholas and Alexandra walked hand in hand through all the rooms of the palace bidding good-bye to the home they had loved so much, and which had seen all their happiness, witnessed all the joys of their married life, the birth of their children, and all that had happened to them, both of good and bad. The little mauve boudoir of the Empress, with its many flowers, had always been a haven of refuge for the Tsar, who had been accustomed to retire to it in order to forget the responsibilities and difficulties of his position; the ballroom had witnessed the first steps of their babies, and in the state apartments sovereigns and their ambassadors had been received and entertained. Now all this was at an end, and they were taking leave of this dearly loved theatre of their grandeur and of their fall. Could anything have been more poignant; could any parting have been more tragic than this farewell to their past happiness, to a home the very walls of which reminded them of all the glory of the Tsar's ancestors, the splendour of their former position, the might and strength of that Russia which had been the first love of their hearts, which, now bruised and bleeding, was witnessing the end of Autocracy?

In the grey light of a summer morning the exiles had to depart. The end of the book had come, the last page had been turned over. Russia and the Romanoffs had parted company for ever.

M. Gilliard, the tutor of the little Tsarevitch, tells, in his interesting book, that the Empress was never so worthy of herself as after the abdication. Her religious faith proved to be her greatest help amid her troubles, and suddenly, under the stress of misfortune, to have transformed into absolute meekness her haughty temper and proud character. This is also to be noticed in some of the letters written by her from Tobolsk, where she shows herself touchingly grateful for small attentions received at the hands of the commissars of the people. One of them had sent her a few trifles she had left behind at Tsarskoye Selo; and what trifles! — four small prints from her mauve room, five pastels from Kaulbach, some snapshots from Livadia, and a small carpet from her bedroom! And these were the things for which the former Empress of Russia, whose slightest wish had been performed and smallest caprice obeyed, was so grateful that she called the man who had returned them to her "kind Commissar Makaroff"!

All the correspondence of Alexandra with Madame Viroubova, part of which was published later by the latter, breathes of the complete resignation with which she met her misfortunes. They are beautiful letters; products of her bruised heart. They breathe the Christian piety that enabled her to face suffering and death with heroic fortitude. Much ought to be forgiven the poor woman who had so sadly blundered, when one becomes familiar with her thoughts and feelings during those weary months.

"God is very near us," she writes in one of her letters; "we feel His support and are often amazed that we can endure events and separations which once might have killed us. Although we suffer horribly, still there is peace in our souls. I suffer most for Russia, and I suffer for you too, but I know that ultimately all will be for the best. Only I don't understand anything any longer. Every one seems to have gone mad."

"It is bright sunshine," she says in another letter, "and everything glitters with hoar-frost. There are such moonlight nights, it must be ideal on the hills. But my poor unfortunates can only pace up and down the narrow yard. How I long to take Communion, We took it last on October 22, but now it is so awkward, one has to ask permission before doing the least thing. I am reading Solomon and the writings of St. Seraph, every time finding something new. Some thoughts one is obliged to drive away, they are too poignant, too fresh in one's memory. All things for ns are in the past, and what the future holds I cannot guess, but God knows, and I have given everything into His keeping. Pray for us and for those we love, especially for Russia, when you are at the shrine of the all-hearing Virgin."

Then come a few poignant lines:

"I am knitting stockings for the small one [Alexis]. He asked for a pair, as all his are in holes. Mine are warm and thick like the ones I gave the wounded, do you remember? I make everything now. Father's trousers are torn and darned, the girls' underlinen in rags. Dreadful, is it not?"

This is the woman who for twenty-three years had had at her command everything she could wish for, who had disposed of millions and millions of roubles. And now she was mending her husband's trousers, and lamenting the rags her daughters had to wear! What an abyss divided her from her happy past!

As time goes on, one can follow the transformation which is taking place in the heart and soul of the captive Empress ; the growing detachment from all earthly things to which she is slowly coming.

"My God," she says, "how Russia suffers! You know that I love it even more than you do, miserable country, demolished from within, and by the Germans from without. Since the Revolution they have conquered a great deal of it without even a battle. ... If they created order now in Russia, how dreadful would be the country's debasement — to Kaye to be grateful to the enemy. . .

"I feel old, oh, so old, but I am still the mother of this country, and I suffer its pains as my own child's pains, and I love it in spite of all its sins and horrors. No one can tear a child from its mother's heart, and neither can you tear away one's country, although Russia's black ingratitude to the Emperor breaks my heart. Not that it is the whole country , though. God have mercy and save Russia!"

And in another letter she says:

"What terrible times you are all living through! On the whole we are better off than you. . . . Soon spring is coming to rejoice our hearts. The way of the cross first — then joy and gladness. It will soon be a year since we parted, but what is time? Life here is nothing — eternity is everything, and what we are doing is preparing our souls for the Kingdom of Heaven. Thus nothing, after all, is terrible, and if they do take everything from us, they cannot take our souls. . . Have patience, and these days of suffering will end, we shall forget all the anguish and thank God. God help those who see only the bad, and don't try to understand that all this will pass. It cannot be otherwise. . . . We live here on earth, but we are already half gone to the next world. We see with different eyes, and that makes it often difficult to associate with people who call themselves, and really are, religious. . . . My greatest sin is my irritability. The endless stupidities of my maid, for instance — she can't help being stupid, she is so often untruthful, or else she begins to sermonize like a preacher, and then I burst — you know how hot-tempered I am. It is not difficult to bear great trials, but these little buzzing mosquitoes are so trying. I want to be a better woman, and I try. For long periods I am really patient, and then breaks out again my bad temper. I long to warm and to comfort others — but, alas, I do not feel drawn to those around me. I am cold towards them, and this too is wrong of me."

On March 13, a few days before she and Nicholas were removed to their last prison in Ekaterinburg, she wrote:

"How I love my country with all its faults! It grows dearer and dearer to me, and I thank God daily that He allowed us to remain here, and did not send us farther away. Believe in the people, darling. The nation is strong and young, and as soft as wax. Just now it is in bad hands, and darkness and anarchy reigns. But the King of Glory will come and will save, strengthen, and give wisdom to the people who are now deceived."

And on March 21, three days before she started with the Emperor on that awful journey which was to lead them straight to Golgotha, she wrote to Anna Viroubova, in the very last letter that the latter was to receive from her, the following words:

"The atmosphere around us is fairly electrified. We feel that a storm is approaching, but we know that God is merciful and will care for us. Things are growing very anguishing. To-day we shall have a small service at home, for which we are thankful, but it is hard, nevertheless, not to be allowed to go to church. . . . Though we know that the storm is coming nearer and nearer, our souls are at peace. Whatever happens will be through God's will."

These words may be regarded as the spiritual last will and testament of Alexandra Feodorovna. Her friend never heard from her again, nor did anyone else in this world. The veil of mystery which for so many months covered the fate of the Tsar and of his family had fallen. They were cut off from everything and everybody, kept in close captivity, and ill-treated in every possible way.

To all those who knew Ekaterinburg, and the spirit of anarchy that had always existed in that city, it was evident that the Emperor's days there were numbered and that he had been taken there for the purpose of being done away with. Yet people hoped his wife and children would be spared. This was not to be. After three months of martyrdom, borne with heroic courage and resignation, the whole unfortunate family was put to death in an atrociously cruel manner — shot down in a dark cellar without having had even five minutes to prepare for the end. Parents, children, and a few faithful servants were all shot by order of the Moscow Soviet, so brutally that even the soldiers who took part in the dreadful deed nearly fainted with horror when it was completed. The bodies were destroyed by fire, after having been hacked to pieces.

The last of the Romanoffs did not even have a decent grave.

CHAPTER X

WHO WAS TO BLAME?

IT is possible, now that some years have passed since the tragedy, to try to pass judgment on those who were its victims. Anna Viroubova, whose restless spirit had been the cause of so much trouble, and who had unwittingly done so much harm to the Empress, rendered her at least one last great service by publishing the letters from which I have given some quotations. These letters, in a certain sense, exculpate their writer from many accusations that were launched against her. They show her as a profoundly religious woman, who in her misfortunes attained a dignity that almost reached the sublime, and who accepted her trials in a spirit of complete Christian meekness and fortitude.

But they, as well as the whole correspondence of Alexandra Feodorovna with her husband during the eventful years of the War, also prove the Empress to have been an hysterical woman who, in her efforts to do the right thing, was continually beating her head against stone walls without ever being able to find a door to get out of the narrow prison in which her mind was confined. She honestly searched for the means of saving Russia, and all her exhortations to her husband to keep firm and not to give into the general wishes of the nation proceeded from a mistaken but absolutely honest conviction that autocracy alone could bring Russia out of its troubles. The idea was an absolutely mistaken one, but, unfortunately for her, the Empress would not see it, nor listen to those who, better than it was possible for her to do, could judge of the situation as well as of its numerous dangers.

She was far too much inclined to believe in flattery of the grossest kind to accept advice which might prove in any way unpalatable to her. And, unluckily for her and still more for Russia, during the last years of her life, before the cataclysm that separated her from those who cannot be called other than false friends, she was surrounded by people who, in their unscrupulous desire to obtain through her the material advantages they craved, toadied to her weaknesses and kept repeating to her that she was a second Catherine the Great, and, like her, strong enough to impose her will upon Russia. In a certain sense she did impose it, because for a few months it was certainly her advice to which the Tsar listened. She overthrew Ministers like M. Sazonoff and others who had believed that they were sitting quite firmly in the place which they occupied, and had filled prior to the outbreak of the War. She made her will felt on all sorts of occasions, and constantly interfered in matters which did not concern her, thus discrediting the husband whom she sincerely believed she was helping.

Without being a brilliant woman, the Empress was far from stupid, and had positive opinions which she aired oftener than was desirable. In her early days she had tried to reform St. Petersburg society; in her maturity she wanted to reform the whole of Russia, to convert it to her own points of view, to make it accept the holiness of Rasputin, the "man of God," as she called him, and she failed in both attempts. This made her bitter, and confirmed her in the opinion, which she had already formed, that the Russian aristocracy and the Russian *intelligentsia* were allied together against the Tsar, a profound error on her part, the consequences of which were to be far more disastrous than she could ever suspect. If she had really known the Russian people, she would most likely have acted differently, but then she did not know them, and this was perhaps her supreme misfortune.

It is impossible to deny that bad luck pursued her from the very first day of her marriage, but then this bad luck was in many cases her own fault, the fault of her pride, of her obstinacy, of the falsely exalted idea which she had of her own importance, and also of the violent dislike she had taken to those of the Russian aristocracy, in whom she saw her direct and personal enemies. Yet, if she had been wise enough to try to propitiate this aristocracy when she first came to reign in Russia, she would most certainly have found her life easier in many respects, and — who knows? — perhaps she might have acquired over it an influence which would have prevented it from joining, in many instances, the ranks of those who were so violently opposed to the Government of Nicholas II that they did not hesitate to make common cause with the worst elements of Russian society in order to overthrow the throne.

The whole catastrophe began, as I have already said many times, with a misunderstanding, which increased as time went on — one of those fatal misunderstandings that nothing can ever clear up, and which was aggravated on both sides by persons eager to profit by it in some way or other. The unfortunate influence of Anna Viroubova consisted in her constantly repeating to her Imperial mistress all the gossip in town and doing her best to make her disapprove of this or that person. What must never be lost sight of in this tragedy is that Anna, as the Emperor and his wife familiarly called her, did not belong to the best social sphere, whatever she herself may tell us to the contrary. She had never been able to obtain the entree of the homes of the smartest St. Petersburg society, nor of the salons of the dowagers who ruled that society with a hand of iron. This angered her, and inspired in her a lust of revenge for the slights which she believed she had received from proud and haughty ladies to whom she had made advances which had been repulsed, not even with good grace. She had not realized that in the eyes of these ladies she represented the much-hated class of bureaucrats, the scourge of Russia, and that although M. Tanieieff, her father, was the head of the private chancery of the sovereign, he was not received by women like Princess Bariatinsky or **Princess Pachkievich or Countess Moussine Pouchkine, who after all were the uncrowned** queens of St. Petersburg society.

The whole tragedy of Anna Viroubova resolves itself into the everlasting duel, which had been going on ever since the days of Peter the Great, between the old Russian nobility and the classes which, under the name of the bureaucracy, had gained entrance into the palace of the sovereign, and in time had made themselves so obnoxious to every true Russian patriot, because they represented graft, favouritism, and base flattery of those in power, as well as chauvinism in its worst form. The curse of Russia has been "Tchinovnikism," as it was called, and it was the Tchinovnik, or bureaucrat, who was the primary cause of the Revolution, just as he had been the reason of all previous attempts of Russian society to emancipate itself from his yoke, far heavier than that of the monarch himself. The Empress believed in the bureaucracy because she had found that it flattered her, bore with her bad temper, and was never offended by her, whatever she might do. She hated the Russian aristocracy because it had refused to toady to her, to kiss the hand she extended to it, and had insisted on its independence and its right to warn the sovereign of the dangers which were besetting his path. She hated also the *intelligentsia* because it wanted to curtail the absolute, autocratic power which was in the hands of her husband, and she hated the *zemstvos* because they represented the Liberal aspirations of the country, tired of absolute monarchy and hungering after a change in the government, and, with it, the possibility for every Russian to assume his share of the many burdens which lay on the shoulders of the whole nation.

After the Great War had disclosed the incapacity of the Government, and the lack of preparedness of the army, the Empress still did not accuse the bureaucracy of the country, nor see that on it, and on it alone, lay the blame for the disasters that had overtaken the land. She refused to admit that it would have been to the advantage of the dynasty to share with the representatives of all classes of Russian society the great burden imposed upon it by the terrific struggle going on. She wanted the Government to do everything, to carry alone this responsibility, and she firmly believed that all that was needed to defeat Germany was the prayers of Rasputin and blind obedience to the advice which he was giving her through Anna Viroubova, who half the time exaggerated his words, or repeated them wrongly, because she was influenced by her feelings against those by whom she imagined she had been personally slighted.

Behind Anna was a whole army of speculators, war profiteers, adventurers of the worst type. They used her as a tool, and brought her every kind of gossip, which she in her turn repeated to the Empress, with the result that the latter kept worrying the Emperor with her complaints against this or that person whom she suspected of disapproving of her conduct. St. Petersburg, or Petrograd, as it bad been named by chauvinists who only saw the German name and forgot that it reminded the country of Peter the Great and of his works, which it was almost a profanation to touch and destroy — St. Petersburg had become a nest of gossip, and it was gossip that caused the Revolution, just as it had been gossip that had brought to light all the abuses that had led to the disasters of the War.

Alexandra Feodorovna fell prey to this gossip, in a sense at least, but, on the other hand, it was she who had set the gossip going, who had furnished it with subjects for discussion and criticism. A misunderstanding, I repeat, but what a tragic, terrible one! Tragic and terrible it certainly was, especially because so many innocent victims perished in consequence.

As for Rasputin, he was a symbol more than anything else. This ignorant peasant was certainly a curious personage, but, admitting even that he possessed the hypnotic faculties attributed to him, he would never have succeeded, had he been alone, in implanting himself in the way he did in the affections and confidence of the Tsarina; it was due to others that he became her adviser, and when he spoke with her, he repeated the words that he had learnt almost by heart from them. There had been men of like power in earlier reigns: history mentions a few of those jesters who in ancient times came to acquire an exceptional position at a royal Court. In ancient Byzantium there, were many, and the Roman emperors also had a few. They are the precursors of the dissolution of empires and of the fall of dynasties.

And the Tsar, what of him? Could he have stopped the *debâcle* which was to submerge him, could he have averted the catastrophe? Undoubtedly, if he had been a strong man, one of those who are not afraid to bring about a revolution "from above in order to prevent it from breaking out from below," to use the words of the Russian publicist, Alexander Herzen. The Tsar's grandfather had been such a man, and had not hesitated before his reforms, nor before the "great adventure" (for such it was) of the liberation of the serfs. His father might have been one had he found himself face to face with a great national necessity. Nicholas II could never lay claim to that strength, and consequently, when he granted concessions, he did so only on paper, and even when he himself decided, after the disastrous Japanese War, to call together a Duma to help him rule his country, it was with the mental reservation that he would never, never allow it to curtail in the slightest degree either his own prerogatives, or his own power. Both he and the Empress were despots, not autocrats, because autocrats can give way to generous impulses, which they absolutely ignored.

The worst about the Emperor was his weakness of character and his indecision, which were to bring him into conflict not only with his people, but also with his wife, who never could understand why he continually changed his opinions and was so often ready to say "no" after he had written "yes." In a certain sense she was far more honest than Nicholas II and had more frankness in her nature. Her whole personality was built on straight, too straight lines, while his was essentially tortuous; and he could never look boldly into a person's eyes. She was too fearless; he feared too many things and too many people.

But the pity of it all! History will undoubtedly clear Alexandra Feodorovna of many a slander and many a calumny. It will give her, in the Russian cataclysm, the place to which she is entitled, and re-establish facts as they really were, not as they are represented by the imagination of her foes. She was a second Marie Antoinette without any of the qualities or the virility of mind of the daughter of Maria Theresa. But in her husband she had to do, not perhaps with a man endowed with the meekness of Louis XVI, but with one just as weak, and just as oblivious of the catastrophe that was going to submerge him.

The fact of the matter was that neither the Tsar nor the Tsarina ever thought it possible that their lives would be endangered after the Revolution, and even in Tobolsk, except just towards the end of their stay there, they believed that no Russian would ever dare to raise a hand against them.

This sense of security probably helped them to bear their misfortunes, together with the deep religious faith which they both possessed, faith in a life everlasting and in the mercy of God. But while relying entirely on Him to save them, they were, at the same time, somewhat afraid of all that was happening to them, of the complete ruin of things they had believed to be everlasting. They had never realized that they were falling ; they had only felt the shock of their fall.

That the Imperial family had good reason to reproach themselves for the disaster which destroyed the old throne of Peter the Great and of Catherine, cannot be denied. The murder of Rasputin gave the signal for other assassinations, other murders, the spilling of more blood ; and the abominable circumstances under which it was conceived and executed, certainly helped to familiarize the Russian people with that contempt for the sacredness of human life which was one of the outstanding features of the upheaval that was to follow. If also destroyed the old Russian idea of the sacredness of hospitality, of the necessity for a host to defend those to whom he has opened the doors of his house, and nothing in the world can excuse the dastardliness of such a deed. Nicholas II was absolutely right when on the back of the petition his kinsmen presented to him, asking him to forgive his cousin the young Grand Duke Dmitri, he wrote : "No one has the right to commit murder." He could not condone the offence, and one of the saddest features in this sad case was that this performance of a sacred duty, the duty of protecting human life, became one of the things most bitterly made an object of reproach to him later on.

On the other hand, those who fanned his anger, and who tried to excite it against his family, committed another crime. Anna Viroubova relates how the Minister of the Interior brought to the Emperor and to the Empress what she describes as suspicious mail which he had seized, and which contained, among other things, a letter written by the Princess Youssoupoff, the mother of Prince Felix, to the Grand Duchess Xenia, sister of the Tsar, in which she congratulated the latter on the part played by her husband in the whole affair, as well as various other correspondence couched in the same style. She adds that when the Empress read these communications and realized that her nearest and dearest connexions were in the ranks of her enemies, her whole countenance seemed to wither and grow old. But it did not strike her how demeaning it was for an Empress of Russia to be reading the private letters of other people, nor how degrading on the part of her husband's Ministers to bring them to her to peruse.

Probably she had never heard the story of the Empress Maria Theresa, of Austria, who, when her chancellor. Prince Kaunitz, informed her that there were in Vienna some people who severely criticized her, asked him how he had come to know it, and when he replied that it was through some of their letters which had been opened by the police, she told him that though he might, as a responsible Minister of the Crown, have to resort to measures of such a disgraceful character as opening private correspondence in questions where the safety of the State was concerned, he had no right to bring their contents to her notice and to make her a party to actions which she could not call other than shameful. Alexandra Feodorovna, had she studied history and especially the lives of its great characters, such as Maria Theresa or Catherine II, might have avoided many fatal blunders.

Of course the fact that the Empress was reading its letters was very soon known to Petrograd society, and one may imagine the indignation that it raised. People found no words harsh enough to apply to her. Nevertheless, there was still some respect left in Russia for the Tsar, the Lord's anointed, among the upper classes of society. It was left to the Soviets, and to the few aliens who were all-powerful among them, to fire the shots which destroyed a dynasty.

Had the prisoners of Ekaterinburg foreseen these shots, or was the whole ghastly tragedy a surprise to them? This is what one would like to know. Did they really believe, when their executioners came to take them down into the cellar on the pretext that there were disturbances in the town and that they would be safer in the basement of their prison house, that the reason was sincere, or did they suspect some treachery? This is one of the questions which will never be answered, but if the consciousness of her approaching doom came to the Empress, what must have been her mental agony when she realized that her innocent children were about to be butchered in cold blood under her very eyes!

Yes, indeed, it had been a misunderstanding all along, a ghastly, terrible misunderstanding, which almost from the first hour of his reign had arisen between Nicholas II and his people. It had begun on the day when he had reproved the *zemstvos*, and it had gone on through the long, yet short years which were to follow. It had been aggravated by the mistakes of the Government during the Japanese War and by the first attempt at revolution which had followed upon if, with all the cruelties that had marked its repression, and had finally been brought to a climax by the unfortunate Rasputin incident and all the disasters of the Great War. Little by little the prestige of the country and the strength of the army had been undermined and destroyed. These misfortunes all resulted from the Tsar's futile clinging to an autocracy entirely out of date, amid the new conditions under which Russia's national aspirations and welfare had to develop, an autocracy which had fixed upon him the responsibility for the deeds of others who sheltered themselves behind his authority and his name, and which wall leave his memory in history branded with crimes that, though he had not personally committed them, he had accepted and endorsed. A misunderstanding, indeed, but one that destroyed Russia and the entire work of Peter the Great.

That the Empress contributed to it to a large extent, it is not possible to deny. But that she took such an important part in politics entirely of her own accord it would also be most unfair to assert. She was simply hurled into the battle by evil advice; flattery; her own resentment against society which she felt had all along misjudged her best intentions; by gossip, of an insidious and misleading nature; by superstition, and by an exaggerated love for her only son, whose incurable disease had **undoubtedly affected her mentality. Her intentions had always been of the best, and** it was not altogether her fault that they never came to anything, and that she never received credit for the good she wanted to do or had done in her own ungracious, curious way. Her greatest defect consisted perhaps in her inability to inspire or retain sympathy, as well as in her inability to sympathize with people for whom she did not care. She was a creature of impulse, moved by impulse, and one who, though endowed with a strong character, yet lacked force of resistance. She never unbent, but she collapsed into a condition of absolute and complete resignation to the misfortunes which befell her and her family ; a resignation that religion alone cannot entirely explain, and which probably was due to her conviction that it was useless to struggle against an implacable fate.

That her cries of agony, uttered from her dreary Siberian prison, were sincere there can be no doubt. "O God, save Russia, this is the cry of my soul day and night," she exclaims. "Have mercy, O God, on our long-suffering country!" It is to be noted that she does not once say: "Have mercy upon us." In her extremity her thoughts were fixed upon Russia, the Russia where she had arrived a lovely bride, in expectation of a Happiness she was never to know; the Russia to which she was devoted in her own strange way, and over which she had hoped her son would reign one day; the Russia which, after having given her a crown, was to refuse her the charity of a tomb.

CHAPTER XI

THE FALL OF A DYNASTY

WHEN recalling the details of the horrible tragedy which came to an end in the dark basement room at Ekaterinburg, the question immediately arises whether it would have been possible in any way to save the unfortunate Tsar and his family. Magistrate Sokoloff has examined it from every possible point of view, and the conclusion to which he came was that nothing short of a miracle could have achieved it, in view of the stubbornness of the Empress and the influence which she exercised over her husband.

While they were prisoners at Tobolsk an escape might have been organized, and, indeed, as Madame Melnik, the daughter of Doctor Botkine, who perished with the family, says, it would even have been relatively easy to do so had one had recourse to Colonel Kobylinsky, the only man who could have managed to bring it about.

Being head of the detachment of soldiers that guarded the captives merely out of devotion to the Emperor, the Colonel had tried to lighten their condition so far as lay in his power. He knew the disposition of the men under him, most of whom were veterans of the War, many decorated with the Cross of St. George for bravery in the field. These men often only acted reluctantly on behalf of the Revolutionary Government in dealing with their former sovereign. This had gone so far that one day the men of the first regiment of Fusiliers of the Imperial family, who comprised the majority of the soldiers of the guard, came to Kobylinsky and declared to him that they would close their eyes when on guard if the Imperial family was driven out of the house where it was confined. But Kobylinsky could not broach the subject of his own accord, and the Empress, and indeed the whole family with the exception perhaps of the Emperor, had taken a violent dislike to him. Alexandra, instead, had fixed her hopes upon a man who, more than anyone else, carries the responsibility for what befell the unfortunate prisoners, because it was through him that an escape was not organized at a time when it would have been possible, and even comparatively easy, to arrange.

This man was named Solovieff; he had been one of the most intimate friends of Rasputin, whose daughter Matrena he was later to marry, and through Anna Viroubova, who In the meanwhile had been released from the fortress where she had spent three miserable months, he managed to get into communication with the Empress, using for the purpose a priest of Tobolsk named Father Vassilieff, who had gained Alexandra's confidence and who, together with Solovieff, brought about the final catastrophe. The Empress was so convinced that a prospective son-in-law of Rasputin must also be a man of God, that she obstinately refused to listen to those who would have brought to her notice serious efforts made by the Russian monarchist party to save her and her family.

Meanwhile Solovieff was entirely the creature of the Bolsheviks, as Magistrate Sokoloff clearly shows, and was allowed by them to remain at Tioumen at first, and at Tobolsk later on, because they knew him to be clever enough to thwart any efforts at escape on the part of the prisoners. The Empress sincerely believed that three hundred officers had assembled at Tioumen and were only waiting for reinforcements to come to Tobolsk and take her away with the Emperor and their children. But in reality there was not even one officer at Tioumen, and the whole story had been invented by Solovieff with the aim and purpose of preventing the Empress from trying to escape from Tobolsk. Thus the tragic influence of Rasputin continued after his death, in the same potent manner as during his lifetime.

The religious feelings of the unfortunate Alexandra were again brought into play, and the hysterical condition into which she had fallen asserted itself once more. It must again be pointed out, as we follow her in the last tragic months of her tragic life, that she was not normal. This cannot be denied; one need only cite as evidence the fact that in the bedroom she had occupied at Tsarskoye Selo, the walls were found to be so completely covered with icons that not one inch of the blue silk with which they were hung could be discerned, except where some of the icons had been taken away by her to her exile. Another peculiarity of hers was her habit of constantly changing the room in which she took her meals, which sometimes were served to her and to her family in her sitting-room, sometimes in her bedroom, and sometimes in her bath-room, while the regular dining-room was used only when there were guests or at official receptions and dinners.

Altogether, these apartments which she had occupied in the palace of Tsarskoye Selo were eloquent witnesses of the singularities of her mind and disposition, even to the rooms occupied by her daughters, which were almost monastic in their simplicity and lack of comfort, with beds that looked like hospital cots, having no pillows and hardly any blankets.

Magistrate Sokoloff also examines, in his remarkable book, the possibility of interference by Germany and of an effort alleged to have been made to have the Emperor and his family given up to the German Government, to be held as hostages. He seems inclined to believe that something of the kind really took place, and that the Bolshevik officer who came to fetch Nicholas II at Tobolsk and officially to take him to Moscow was a German emissary, but that the Bolsheviks thwarted his purpose by causing the Emperor to be arrested at Ekaterinburg, ostensibly by the local Soviet, but actually in accordance with orders dispatched from Moscow.

As Magistrate Sokoloff proves beyond the shadow of a doubt, the murder was arranged and executed according to instructions sent from Moscow. Yourovski, the commandant of the Ipatieff house, where the family met its doom, was but an instrument of other people, some of whom are known, while others have succeeded in keeping their names secret. Sokoloff says this quite plainly when he writes that "there were other persons who, together with Sverdloff, the head of the Tzik in Moscow, and Goloshokin, who occupied the same position at Ekaterinburg, had organized and ordered the crime; but," he adds, "I do not know who they can be."

Vanitas vanitatum! — this is the summing up of this tragic story. *Vanitas vanitatum!* Where have all those great and mighty Tsars gone? What has become of Ivan the Terrible, and of Boris Godunov, the usurper, and of the first Romanoff, the boy Michael, whom the Muscovite Boyars fetched from the Ipatieff monastery of Kostroma, to take his place on the throne of the Ruriks? Where are Peter the Great and his Streltsis, and the Tsarevna Sophia, and Menchikoff, and the beautiful Elizabeth Petrovna, and Catherine, the magnificent Empress? Where have they all gone? Have they seen the destruction of their immense work, and the end of their race? Do they know that the bells of Ivan Veliki will never again call upon the Russian people to welcome its Tsars, that the sanctuaries where they once worshipped have been profaned, the palaces where they once lived, given up to a hungry and sacrilegious mob? Do they know all they sleep undisturbed under their shrouds of ermine, in the dark churches in which they were laid to rest?

It is difficult to realize the extent of the destruction that has overtaken the work of all these brave, cruel, cowardly, or noble potentates. They were, for the most part, strong men; they believed that the edifice which they were building would last, if not for ever, at least for many, many centuries; they hoped that their successors would add stone upon stone to the vast monuments of their ambition, but a few days annihilated what it had taken centuries to create.

And now it is all over. The work of destruction has been accomplished, and not one survivor has escaped the catastrophe to tell us how it really happened in all its tragic details. Nicholas and Alexandra have passed into history, and let us hope that to her, at least, history will be merciful as well as kind, because if she erred deeply, that beautiful, capricious, wayward woman suffered much.

After her one hour of supreme triumph on her wedding day, very soon, too soon, clouds had come to obscure her horizon; grief, sorrow and anxiety had become her portion; the tide of unpopularity had risen around her and engulfed her in its cold waves; the cheers had changed into hisses, the acclamations into howls of rage and fury. And then had come disaster, ruin, her crown wrenched away from her; captivity, exile — exile bleak and dark — privation, poverty, suffering, humiliations without number, insults without end, until at last, in the middle of a summer night, eleven men had appeared and stood before her,— men with revolvers; men sent to slay, men under whose shots she fell, while seeing her children and her husband die.

APPENDICES

I

TITLE OF RUSSIAN HEIR APPARENT

IN old Russia, the title of Tsarevitch, as here used and as one generally writes it abroad, was written Cesarevich. It belonged to the eldest son of the sovereign, or to his heir presumptive in certain cases. For instance, during the reign of Alexander I his eldest brother, Constantine, was called Cesarevich, and the title remained his property even after the accession to the throne of Nicholas I, whose son, Alexander II, was also called Cesarevich.

When Nicholas II ascended the throne, his brother George received the title of Cesarevich as heir presumptive, but after the latter's death it was not granted to the Grand Duke Michael Alexandrovitch, who took his place, in spite of the fact that the Empress had not yet borne a son, as the Emperor did not care to raise any complications in case his marriage ended by being blessed with the birth of an heir, for which he was always hoping.

The name, not title, of Tzarevitch and Tzarevna belonged in old Russia to all the children of the sovereign; it did not refer to the heir to the throne alone.

As for the spelling of the word Cesarevich, the Russian Court was very particular about it.

II

TEXT OF THE ADDRESS PRESENTED BY THE *ZEMSTVO* OF TVER TO NICHOLAS II ON HIS ACCESSION

MAY it please Your Imperial Majesty:

In these memorable days which see the beginning of your services in the cause of the welfare of the Russian nation, the *zemstvo* of the Government of Tver greets you with feelings of fervent loyalty. We share your sorrow. Gracious Sovereign, and we hope that you will find some consolation in this sad hour, when an unexpected misfortune has befallen you, as well as the whole of Russia, in the love of your people, as well as in the hopes and trust that the nation has put in you; and that you will find in those feelings a firm support in the fulfilment of the difficult task that has been imposed upon you by Divine Providence.

The Russian nation has listened with gratitude to the solemn expressions uttered by Your Imperial Majesty upon your accession to the throne of all the Russias. We have also shared these feelings of gratitude together with the rest of the nation, and we are sending fervent prayers to the Almighty for the success of the important task that lies before you, and for the fulfilment of the high aims you have put before you, namely, the happiness and welfare of all your faithful subjects. We allow ourselves to indulge in the hope that on the height of the throne the voice of the nation and the expression of its desires will be heard and listened to. We are firmly convinced that the welfare of Russia will improve and fortify itself under your rule, and that the law will henceforward be respected and obeyed, not by the nation alone, but also by the representatives of the authority that rules it, because the law, which in Russia represents the wishes of the monarch, must stand above the personal opinions and views of these representatives. We earnestly believe that during your reign the rights of individuals, as well as those of already existing representative bodies, will be protected permanently and energetically.

We expect, Gracious Sovereign, that these representative bodies wilt be allowed to voice their opinions in matters in which they are directly concerned, in order that the expressions of the needs and thoughts, not only of the administration, but also of the entire Russian nation, may reach the throne. We expect, Gracious Sovereign, that under your rule Russia will advance on the path of civilization and progress, as well as on the road of a peaceful development of its resources and needs. We firmly believe that in the close union of all the elements and classes that constitute the Russian people, who are all devoted to the throne as well as to their country, the power which Your Majesty wields will find new sources of strength and stronger chances of success towards the fulfilment of the high aims Your Imperial Majesty has in view.

III

LETTER ADDRESSED BY THE REVOLUTIONARY EXECUTIVE COMMITTEE OF GENEVA TO NICHOLAS II

YOU have spoken, and your words are at present known everywhere in Russia; aye, in the whole of the civilized world. Until now you were unknown, but since yesterday you have become a definite factor in the situation of your country, in regard to which there is no room left for *senseless dreams*. We do not know whether you understand or realize the position which you have yourself created with your "firm words," but we believe that people whose position is not so high as yours or so remote from the realities of life, and on that account are able to see what is going on in Russia just now, will easily understand what is your position and what is theirs.

First of all, you are badly informed about these tendencies against which you decided to raise your voice in your speech. There has not been heard in a single assembly of any *zemstvo* a single word against that autocracy which is so dear to your heart; nor has one member of a *zemstvo* ever put the question on the basis upon which you have placed it. The most advanced thinkers among them have only insisted, or, rather, humbly begged, that a closer union be inaugurated between the monarch and his people; for the right of the *zemstvos* to have free access to the throne without anyone standing between it and them; for the right of public debate, and for the assurance that the law should always be observed and stand above the caprices of the administration.

In a word, the only thing that was in question was the desire to see fall and crumble to the ground that wall of bureaucracy and courtierdom which has always parted the sovereign from the Russian nation. This was the desire of those people whom you, who have only just ascended the throne, inexperienced and ignorant of the national needs, have seen fit to call "senseless dreams."

It is clear to all the intelligent elements of the Russian people who has advised you to take this imprudent step. You are being deceived; you are being frightened by that very gang of bureaucrats and courtiers to whose actual autocracy not a single Russian man or woman has ever been reconciled. You too have reproached the *zemstvos* for the feeble cry that has escaped their lips against the tyranny of the bureaucracy and of the police.

You have allowed yourself to be carried so far in your ideas of protecting that autocracy — your own — against which no one thought of rising, that you have regarded as a danger thereto the participation of the *zemstvos* in the government of the country as well as of local needs. Such a point of view does not correspond even to that position in which the *zemstvos* found themselves confirmed by your father's wishes; a position in which they appear as an indispensable organ and participate in the internal government of the country.

But your unfortunate expressions not only are a mistake in the way in which you have worded them, but appear as the definition of a whole system of government: and Russian society will understand quite well that on the 17/30th of January it was not at all that ideal autocracy of which you believe yourself to be the representative that spoke through your mouth, but the omnipotent and jealous guardian of its own privileged *bureaucracy.*

This bureaucracy, which begins with the committee of ministers and ends with the meanest policeman, is odious to all those who desire the extension of real autocracy, even the one that is maintained by the present order of things. This it is that keeps the monarch removed from free communion with the representatives of the nation. And your speech has proved once more that every desire on the part of the nation to be other than slaves kissing the ground before the throne, and to bring to its notice the needs of the country — the most urgent needs — in a submissive form, is met only with a brutal rebuff.

Many fundamental questions concerning the welfare of the nation have yet to be placed upon a satisfactory basis. Questions of moment have arisen since the great epoch of reforms initiated by your grandfather, and these lately have come to the front more acutely owing to the great famine which has weakened the country.

Russian public opinion has been, and is, working hard and with painstaking efforts towards the solution of these; and it is just at such a time that, instead of words of comfort promising a real and beneficial union between the Tsar and his people, and of an acknowledgment from the heights of the throne that in future public discussion and a strong upholding of the law will mark the beginning of a new era in the public life of the country, the representatives of the different classes of society, gathered before you from all the corners of Russia, and expecting from you help and consolation, only heard from you a new expression of your attachment to the old system of an outworn autocracy, and carried away the impression of the total separation of the Tsar from his people.

Do believe that even for the mildest of men such a declaration, ill-timed as it was, could only produce a crushing feeling of betrayal. The 17th of January has done away with that halo with which so many Russians had surrounded your young, inexperienced head. You have laid your own hand on your popularity, and you have destroyed it.

Unfortunately, the question does not touch your popularity alone. If in words and with deeds autocracy identifies itself with the all-powerful bureaucracy ; if its existence is possible only when every expression of the public need is crushed, and if it can live only when surrounded by an extra guard of police, then indeed it has outlived its time and lost the game. It has dug its own grave with its own hands, and sooner or later, but at all events at a none too distant period, it will fall under the weight of the real and vital forces of the nation. You have yourself, by your own words and conduct, put before society one clear question, which in itself alone is a terrible threat to the system of autocracy. You have challenged not only the *zemstvos*, but the whole of Russian society, to a mortal duel, and they have now nothing left them except to choose deliberately between a forward movement in the cause of civilization and blind obedience to autocracy. True, you have strengthened by your speech the detective-like proclivities of those who see the only possibility of serving their sovereign in the crushing of every expression of public feeling and in disregard of the law. You have appealed to the enthusiasm of those who are ready to give their services to every kind of master, and who do not give a single thought to the public welfare, finding that tyranny serves their own narrow-minded views. But you have turned against you all those who want to lead the country forward in the road of progress and civilization.

And what will become of all those who are unable to reconcile themselves to the concessions required of them, and to a long and largely hopeless struggle with the present order of things? After your sharp reply to the most humble and lawful demands that have been addressed to you, by what and through what means will Russian society be able to keep in quiet submission to your will those of its members who wish to proceed farther and farther on that road which leads to the amelioration of the nation's fate? Yet this is the impression created for Russian public opinion and the Russian people Ivy your first words to it and your first reply as a sovereign to the humble demands of its representatives.

Without mentioning the feelings of discouragement and helplessness of which you will very soon be convinced, your speech offended and revolted some who, however, will soon recover from their present depression, and will begin a peaceful, quiet, but none the less determined struggle to obtain the liberties which they require.

Likewise it has strengthened in others the determination to fight to the bitter end against a hateful order of things, and to fight it with all means they have at their disposal and in their power. You have been the first to begin the struggle, and it will not be long before you find yourself entangled in it.

St. Petersburg, January 19, 1895.

IV

PRINCE ORLOFF AND GENERAL ORLOFF

THERE were two Orloffs at the Court of Nicholas II. The elder of the two, General Orloff, had commanded the Regiment of Lancers of the Empress Alexandra, and became her great favourite. He died at Cairo in Egypt about the time little Alexis was born, and his body was brought back to Tsarskoye Selo and buried near the church the Empress had built near the Imperial palace, which was called the church of Znamenia, after a miraculous image of the Virgin which it contained, and which had been brought there from a little provincial town called Znamenia. The Empress used to go every day to pray at the grave of her friend, a fact that gave rise at one time to much talk and criticism.

The other Orloff, whom Alexandra could not tolerate, because he had always opposed Rasputin, was Prince Vladimir Orloff, a son of the former Russian Ambassador to France. His family had always ranked among those who were considered personal friends of the sovereign, and he himself occupied for a number of years the position of head of the Emperor's military cabinet. He was married to Princess Olga Belosselski. He had repeatedly warned the Emperor against the growing influence of Rasputin, and entreated Nicholas not to assume the command of the army during the war. When the Grand Duke Nicholas was sent to the Caucasus as Viceroy, Prince Orloff also was dismissed by the Emperor and appointed a member of the Grand Duke's staff in Tiflis. He contrived to escape from the Bolsheviks to the Crimea and made his way to Paris, where he died about a couple of years ago. He was a very noble character and a type of the old Russian nobleman.

Prince Orloff and General Orloff, who were not at all related, are often confused with each other: hence this explanation.

V

REPORT OF JUDGE RUDNEFF

THIS document was translated into English, by Judge Rudneff himself, and his style and spelling have been preserved almost entirely, which explains its foreign construction of phrases. He wanted to publish it in London, but died before he succeeded in doing so. His spelling of names and places have also not been changed.

This report differs in many respects from what we had heard from other sources. It may nevertheless be accepted as embodying the truth about Rasputin as Judge Rudneff saw it. St. Petersburg's society declared the former to have been much blacker than he is represented in the Judge's narration. And very likely Rudneff might have changed it had he read the letters of the Empress Alexandra to her husband which were found after their assassination and published later, letters to which he did not have access. Rut in spite of this lack of knowledge on his part, I think that the Judge had greater means of ascertaining the truth about Rasputin than persons such as M. Rodzianko, the President of the Duma, whose report to the Emperor was later found to have been based in part on the current gossip which he had heard here and there, and which rested largely upon imagination.

Text of Judge Rudneff's Report

As an investigating Judge, I had access to all documents, and the right to be present at the examination of all witnesses, with the view of establishing impartially the part played by persons accused by society and the public press, of exercising influence on foreign and domestic politics. I was ordered to read all the papers and letters found in the Winter Palace, the palace of Tsarskoye Selo, and at Peterhof, especially the private correspondence of the Emperor and Empress, certain of the Grand Dukes, and also the correspondences seized in the houses of Archbishop Varnava, also of Countess S.S. Ignatieff, Dr. Badmaeff, Voyeikoff, **and Anna Wyroubowa, and also to ascertain what relations had existed between the Imperial** Family and the German Imperial House. Being aware of the importance of my inquest in the matter of throwing light on historical events preceding and following the Revolution, I made **copies of all documents and letters, dossiers and statements of witnesses. In leaving** Petrograd I took with me all these copies, concealing them in my home at Ekaterinoslaw, but it is probable that these documents were destroyed when the Bolschewiki raided my house. If by happy chance I find that they still exist, I shall certainly publish them in full, without any comments of my own.

In the meantime I consider it my duty to write a short account of the principal persons who were accused of being Dark Forces. I must however warn the reader that as I write from memory some details may escape my mind. When I went to Petrograd to begin my work with the High Commission I admit that I was influenced by all the pamphlets and newspaper articles on the subject of the Raspoutine influence, and other rumours and gossip, and I began my work under preconceived prejudices. But a careful and impartial investigation soon forced me to come to the conclusion that these rumours and newspaper accounts were based on very slender foundations.

The most interesting person charged with exercising a malign influence on political affairs was Gregory Raspoutine, therefore this person was the central figure of my investigation. The account of the surveillance under which he lived, up to the very day of his death, is of great importance. This surveillance was exercised by the ordinary as well as the secret police, special agents noting all his goings and comings, some of these agents being disguised as policemen or as servants. Everything concerning the movements of Raspoutine was carefully recorded every day. If he left his house, even for an hour or two, the moment of his departure and of his return was noted, and also every person he met while away.

The secret agents kept a strict account of all people he met, and of all who visited him. In cases where the names of these persons were not known, their full descriptions were taken. After having read all these papers, and examined many witnesses, I reached the conclusion that Raspoutine was a person more complex and less comprehensible than had been previously represented. In studying his personality I naturally paid attention to the chronological order of circumstances which finally opened to the man the doors of the Tsar's Palace, and I discovered that the first preliminary was his acquaintance with the well-known, pious, and learned churchmen Bishops Theofan and Hermogene. I noted also that it was afterwards due to the influence of Raspoutine that these two great pillars of the Orthodox Church fell into disfavour. He was the cause of the relegation of Hermogene to the Monastery of Saratoff, and of the disgrace of Theofan, after these two archbishops, discovering Raspoutine's low instincts, openly turned against him. All the evidence I could collect pointed to the conclusion that in the inner life of Raspoutine, a simple peasant of the government of Tobolsk, there occurred suddenly a complete change transforming him and turning him toward Christ. Only in this way can I explain to myself his intimacy with these two remarkable bishops. This hypothesis is moreover confirmed by Raspoutine's story of his journey to the Holy Land. This book is marked by extreme naivety, simplicity, and sincerity. On the recommendation of the exalted churchmen mentioned, Raspoutine was received by the Grand Duchesses Anastasia Nicholaiewna, and Militza Nicholaiewna, and it was through them that he made the acquaintance of Madame Wyrouhowa, *née* Tanieieff, then a maid of honour, lie made a deep impression on this very religiously inclined woman, and gained at last an entry to the Imperial Palace. It was then that awoke in him his worst instincts, hitherto repressed, and it was then that he began adroitly to exploit the religious fervour possessed by very highly placed personages. It must be admitted that he played his part with astonishing cleverness. Correspondence bearing on the subject and the testimony of various witnesses prove that Raspoutine refused all gratuities, subsidies, and even honours which were freely offered to him by their Majesties, indicating thus his integrity, his disinterestedness, and his profound devotion and attachment to the Throne, insisting that he was an intercessor for the Imperial Family before God. He alleged that every one envied him his position, that he was surrounded by intriguers and slanderers, and therefore evil reports concerning him were unworthy of belief. The only favour he accepted was the rental of his lodgings, paid by the personal Chancery of His Majesty. He also accepted presents made by the hands of the Imperial Family, such as shirts, waistbands, &c.

Raspoutine had free entry to the apartments of the Emperor, saying there his prayers, addressing the Emperor and Empress with the familiar "thou" and greeting them in the Siberian peasant manner with a kiss. It is known that he warned the Emperor "My death shall be thine also," and that at Court he was regarded as a man gifted with the power of foreseeing events. His predictions and prophecies were couched in mysterious phrases like those of the sibyls of antiquity.

Raspoutine's income was derived from numerous persons who desired positions and money, and used him as their intermediary with the Emperor. Raspoutine asked favours for his clients, promising, if these were granted, all kinds of blessings to the Imperial Family and to Russia.

206

To this must be added that Raspoutine possessed a strange power by which he was able to exercise hypnotic suggestion. I have been able to establish the fact that he cured by hypnotism the disease of St. Vitus's dance which afflicted the son of one of his friends, **Simanowitch. The young man was a student in the College of Commerce, and his illness** completely disappeared after two *séances* during which Raspoutine plunged the patient into hypnotic slumbers.

Another case establishing the hypnotic power of Raspoutine may be noted. During the winter of 1914—1915 he was called to the house of the superintendent of railways in Tzarskoyé Sélo where lay, entirely unconscious, Anna Alexandrowna Wyroubowa, who had been seriously injured in a railway accident. She was suffering from broken legs and a fracture of the skull. Their Majesties were in the room when Raspoutine arrived, and he, simply raising his arms, said to the unconscious woman: "Anouchka, open your eyes," which she instantly did, looking intelligently around her. This naturally made a deep impression on every one present, including their Majesties, and it served to increase the prestige of Raspoutine. Although Raspoutine could barely read and write, he was far from being an inferior person. He had a keen and observant intellect, and a rare faculty of reading the character of any person with whom he came in contact. The rudeness and exaggerated simplicity of his bearing, which lent him the appearance of a common peasant, served to remind observers of his humble origin and his lack of culture.

As so much had been said in the public press about the immorality of Raspoutine, the closest attention was given by me to this phase of the question. From the reports of the secret police it was proved that his love affairs consisted solely in night orgies with music hall singers and an occasional petitioner. It is on record that when he was drunk he sometimes hinted of intimacies in higher circles, especially in those circles through which he had risen to power, but of his relations with women of high society no thin g was established, either by police records or by information acquired by the commission. In the papers of Bishop Vaxnava was found a telegram from Raspoutine as follows; "My dear, I cannot come, my silly women are shedding tears and won't let me go. As for the accusation that in Siberia Raspoutine was accustomed to bathe in company with women, and that he was affiliated with the sect of the "Khlysty," the Extraordinary Commission referred these charges to Gramoglassoff, professor in the Ecclesiastical Academy of Moscow, who, after examination of all the evidence, testified that among peasants of many parts of Siberia the common bath was a usual custom, and that he found no evidence in the writings or preachings of Raspoutine of **his affiliation with the**

"Khlysty" doctrines.

Raspoutine was a man of large heart. He kept open house, and his lodgings were always crowded with a curiously mixed company living at his expense. To acquire the aureole of a benefactor, to follow the precepts of the Gospels according to which the generous hand is always filled, Raspoutine took the money offered by his petitioners, but he gave generously to the poor and to people of the lower classes who begged his assistance. Thus he built up a reputation of being at once a generous and a **disinterested man. Besides these alms Raspoutine spent large restaurants,** *cafés*, music halls, and in the streets, when he died, he left practically nothing. The **investigation disclosed an immense amount of evidence concerning the petitions carried by Raspoutine to Court, but all these, as has been** said, referred merely to applications for positions, favours, railway concessions, and the like. Notwithstanding his great influence at Court not a single indication of Raspoutine's political activity was discovered.

Many proofs of his influence were found in the papers of General Voyeikoff, Commandant of the Palace, as for instance the following: "My dear, arrange this affair. Gregory." These letters were annotated by Voyeikoff, with the names and addresses of the petitioners, the nature of their demands, the results of their applications and the date of the replies. Many letters of the same kind were found among the papers of the President of the Council of Ministers, Sturmer, and of other high personages. All the letters concerned themselves exclusively with favours and **protection for the people in whom Raspoutine interested himself, he had special names for various persons with whom he was in frequent contact. Sturmer was called "The Old Man," Archbishop Varnava "Butterfly," the Emperor "Papa," and the Empress "Mama." The nickname of Varnava, "Butterfly," was found in a letter to Madame Wyroubowa.**

The inquiry into the influence of Raspoutine on the Imperial Family was intensive, but it was definitely established that this influence had its source in the profound religious sentiments of their Majesties, joined to the conviction that Raspoutine was a saint, and was the sole intermediary between God and the Emperor, as well as of all Russia. The Imperial Family believed that they saw proofs of his sanctity in his psychic powers over certain persons of the Court, such as bringing back to life and consciousness the desperately injured Madame Wyroubowa, whose case has been described; also in his undoubtedly benign influence over the health of the heir, and on a whole series of fulfilled prophecies.

It is evident that sly and unscrupulous people did everything in their power to profit by Raspoutine's influence on the Imperial Family, thus waking up in the man his worst instincts. This is particularly true of the former Minister of the Interior, A.N. Khwostoff, and of Belezky, Director of the Police Department. To consolidate their position at Court, they came to an understanding with Raspoutine whereby they agreed to pay him out of the private funds of the Police Department the sum of three thousand rubles monthly, besides other sums that he might require, provided he helped them to place candidates agreeable to them. Raspoutine accepted these conditions, and for three months filled his engagements, but finding that the arrangement was not advantageous to himself, returned to his independent manner of work. Khwostoff, fearing that Raspoutine would betray him, began openly to oppose him. He knew that he stood well with the Imperial Family, and he counted also on the co-operation of the **Duma, of which he was a member, and in which Raspoutine was cordially hated. This put Belezky in a difficult position, because he doubted Khrwostoff's power at Court, and he had no doubt whatever concerning Raspoutine's power and influence. Belezfcy decided therefore to betray his chief, and range himself on the side of Raspoutine. His object was to use the words of Raspoutine himself, to throw down the Khwostoff ministry. The struggle between these two officials culminated in the famous plot against the life of Raspoutine, which** created such a sensation in the press during the year 1916. The plot was laid by Belezky in the following manner. An engineer called Heine, owner of several private gambling houses in Petrograd, was hired to go to Christiania to meet the unfrocked monk, Illiador Troufanoff, a former friend of Raspoutine. The result of this journey was a series of telegrams addressed to Heine, and signed by Illiador, covertly alluding to a conspiracy against the life of Raspoutine. In one of these telegrams it was stated that the forty men engaged in the conspiracy were dissatisfied to wait any longer, and that it was necessary to send them immediately thirty thousand rubles. These telegrams, coming in war time from a neutral country, were delivered to the police, and only after having been read, passed on to the person addressed. Finally after receiving all the telegrams, Heine presented himself to Raspoutine in the guise of a repentant sinner, giving him full details of the plot, in which he owned himself concerned, but of which he vowed that Khwastoff was the leading spirit. The result was that Raspoutine took the story to the Imperial Family, and the dismissal of Khwastoff quickly followed. It is an interesting fact that Heine's telegrams from Christiania mentioned a number of persons living in Tzaritzyne, former friends of Illiador, who were supposed to be in Christiania busy with the details of the plot. The evidence given at the inquiry proved beyond doubt that the persons referred to had never left their homes.

Personally Khwostoff was highly esteemed by both the Emperor and the Empress, they believing him to be sincerely religious and devoted to the interests of the Imperial Family and to Russia, but the evidence shows that he was really devoted only to his personal interests. But for the time he remained in power Khwostoff was the closest to Raspoutine of all the ministers. Rumours of the latter's intimate relations with Stunner have been found to be without foundation. There was between them, it is true, a sort of friendship. Sturmer understood Raspoutine's great influence, and did what he could to advance the interests of his clients. He sent fruit, wine and delicacies to Raspoutine, but there is no evidence that he allowed him to influence political affairs. The relations between Raspoutine and Protopopoff, who, for some reason, Raspoutine called "Kalinine," were not more intimate, although Protopopoff liked Raspoutine, and it is certain that Raspoutine defended Protopopoff when the position of the latter was threatened. This was done usually in the absence of the Emperor, Raspoutine addressing himself to the Empress, at the same time uttering predictions.

Among Protopopoff's papers were found intimate and even affectionate letters from Raspoutine, but not one letter contained anything more than recommendations in favour of different persons. Both the press and the public seem to have been persuaded that Raspoutine was very intimate with two political adventurers, Dr. Badmaeff and Prince Andronnikoff, and that through him these men were able to exercise wide political influence. Evidence has established, however, that these rumours were without any foundation. The two adventurers were, in fact, nothing more than the hangers on of Raspoutine, glad to gather up the crumbs from his table and falsely representing to their clients that they had influence over Raspoutine, and through him influence at Court.

Dr. Badmaeff was the physician of Minister Protopopoff, but the Imperial Family had no confidence in his methods — any more than had Raspoutine — and in an examination of the servants of the Imperial Household, it was clearly proved that the Thibetan doctor had never been called in his professional capacity in the apartments of the Emperor's children.

The character of the Empress Alexandra was shown clearly in her correspondence with the Emperor and with Madame Wyroubowa. This correspondence, in French and English, is filled with sentiments of affection for her husband and children. The correspondence reveals also the deep piety of the Empress. In her letters to her husband she often describes her emotions during religious services, and speaks of the peace and tranquillity of her soul after prayer. In passages in which Raspoutine is mentioned she speaks of him as "that holy man" and shows that she considers him one sent by God, a prophet, and a man who prays sincerely for the Imperial Family. Through the whole correspondence, which covers a period of ten years, I found not one single letter written in German. According to the testimony of Court adherents, I have proof that before the war German was never spoken at Court. Because of the public rumours of the sympathy of the Empress for Germany, and of the existence in the Palace of Tzarskoye Selo of private wires to Berlin, I made a careful examination of the apartments of the Imperial Family, and I found no indications at all of communications between the Imperial Household of Russia and the Imperial Household of Germany. I also examined the rumours concerning the beneficence of the Empress towards the German wounded and prisoners of war, and I found that the Empress showed compassion for the sufferings of Germans and Russians alike, without distinction, desiring to fulfil the injunctions of Christ who said that whoever visited the sick and the suffering also visited Himself.

For these reasons, and above all on account of the frail state of health of the Empress, who suffered from a disease of the heart, the Imperial Family led a very retired life, which favoured the development, especially in the Empress, of extreme piety. Inspired by her devotion, the Empress introduced into certain churches attached to the Court, a regime of monastic services, and followed with delight in spite of her bad health, up to the very end, masses which lasted for hours at a stretch. This same excessive religious zeal was the foundation for her admiration for Gregory Raspoutine, who possessing an extraordinary power of suggestion, exercised an undeniable salutary effect on the invalid Tsarevitch. Because of her extreme piety the Empress was in no proper state of mind to understand the real source of the amazing influence of Raspoutine on the health of the Heir, and she believed the explanation of it to be due, not at all to hypnotism, but to the celestial gifts which Raspoutine owed to the sanctity of his life.

In terminating this inquiry, I believe it necessary to repeat that Bishops Theofan and Hermogene contributed in an important manner to the introduction of Raspoutine at Court. It was because of their recommendations that the Empress in the beginning received Raspoutine cordially and confidently. Her sentiments towards him were fortified only by the reasons indicated in the course of this document.

The reader will notice the different way of spelling certain names Rudneff employs. We thought, however, it would be better to reproduce his report with practically all its mistakes, considering the fact that it is not a translation by the author but one made by Rudneff himself.

VI

OPRITCHNIKIS

THE Opritchnikis were a bodyguard of Tsar Ivan the Terrible, whom he employed as spies and executioners. They were both dreaded and detested by everybody, and, on account of their numerous atrocious cruelties, were regarded in Russia much as were the Spanish Inquisitors in the Netherlands and other countries. To this day the word *Opritchnik* is one that is used only when one wishes to brand a person as something worse than a brigand.

The Russian political police under the last Tsars (the famous Third Section) were supposed to be modern Opritchnikis and to have derived from the original body.

VII

THE PRESIDENT OF THE DUMA'S WARNING TO THE TSAR

BEFORE the war, when the Rasputin scandal was already at its height, the president of the Duma, Michael Vladimirovich Rodzianko, took it upon himself to warn the Tsar of the different rumours in regard to the presence, in the imperial palace, of Rasputin. Unfortunately he laid particular stress on the fact that Rasputin belonged to the religious sect called Khlystys, which, though common talk, was proved later on not to have been the truth. This fact considerably weakened the impression M, Rodzianko's talk had at first produced upon Nicholas II.

In his memoirs the late president of the Duma relates that among other things he said the following in the course of the conversation he had with the Emperor on the subject of Rasputin: "It is my duty. Sire, as a Russian and as Your Majesty's loyal subject, to warn you that our enemies are striving to undermine the throne and the Church, and to cast a shadow on the beloved name of the Tsar. In the name of all you hold sacred, in the name of Russia, and for the sake of the welfare and happiness of your successors, I implore you to banish this villainous rogue, and so dispel the fears which assail those who are loyal to the throne."

M. Rodzianko here makes an allusion to the suspicions which existed in certain circles of Russian society that Rasputin had been placed by secret anarchist societies in his position of adviser to the Imperial family in order to destroy the prestige of the sovereign not only among educated people, but especially among the peasants to whom it was represented that the Tsar was protecting sectarians, whose creed was an abomination in the eyes of all pious members of the Orthodox Church. This was why Rodzianko, in his report to the Emperor, laid such stress on the charge that Rasputin belonged to the sect of the Khlystys.

Later on, Rodzianko used his best efforts to persuade Nicholas II to grant Russia the constitutional government for which all classes of society were clamouring. He actually found the courage to tell his sovereign that he ought to find some way of preventing the Empress from exercising any influence on politics. "Your Majesty," he said at last, "do not compel the people to choose between you and the good of the country. So far, the ideas of Tsar and Motherland have been indissoluble, but lately they have begun to be separated."

It was then that there happened the incident which impressed the president of the Duma more than anything had ever done before. The Emperor pressed his head between his hands, then said: "Is it possible that for twenty-two years I have tried to act for the best, and that for twenty-two years it has all been a mistake?"

It was a hard moment. But with a great effort at self-control, Rodzianko replied: "Yes, your Majesty, for twenty-two years you have followed a wrong course."

After this conversation the president of the Duma saw Nicholas II only once more, when he made his last appeal to the monarch in favour of the establishment of a constitutional government.

"There is still time," he said; "it is still possible to change everything and grant a responsible ministry. That, apparently, is not to be. You, your Majesty, disagree with me, and everything will remain as it is. The consequence of this, in my opinion, will be revolution and a state of anarchy which no one will be able to control."

These words were the writing on the wall which Nicholas II refused to read.

VIII

LETTERS OF THE EMPRESS

THE letters from the Empress to her husband and to her friends during her captivity in Tobolsk have been reproduced practically as she **wrote them.** Alexandra Feodorovna preferred the English language to any other, and, strange to say, spoke both French and German indifferently, but this does not mean, as the reader will be able to judge, that she knew English well or invariably wrote it correctly.

Also available in this series

Life of Alexander II, F.E. Grahame

Alexander III, Tsar of Russia, Charles Lowe

Collected Works: Once a Grand Duke; Always a Grand Duke; Twilight of Royalty, Alexander, Grand Duke of Russia

Between two Emperors: The Willy-Nicky telegrams and letters, 1894-1914

Frederick, Crown Prince and Emperor, Rennell Rodd

Letters of the Empress Frederick, edited by Sir Frederick Ponsonby

Potsdam Princes, Ethel Howard

The Complete Works: The Journal of a Disappointed Man; A Last Diary; Enjoying Life and other literary remains, W.N.P. Barbellion

CPSIA information can be obtained
at www.ICGtesting.com
Printed in the USA
LVOW10s1720150418
573554LV00036B/1734/P